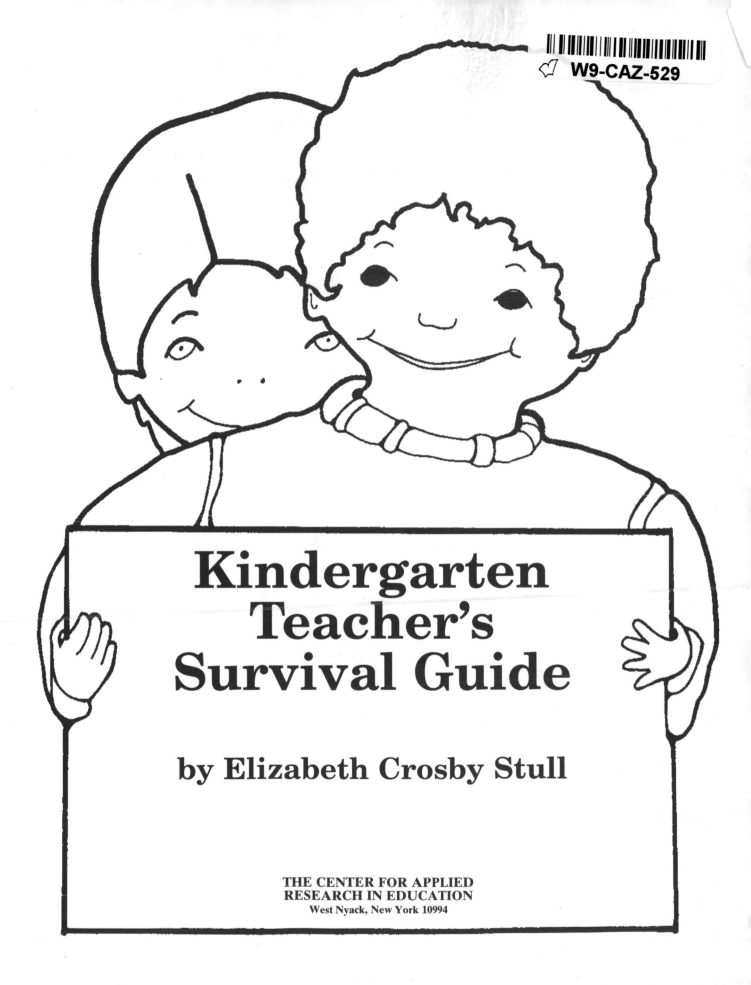

Kindergarten Teacher's Survival Guide

by Elizabeth Crosby Stull

THE CENTER FOR APPLIED
RESEARCH IN EDUCATION
West Nyack, New York 10994

Library of Congress Cataloging-in-Publication Data

Stull, Elizabeth Crosby.
    Kindergarten teacher's survival guide / by Elizabeth Crosby Stull.
        p.   cm.
    Includes bibliographical references (p.   )
    ISBN 0-87628-499-3 (spiral wire).—ISBN 0-87628-495-0 (pbk.)
    1. Kindergarten—Curricula. 2. Kindergarten—Activity programs.
3. Classroom management. I. Title
LB1180.S79 1997
372.19—dc21   97-20371
                                                              CIP

Printed in the United States of America

10 9 8 7 6 5 4
ISBN 0-87628-499-3 (S)

10 9 8 7 6 5
ISBN 0-87628-495-0 (P)

THE CENTER FOR APPLIED RESEARCH
IN EDUCATION
West Nyack, NY 10994

On the World Wide Web at http://www.phdirect.com

To Lorren

Who, like The Little Red Hen,
            cut the wheat
            baked the bread
            set the table
And, unlike The Little Red Hen,
            he happily shared all.

Thanks, also, to the second graders who drew the charming teachers who are in charge of each section.

And many thanks to Susan Kolwicz, editor, for her care and help with this book.

E.C.S.

About the Author

Elizabeth Crosby Stull, Ph.D. (The Ohio State University) has over 30 years of experience in education as a primary teacher and teacher educator. She began her career as a teacher of grades 1, 2, and 4 in the public schools of Greece Central, Camillus, and Pittsford in upstate New York, and is currently teaching part-time for Ohio State at Marion.

Dr. Stull has published many articles in professional journals such as *Instructor* and *Early Years* and is coauthor, with Carol Lewis Price, of *Science and Math Enrichment Activities for the Primary Grades* (The Center, 1987) and *Kindergarten Teacher's Month-by-Month Activities Program* (The Center, 1987). In addition, she has written *Children's Book Activities Kit* (The Center, 1988), *First Grade Teacher's Month-by-Month Activities Program* (The Center, 1990), *Alligators to Zebras, Whole Language Activities for Primary Grades* (The Center, 1991), *Second Grade Teacher's Month-by-Month Activities Program* (The Center, 1992), and *Multicultural Discovery Activities for the Elementary Grades* (The Center, 1995).

Dr. Stull is a member of the National Association for the Education of Young Children, The International Reading Association, as well as Phi Delta Kappa and Delta Kappa Gamma, two education societies.

About This Book

The *Kindergarten Teacher's Survival Guide* serves as a one-stop resource to help you plan a successful kindergarten program filled with learning and fun for the entire school year. With its unique mix of activities, tips and strategies, and reproducibles, the *Guide* helps you create a program that takes into consideration the following critical areas:

- **Philosophy:** Are you, the teacher, well grounded in child development? What are the state and district philosophy and guidelines for a successful kindergarten program?
- **Goals:** What forms of assessment are available to you? Are the goals realistic? How are they determined and evaluated?
- **Curriculum and Instruction:** Kindergarteners thrive on a schedule and, yet, a measure of flexibility needs to be built into the day. Does the classroom meet the needs of different types of learners? Does it foster exploration, questioning, and active learning? Do you have adequate materials for instruction?
- **Evaluation:** Are children learning and progressing in a safe and comfortable atmosphere? Do you reteach and reinforce in a variety of ways? Are the children eager to come to school each day? Does the classroom look visually appealing, and thus invite learning? Are the children making progress?

Organized into twelve information-packed sections and featuring a teacher* on each section-opening page to serve as your guide, the *Kindergarten Teacher's Survival Guide* includes the following:

Welcome to Kindergarten

This section is designed to get you off to a good start with tips for getting the kindergarten room ready for the first day of school, how to set up the typical classroom with the help of a useful diagram, and sample schedules for half-day and full-day classes. There are sample forms for use with an I.E.P., and a field trip and general parent letters. Information is available on learning styles and multiple intelligences as well as on portfolios for each learner. Along with this, the emotional, physical, social, and intellectual characteristics of kindergarteners are reviewed here. And, 40 succinct tips for making the day go smoothly should be helpful. On the lighter side, there are "30 Things That Go Wrong When There's a Full Moon," since a bit of humor is essential for the kindergarten teacher.

*The teacher drawings were made by second-grade students.

Classroom Management

Since classroom management is critical for the well-being of the children and for the success of any program, there are suggestions for setting up rules and consequences, for managing the group during special events, for traffic control, and much more. Suggestions for using puppets, the mystery apron, clapping patterns, and ways to prepare for transitions are all designed to assist the teacher, along with a list of 45 specific survival tips and six reproducible pages.

Reading

One of the many keys to reading success is repetition and drill, but that does not automatically mean drudgery. Many opportunities for games and chants are provided, and suggestions for maintaining a print-rich environment. Practice letter/sound relationships by nibbling your way through the ABC's like a mouse, or taking an alligator to the dentist. Picture books, poetry, journals, graphing favorite storybook characters, and making books are among the numerous ideas presented in this section along with 19 activity pages for reinforcing reading skills and making an *ABC Book*.

Writing

Tips for setting up a Writing Center, picture books that invite writing , making a story burger, roping off a story, and writing in a journal are all detailed in this section. Children will enjoy the Teddy Bear Writing Paper and eight other activity sheets.

Speaking

Some picture books invite speech, such as wordless books and cumulative tales. Assistance through stories for the shy child and tips for enjoying our voices are included, along with eight reproducible pages of puppets, story cards, and a fairy tale concentration game.

Listening

Go on a Listening Walk, listen to teacher directions on tape recordings, set up conditions for good listening in the classroom, and "Close Your Eyes and Listen for the Cat." (Listening is also addressed in the Music and Movement section.) Seven reproducible pages complete this important section.

Mathematics

The first part of this section works through the thirteen standards set forth by the National Council of Teachers of Mathematics (NCTM) and gives numerous teaching suggestions for each. Active learning is the philosophy in this section and many activities are provided for patterning, working with shapes, graphs, categorizing, and even singing about pennies. Many children's picture books are listed, and opportunities for counting and singing in different languages are provided. A helpful section on computers is included. Children will like the number rhymes in "Counting with Mother Math Goose." There are 25 succinct survival tips, as well as 22 activity pages to help with weighing, body measurement, graphing, fractions, patterns, and a "Celebration of 100."

Social Studies

We live in a complex world and children need to feel secure, so we begin with the family study and branch out to the school family and the first family. We explore our surroundings in terms of birds and animals, the four seasons, and learn about communication in our world. There is a multicultural approach to holidays throughout the school year with guided activities and recipes, and suggested folktales to use as a springboard to understanding ourselves and others. We learn about the American flag, and the Pledge of Allegiance. Included are 37 survival tips and 25 activity pages in this busy section.

Health and Science

Activities for learning about and with the five senses start off this section. Like math, science takes a hands-on approach to learning and we plant seeds, investigate simple machines, work with rocks, explore similarities and differences via the Venn Diagram, try healthy snacks, and learn to take care of ourselves especially during Dental Health Month. A specific list of survival tips and 14 activity pages help us to act like real scientists by investigating, predicting, categorizing, collecting, estimating, and problem solving.

Art

In this stage of development, children need to explore with a variety of media since they are process rather than product oriented. Many suggestions are provided for working with clay, making mosaics, bark rubbings, and enjoying art from many cultures. There are art recipes, and a special section on "Color" provide many learning opportunities. We will make a "Teddy Bear Vest Book of Colors" (English and Spanish) and then make the vest, too! Our survival list contains 21 tips and there are 17 helpful activity pages.

Music and Movement

Rhythms and rhymes and chants and make-believe stories for hand, foot, and whole body movement, as well as an exercise regimen, keep us happy, healthy, and fit. Children will enjoy doing the "Humpty Dumpty" and the "Jungle Make Believe" activities. Survival tips are included and the 20 reproducible pages provide the class with masks for storytelling as well as a "Fairy Tale Puppet Set" and more!

More Information for the Teacher

This includes five short sections on important matters accompanied by more than 50 specific activities and useful bits of information on "Keeping the Kindergartener Happy," "Keeping the Kindergartener Healthy and Safe," "The Home/School Connection," "Transitions After Vacations," and "End-of-Year Assessments."

Bibliography

Although there are hundreds of children's books and resources listed in the *Guide,* it's simply not enough! This extensive bibliography, which includes media and computer information, is here at your fingertips to provide you with even more resources for your teaching needs.

I hope you find that the *Kindergarten Teacher's Survival Guide* helps you! Write and tell me if it did. Enjoy your year, it goes by fast. The children deserve the best you've got to offer and it's difficult to let them down. Most of my college students remember their kindergarten teacher . . . . so your effort will not go unnoticed. They don't necessarily remember the mechanics of what you taught as much as how you did it, what you said to them, and how you handled yourself. You're being watched daily by experts.

Elizabeth Crosby Stull

Contents

READING
55

WRITING
107

SPEAKING
129

SOCIAL STUDIES
227

HEALTH and SCIENCE
291

ART
337

MUSIC and MOVEMENT
385

BIBLIOGRAPHY
453

WELCOME TO KINDERGARTEN!

Ms. Mustafa

Welcome to Kindergarten!

Welcome to the child's world of work and play. Kindergarten is the German word for "children's garden." This term is appropriate for there is much growth and development taking place in this garden—physical, mental, emotional, social, to name a few areas to be tended.

The curriculum can be likened to the garden soil, in that it must be rich and nourishing. And since children learn best by doing, they can dig and plant and pull up and water and sing in their secure and happy place under the guidance of a warm and caring gardener, the teacher, who provides a model or serves as a model in all areas of development.

The garden contains turnips, cabbages, plums, grapes, and roses—each requiring the same yet different measures of care, and each deserving a teacher with a green thumb who enjoys the variety of a rich garden.

So, as the kindergarten caretaker, gather your hoe and rake and growth manuals, your tools of the trade, and tend your garden well each day—for you have the awesome task of providing the foundation for the day when each child will have to tend a garden of his or her own.

Characteristics of the Five-Year-Old

General Information

A normal, healthy five-year-old child is filled with exuberance and bubbles over with stories to tell when he or she charges in through the doorway of the classroom each day—stories about pets, a baby brother who cried all night, a new haircut, a schoolbus that broke down. You might hear, "Hey everybody, don't get near me! My sister's got pink eye!" or "We got a new dog. He's just like

Paddywack, only he's down lower," or "Maryanne ran off the bus before Mrs. Dolly said OK."

Some children are in a rush to get to an activity that was only partially finished the day before. Some come in and stay by the teacher's side until they get a chuck under the chin and a word of encouragement before they skip off. Some come in quietly, shyly, until things get started and then they, too, join in the busy, active world of learning in the kindergarten environment. During the day, though, the scene will shift, the rhythm will change, and the sounds will vary. The teacher cannot lose sight of the individuals with varying needs who make up this group. These fragile youngsters who enter the classroom daily as they begin their formal school experience need a teacher with sound emotional health, a solid background in child development, the wisdom of a sage, the patience of a saint, a high energy level, and a reverence for the innocence and beauty that shines through the eyes of the young child. As one kindergarten teacher put it, "I am surrounded each day by the best company in the world!"

The child is a work of art in progress, much like a weaving—and the teacher needs a wide variety of threads, textures, colors, and techniques to provide and guide children through a rich kindergarten tapestry of experiences.

Emotional Characteristics

- egocentric; sees things from a personal point-of-view
- dependable
- obedient; wants to please
- happy and satisfied when made to feel important
- able to handle some responsibility
- angry if a job proves too challenging and success isn't within reach
- one who thrives on praise
- able to use dramatic play as a vehicle for working out problem situations

Physical Characteristics

- continuing to develop small-motor coordination
- likes to be in motion—actively engages in hopping, skipping, throwing, kicking, running
- handedness has usually been established

- can grasp a pencil and make letters and numerals (does better with large spaces rather than small, lined paper)
- bumps into things; doesn't always accurately calculate physical space
- is in a period of slow physical growth

Social Characteristics

- likes to finish a job, so will need advance notice when time is running out
- wants to care for self—buttons, zippers, snaps, laces
- will follow rules and conform to the group
- is eager to please adults
- likes others
- will give and receive affection
- can be shy
- can be uninhibited

Intellectual Characteristics

- concrete thinker; will take things literally
- curious about the natural world
- investigates; likes to take things apart, likes to open doors and look around corners
- communicates using full sentences
- enjoys books and listening to stories
- can learn through observation and imitation, but learns best with a hands-on approach

- can recognize colors, letters, shapes
- highly imaginative; inventive in dramatic play and storytelling
- likes to explore with new materials (clay, sand, media)
- vocabulary is rapidly increasing
- can reflect experiences with words, play, and visual art
- is in a "peak" learning period, so needs a rich environment
- can learn a foreign language with ease
- has a natural interest in rhythm and rhyme
- is in the Piagetian Preoperational Stage of Development (ages 2–7 years)

General Kindergarten Information

At what age can children be admitted to kindergarten?

In the public school setting, rules regarding age do vary from state to state. In some states, the child must be age 5 by the first of December of the new school year. In others, the child must be age 5 when entering kindergarten, or age 5 by the end of September. Private schools may have their own rulings, as long as they comply with state law. Proof of age (birth certificate) is required.

Is health an issue?

A parent will need to give a factual background history of the child's health record. Has the child had the required inoculations and check-ups? Is the child disease-free? Has the child seen a dentist regularly? Does the child require medication as prescribed by a family physician and, if so, how is it to be administered during the day? This information needs to be made clear, in the best interests of the young child.

Are there kindergarten prerequisites?

If the child has attended preschool, request the necessary records from the director and/or staff regarding the child's emotional, social, and academic development.

Is there a "Kindergarten Day" sponsored by the school district during the previous spring, or summer, or first week of school, when child and parent spend a morning at school to become acquainted with the environment? In some districts, the parents and students are directed to go to the library (or cafeteria). They sign in, and both parent and child each receive a name tag. Children go to the classroom for their orientation to the room by the teacher, and parents stay in the library for an orientation to the school by the principal or supervisor. Children are brought back to the library to meet their parent again—perhaps cookies are served.

Is there a Kindergarten Screening Assessment Day sponsored by the school district during the previous spring, when children are asked to perform a variety of skill tasks to assess their developmental level (e.g., ability to listen and follow simple directions, ability to speak clearly, ability to recognize shapes, colors, numerals, and so on)? See the ASSESSMENT FORMS in this section for some ideas.

Does the kindergartener have "special needs"?

For the health and safety of all students, it is generally required that students should have control of bodily functions, and be able to go to the bathroom with no assistance. Is the student able to button and zip clothing, tie shoes, and get dressed to go home without assistance?

Hearing—Does child require a hearing apparatus, and will the teacher be required to use a microphone?

Seeing—Does child with less than normal vision wear corrective glasses? Will special accommodations need to be made for children for whom glasses do not solve the problem (blurred vision, loss of sight in one eye, dim vision, no vision)?

Speech—Does child stutter or show overt signs of not being willing or able to communicate verbally? If so, how does this child make known his or her needs?

Body movement—Does child wear leg braces, or walk with crutches, or move about in a wheelchair? What accommodations will have to be made for this student?

Behavior disorder—Does child have a mild to severe behavior disorder and, if so, what is the nature of the disorder? Have parents sought the help of a professional? If so, what records are available to the school? If not, is parent willing to seek professional help? How can this child be accommodated in the average kindergarten classroom so that disruptions are kept to a minimum?

Daily Schedule

Kindergarteners thrive on routine and like to have a daily schedule of events. They count on certain experiences that only the school can provide, and while they can take variation in their routine, there does need to be an underlying structure. They are teacher-dependent and deserve the best models, for they are, in fact, modeling speech, attitudes, behavior, and values of the one in charge. The kindergarten teacher has a tremendous responsibility to these youngsters, and needs to remain emotionally and physically fit.

Begin the business of the day by taking attendance and lunch count (if appropriate). You will want to have the children say the Pledge of Allegiance, standing tall, facing the flag, with their right hand across the front of their body and placed on their heart. Check this by moving through the group, making corrections.

Initially, to learn the Pledge of Allegiance, the teacher says a line and has the children repeat it after her or him. Do this regularly until a number of children have most of it, and then say it in unison daily. Occasionally, go back over it line by line, but a chorus of voices will usually carry those still struggling to learn it. The teacher's strong voice is needed for this experience, and children will soon follow the inflection and the wording.

The Pledge of Allegiance

I pledge allegiance
To the flag
Of the United States of America.
And to the Republic
For which it stands
One nation under God,
Indivisible
With liberty and justice for all.

Sample Schedule (half day)

(Approximately 3 hours with the children, repeat for the afternoon schedule.)

8:00 A.M.	Teacher goes over plans and last-minute preparations
8:30–8:45	Greet children on arrival Children take items to their hook or cubbie Quiet activities and browsing through books before school begins
8:45–9:00	Opening (attendance, Pledge, song) Calendar activities and weather reporting Sharing and discussion time
9:00–9:20	Circle time (instruction) Planning for day's activities
9:20–10:00	Work period (individually or in small groups at stations)
10:00–10:15	Clean up and get ready for recess
10:15–10:30	Recess (indoor, or outdoor if at all possible)
10:30–10:45	Toilet, wash hands, snack time, rest
10:45–11:10	Story time (discussion, instruction, dramatization)
11:10–11:25	Music: group singing, rhythms, marching
11:25–11:40	Evaluation and preparation for leaving
TEACHER	Lunch, clean-up, ready the room for the P.M. session. (Enlist the aid of older students to help get the stations ready.) P.M. session enables teacher to make modifications.

Sample Schedule (full day)

(Approximately 6-3/4 hours with the children.)

8:00 A.M.	Teacher goes over plans and last-minute preparations
8:30–8:45	Greet children on arrival Children store their items in the cubbies provided, or hang clothing on hooks Quiet book-browsing time before school begins
8:45–9:00	Opening (attendance, Pledge, singing) Calendar activities, weather reporting, and experience chart Sharing and discussion time
9:00–9:15	Planning for the morning
9:15–10:15	Activity time (small groups working at centers in the room; may be theme related)
10:15–10:45	Snack time and socialization (some teachers read aloud during this time)
10:45–11:15	Play period (indoor—blocks, housekeeping, special centers of interest, individual book browsing)
11:15–11:45	Story time and literature study
11:45–12:30	Lunch and recess (outdoor if weather permits)
12:30–1:15	Rest period (varies by group; some require an hour)
1:15–1:30	Music and rhythm time
1:30–1:45	Circle time (planning for afternoon, some instruction)
1:45–2:15	Activity time (continuation of A.M. activity or a different activity)
2:15–2:45	Special (library, art, music, physical education, or computers)
2:45–3:00	Evaluation of the day
3:00–3:15	Dismissal (unhurried and end on a happy note)

Getting the Kindergarten Room Ready for the First Day

On the next page is a diagram of a kindergarten classroom that may help to give you some ideas.

Here are some helpful hints to use BEFORE school begins:

- Check the cupboards to see what is already available for use.
- Put high activity areas near each other, and separate them from low activity areas.
- Have your room rules listed and posted (rules/consequences).
- Have colorful bulletin boards on display to help create a warm, welcoming environment.
- Have colorful books arranged for display in your library area.
- Have at least fifty picture books in the classroom ready to go (visit your local library and school library).
- Obtain a supply of junk mail, magazines, newspapers.
- Have name tags made for each child (pin on, or wear as name necklace).
- Have name tags placed above coat hooks and cubbies.
- Label items in the room (sink, drink, door, clock, shelves, etc.).
- The Math, Science, Work, and Art tables may be used initially as the child's own desk area (and later set up as Areas of Interest); if so, put name tags on the tables.
- If you plan to have Areas of Interest immediately, then equip them with only a few items at the beginning, such as:

  —math center with one or two manipulatives

  —science center with bark samples and rocks or seashells

  —writing center with pencils and paper

  —listening center with story tapes

  —music cassettes/records for the music area

  —housekeeping corner with kitchen supplies

  —clothing for dress up

  —easel with paper and crayons (not paint)
- Make a large room calendar that you will be using daily.
- Have chart paper available for daily group writing.
- Make sure you have chalk and erasers, scissors, glue, crayons, paint, rulers, pencils, felt-tip pens.
- Make a "stop" and "go" sign for the bathroom.
- Check to see if there is toilet tissue.

Sample Room Diagram

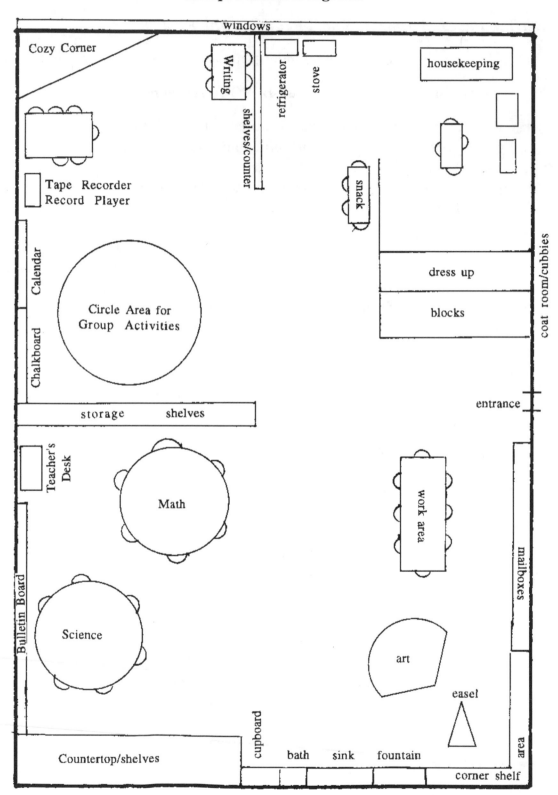

- Check to see if the toilet flushes properly.
- Make sure there is paper toweling in the container by sink.
- Make sure there are sponges for clean-up of tables and sink.
- Have a box of tissues available for runny noses.
- Have your letter photocopied and ready to go to parents if you have not already done so (include schedule, class rules and consequences, school phone, and ask for donations for the room).
- Join a children's book club to stock your bookshelves with a variety of books.
- Go to garage sales and look for items for the class (costumes, a mirror, an alarm clock, rugs, a big carpet, bathroom scale, books, and so on).
- Settle your desk with what you want in the drawers, and what you want on top.
- Select the books you will read aloud the first day and have them ready to go.
- Select the music materials for use the first day.
- Make a bus list and hang it by the door.
- Arrange to have lunch with an experienced kindergarten teacher for "tips."
- Read District and School manuals from cover to cover.
- Get plenty of rest, and start taking vitamins.
- Contact your room mother re: party procedures, classroom assistance.
- Learn the layout of the building.
- Print your name on the chalkboard.
- Have a list of students' names available so you can check them off the first day.
- Learn the procedure for notifying the office of child absence, child illness.

Keeping a Kindergarten Portfolio

What is a portfolio?

It is a record of progress made by the student.

What is in a portfolio?

A wide variety of items and samples of the child's work that shows his or her development throughout the year. For example:

- a monthly sample of drawing (perhaps a self-portrait)

- a monthly sample of writing
- a monthly sample of the child's printing (first and last names)
- samples of number work
- photographs of the child's three-dimensional work
- photograph of the child at work or play
- sample of art work

Where do you keep a portfolio?

- Keep it in a file drawer by your desk.
- Keep it in a large box in the classroom.
- Keep it in a cupboard.

Should children be allowed to see their portfolio?

Yes. It is a good means for you to hold individual conferences with children and to show them the progress they are making, or where they need to focus their attention.

Should parents be allowed to see the portfolio?

By all means. This is a good reference for parent-teacher conferences. Often a child's work gets home in crumpled condition, or it's whisked out of the child's hand by the wind and doesn't reach home. This is an opportunity for you to discuss the child's individual progress.

Should parents be allowed to see other children's portfolios?

That's not the purpose of a portfolio. However, there are times when you may want to show the parent a sample of work, for example, that is not so good as and/or far superior to their child's work to make your point. NO NAMES are to be given. This "educates" the parent as to what you are talking about when you are referring to *average*, *below average*, and *above average*.

Can children have unlimited access to their portfolio in the classroom?

At this age, *unlimited* access does not work well because the work gets all mixed in together and valuable portfolio information can be lost or misplaced.

It is a good idea to conference with each child, and to ask the child what he or she would like to have in the portfolio. It gives the child a sense of ownership and pride in their work and shows you what they consider to be of value. However, maintaining the portfolio is the responsibility of the teacher.

By the end of the year, isn't the portfolio stuffed?

Keep sorting and deleting items throughout the year. You are aiming for representative work, for work that shows change and progress, but not *all* work.

Learning Styles

The term "learning styles" has been used to describe how one deals with ideas, concepts, day-to-day information, and the **preference** that one shows for learning—visual, auditory, global, tactile/kinesthetic. This would be the way that one best processes information. This material would apply to all learners—the average learner, delayed learner, gifted learner, and learners with special needs. The following is from the work of Rita and Kenneth Dunn in their book *Teaching Students Through Their Individual Learning Styles: A Practical Approach.*

For example, let's take a look at *silk* material. When the teacher is discussing silk and showing silk, the learner may be focusing upon the following aspects:

Visual learner—benefits from seeing the shimmering silk

Auditory learner—benefits from listening to the *words that describe* the smooth, silky cloth

Tactile/kinesthetic learner—wants to feel the silk material with the fingertips or palms of the hand

Global learner—wants to see/touch the silk first, then hear details about it (from whole to part)

When it comes to reading and the printed word, the **visual learner** needs a print-rich environment, and one that has a variety of items to see, watch, observe. Photographs, pictures, diagrams, charts, murals, and maps are all examples of visuals that enrich a learning experience. When talking about graphs, the visual learner benefits by having the class construct a graph and then can "see" the results. Working with the overhead projector, using different colored chalk on the chalkboard, and highlighting charts with drawings and different colored pens is helpful for the visual learner.

This learner, being visually curious, also likes to have new and different items in the classroom, or *realia,* that can make an idea or concept come to life. A high percentage of children are visual learners.

The **auditory learner** can gain information by listening to stories and tapes, as well as to music. Discussions are helpful. Often, when information is being verbalized, this learner can easily pick up the idea being communicated.

When information and instructions are given to the student body over the inter-com system in the school, chances are the auditory learner can get the message without having to have it repeated. This learner is often a good line leader during fire drill practice and trips to the lunchroom because verbal instructions do not pose the problem that they do for some children.

To strengthen this skill, and for the ADD/ADHD learner, the teacher can record directions and information on a cassette tape, and teach the children how to access them.

The **tactile/kinesthetic learner** is the one who benefits from being able to "feel" or touch items. This person benefits, as do all children, from handling materials and learning by a hands-on approach. *This is the best way for all children to become familiar with math concepts, by counting actual items and using "manipulatives."*

The kindergarten classroom should be a veritable wonderland of tactile experiences for the young learners. Real items to touch, handle, lift, turn over in their hands, stroke, scrunch, twist, and bend are all ways in which children learn the properties of items. Notice that kindergarteners naturally want to "touch" everything, as this is a perfectly normal way that the five-year-old gains information and learns.

The **global learner** benefits from seeing the end product, or the whole picture, before delving into the parts. This learner likes to know outcomes.

Say, for example, that you plan to bake muffins with the students. It is best for this student to know what a muffin actually looks like, so that the mixing, sifting, and stirring make sense, and he or she doesn't go through the process in a state of confusion.

All lessons should have elements of the above, so that the students gain understanding in a variety of ways. For some students, it is helpful to strengthen areas that are weak, at the same time that you are playing to their strengths.

Working with individuals, with peers, in small groups, and in large groups gives the students opportunities to learn in a variety of ways.

In addition, there are a number of specific elements that need to be taken into account when addressing a person's learning style, especially in the kindergarten environment. The following four elements are addressed: *environmental, sociological, emotional,* and *physical*.

Environmental Elements

Sound—Note the sound level in your room. Some children are bothered by noise, whereas others seem to be oblivious to loud noise. Let children know what level of sound is appropriate for indoors/outdoors.

Light—Some children are bothered by bright lights. Make sure children sit with their backs to the windows. Also, change the lighting in the room periodically; this can be done by having several lamps available to switch on when the overhead lights go off. The warm glow is especially comforting when children enter the room, and during storytime.

Temperature—Keep a moderate temperature in the classroom and extra sweaters for children who feel a chill. To cool a room, open the windows and keep the hallway door open in order for fresh air to move through. When it is extremely hot, with no air conditioning, allow children to have a water thermos available.

Design—This refers to the arrangement of your furnishings, and here the teacher becomes the designer. In the kindergarten classroom, make sure noisy areas (blocks) are not next to your quiet book area. Do you plan to have a rocking chair for reading? Comfy pillows?

Sociological Elements

It is a good idea to have children work in *pairs* or with *peers* for some of your activities. Also, plan to have *independent* activities, as well as *team* activities.

Emotional Elements

Some children come to school *motivated* to learn, whereas others need to be motivated by the teacher. This is where puppets, storybooks, art activities, and field trips help to get children hooked on learning. The amount of *persistence* in completing a task varies from child to child, often depending upon her or his background training. The amount of *responsibility* that each child can be given or that can be expected, is another factor that the kindergarten teacher needs to be aware of. Finally, some children require more *structure* in their environment than do others. A child likes to know what to expect, what is coming next in the daily routine.

Physical Elements

These include *time of day* (some children are at their best in the morning, whereas others are slow to awaken), and some afternoon kindergarteners who are morning persons are just winding down. Another element is the *need for intake* (eating/drinking) during school hours. Some teachers have solved this by having food (carrot sticks, celery, crackers) available in addition to snack time. The *need for mobility* is another element, which is why the teacher must give children an opportunity to move and exercise. Also, never take away a play period as punishment, for exercise may be just what the child needs to settle down. Finally, *perceptual strengths (visual, auditory, tactile, kinesthetic)* constitute another element that has previously been discussed.

Teacher Resource: Rita Dunn, "Introduction to Learning Styles and Brain Behavior: Suggestions for Practitioners." *The Association for the Advancement of International Education,* Vol. 15, No. 46, Winter (1988), p. 6.

Multiple Intelligences

In his book *Frames of Mind*[*], Howard Gardner identifies seven distinct intelligences and styles of learning. The claim is made that we should not be asking the question, "How smart are you?" but, rather, "HOW are you smart?" meaning, what is your strength.

Here is a listing of the seven intelligences we should be looking for in the kindergarten classroom. We can make our teaching rich and varied so that we are teaching to all children—not just to one or two modes of learning. Some samples are given below:

Visual/Spatial Learner

Needs to see the items: can work well with puzzles, colors, shapes, pictures. This learner will benefit from having the teacher print on the chalkboard, or on

[*]**Source:** Gardner, Howard. *Frames of Mind: The Theory of Multiple Intelligences.* NY: Basic Books, A Division of HarperCollins, 1983.

an experience chart. Needs to *see* the calendar and the weather chart. Use the overhead projector for the learner who is challenged.

Linguistic Learner

Readily participates in verbal activities. Likes to say, hear, and see the words. Is eager to memorize poems and chants. Enjoys vocabulary games.

Logical/Mathematical Learner

Learns best by categorizing and classifying, and working with patterns and relationships. All children benefit at this age from working with manipulatives and a "hands on" approach, but this child will select activities of this sort during free-choice time. Likes to build. Is able to make connections quite readily.

Musical Learner

Learns best through rhythm, repetition, chanting, music, melody. This child is at home with music and is not inhibited when it comes to singing out—this is your marching band leader type! Rhyming and chanting work well in the math area as well as with reading activities.

Bodily–Kinesthetic Learner

Wants to touch items being described and discussed for a better understanding. For example, sees the word "rough" printed on the chalkboard, hears the word "rough," but really gets the sense of roughness by *touching* a piece of rough material along with a sample of smooth material for contrast. This learner is physically active—so jumping to a number count, or bouncing a ball while chanting the ABC's are valuable activities for this learner.

Interpersonal Learner

Likes the company of others and is generally cooperative, willing to share, and enjoys working with a partner or in a small group.

Intrapersonal Learner

Can work well independently; has a strong sense of self. Will pace herself/himself for task completion, and may prefer to work alone.

Sample I.E.P.

INDIVIDUAL EDUCATION PLAN (I.E.P)
FOR SPECIAL NEEDS LEARNER

Name_____Date _____

School Diagnosis _____Made by _____Date _____

Professional Diagnosis _____Made by _____Date _____

SPECIFIC COMMENTS DURING MEETING HELD WITH THE FOLLOWING
TEAM MEMBERS:

Teacher Comments:_____(name)

Parent Comments:_____(name)

Principal Comments: _____(name)

Nurse/School Psychologist Comments:_____(name)

Special Teacher (Speech, Phys. Ed, etc.) Comments: _____(name)

Child: (if present)

PLAN OF ACTION: (Goals/Objectives; Behaviors to Work On)

Timeline for Assessment

Next Meeting Date

Sample Parent Letter

Date _____

Dear Parents,

Greetings from Kindergarten! We are going to be working on a unit on COLORS for the next three weeks, and we could use your help.

We plan to set up a color display for each color (red, orange, yellow, green, blue, purple). So, if you have something to loan us for our display, we would appreciate it. It could be a placemat, a swatch of material, a plastic dish, plastic utensils, a mixing bowl, an article of clothing or jewelry, socks, or something else you have that is colorful and bright.

Please send the item(s) in a bag, and stick masking tape with your last name on the bottom of the item, so we can return it to you.

****

HOW CAN I HELP MY CHILD AT HOME:

- At home, you can help your child by going on a color walk through your house. Find three items that are green, yellow, red, and so on.
- When you have your child help you put away the groceries, identify the colors on the labels.
- At breakfast, identify the colors on your cereal box. What color is your child's juice today?
- Have your child help you match the socks from the clothes dryer—all the blue ones, the white ones, the red ones, and so on.
- What color jacket or sweater does your child wear? What color cap or hat? Have your child locate it among other clothing items.
- Do you have flowers growing in your yard? What color are they? Do you have plants growing in your home? What color are they? Do you have a pet? What color is it?
- What colors are the traffic lights? What color is the stop sign?

We are surrounded by colors! An awareness of colors helps make children aware of other things in the environment. This awareness promotes curiosity and encourages questions, which help your child to learn and do well in school.

Thanks for your help!

_____
Teacher

Sample Parent Letter/Field Trip Form

(Date)_____

Dear Parents,

We're planning a field trip! This trip is in conjunction with our Kindergarten course of study on
_____. In order for your child to go on this trip, your written permission is
required. Therefore, please sign this form, detach it, and return the permission slip with your child
as soon as possible.

We need three parent volunteers to accompany us on this trip. If you are interested in going with
us and looking after a small group of children, you can join in the learning and the fun! Please call
me at school or call our Kindergarten room mother.

If you have any questions or concerns, do not hesitate to contact me. We'll do everything possible to
ensure your child's safety and well-being during this trip, and look forward to it as a pleasant learning experience.

TRIP TO: _____

DATE:_____

Sincerely,

_____

(teacher)

· ·

Yes. I give permission for my child, _____, to go on this field trip
with the Kindergarten class.

TRIP TO_____

DATE _____

SIGNATURE _____

TODAY'S DATE _____

30 Things That Go Wrong When There's a Full Moon

1. More pencil points break.
2. More paint gets spilled.
3. More toilets won't flush.
4. More sinks get clogged.
5. More crayons get crunched into the carpet.
6. More water gets spilled.
7. More erasers disappear.
8. More glue won't stick.
9. More scissors get rusty.
10. More sneaker laces get knots.
11. More dormant flies begin to come to life and become divebombers.
12. More overhead fluorescent lights begin to flicker and buzz.
13. More parents call you at night.
14. More kids get red spots.
15. More fingernails get slivers.
16. More chairs topple over.
17. More clay gets stepped on.
18. More noses get runny.
19. More paintbrushes get lost.
20. More doorknobs won't turn.
21. More cupboard doors stick.
22. More kids lose their money.
23. More lunchpails crash to the floor.
24. More bare knees get scraped.
25. More children get coughs.
26. More piano keys stick.
27. More buttons fall off.
28. More zippers won't zip.
29. More special classes get canceled.
30. More swings come unhinged.

HANG IN THERE!
The Moon is on the wane and soon things will be normal again.

The Big 4-0

Forty Tips for Making the Day Go Smoothly

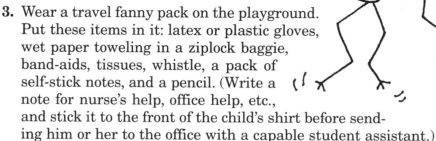

1. Wear a carpenter's belt during your arts/crafts period—the type with many pockets in a row. In these pockets keep extra felt pens, a pair of scissors, a stapler, paper clips, a bottle of glue, and tissue.

2. Noisy boys and girls are often tired boys and girls. Take a rest before starting the next job (especially on Mondays).

3. Wear a travel fanny pack on the playground. Put these items in it: latex or plastic gloves, wet paper toweling in a ziplock baggie, band-aids, tissues, whistle, a pack of self-stick notes, and a pencil. (Write a note for nurse's help, office help, etc., and stick it to the front of the child's shirt before sending him or her to the office with a capable student assistant.)

4. Laminate colorful cards with school name and phone number on them. Have children wear them when going on a field trip.

5. Make friends with the children's librarian at the public library, and visit there on your way home from school once a week, or once every ten days. The colorful picture books you bring to the classroom will enrich your story time.

6. Have story time daily. If one story gets the children very excited, follow that one with a quiet story that settles them back down.

7. Have each student bring in a favorite pillow so they can curl up with a good picture book.

8. Computer programs at this level should be enjoyable for the child, and not necessarily skill oriented.

9. Have a comfortable "Time Out" area where a child can go when he or she is out of sorts.

10. Ask parents (monthly) to send in items for the housekeeping corner so that the play is enriched with a new hat, shoes, cape, and so on.

11. Shop during "After Halloween Sales" to purchase costumes that will enrich storytelling, play period, and writing time.

12. Wear comfortable shoes. Keep an extra pair in your desk drawer and change when you get to school, if you need to wear dress shoes for an after-school appointment.

13. Link up with a teacher at an upper-grade level, and arrange to enlist the aid of a "teacher's assistant" group of capable student volunteers. Set up a schedule for them to come to the kindergarten classroom to help during busy times (snack time, outdoor and indoor recess, and during arts/crafts time).

14. Keep a package of "kitty litter" under the sink. If a child gets sick and vomits in the classroom, cover it with this material and call for custodial help for clean-up.

15. Wear a snap-on belt, with a pair of latex gloves clipped to the belt. If a child has a nose bleed, gets a knee scrape, or has a problem at anytime where blood is involved, immediately put on the gloves and then go into action.

16. Cold water on paper toweling works wonders for minor complaints. If a child complains of a sore elbow, sore finger, and so on, treat the complaint seriously. Go to the sink, pour cold water on the folded toweling, press out excess water, and give it to the child to put on the spot that hurts. Let the child hold this on as long as he or she needs to do so. It usually makes the hurt go away.

17. Get a red rope (dye a piece of clothesline). Red signifies danger. Encircle an area where you do not want children to go. (For example, if glass breaks, mark off the area.)

18. Keep a mop, extra large sponge, pail, broom, brush broom, whisk broom, and dustpan handy.

19. Ask each parent to donate a box of tissue and liquid hand soap (regular or antibacterial). When supply is running low, send home another request.

20. Ask each parent to donate a box of snack crackers. When supply is running low, send home another request. Use this supply if a child forgets his or her snack, or complains of being hungry. Also, let parents know in writing what you consider to be a daily healthy snack, e.g., apple or grapes, peanut butter/crackers, vegetables such as carrot sticks or celery sticks.

21. Keep a flashlight handy in case of power failure.

22. Keep a battery-operated radio in the classroom (for weather updates, news, or even as soothing background music).

23. Give children praise for a job well done . . . a special badge, certificate, sticker, or rubber stamp on the hand.

24. Institute a "Please and Thank You" Day. Children need to practice these words in appropriate situations.

25. Put a bird feeder outside your window. It invites nature study.

26. Put an outdoor thermometer outside your window. It invites awareness of the environment and seasonal changes.

27. Have a "Substitute Packet" available in case of absence. Get a tote bag and include your daily schedule, list of good helpers, storybooks, and worksheets

that students have already done (it will serve as review). The less the students' schedule is interrupted, the better your day will be when you return.

28. Don't take it personally. If a child is out of sorts, chances are it's something that happened outside of the classroom. If it persists, contact parents.

29. Deal with fear. If there has been trouble in the neighborhood or if someone is ill, talk about it.

30. Place stuffed animals or puppets way up high, and use them to help with classroom management. Magically, a note appears tucked underneath them—it may be complimentary ("Nice job coming in from recess!") or it can be instructive ("Yoo-hoo! Too noisy in the hall. You woke me up out of a sound sleep!").

31. Take a cellular phone with you on a field trip in case of an emergency when you're out in the middle of nowhere.

32. Replenish your chalk supply regularly, and use different colors.

33. Check the room temperature—not too hot, not too cold.

34. Make an arrangement with the school nurse so that extra underpants are available "just in case." If you don't have a full-time nurse, keep these available in your room.

35. Keep extra child's sweaters available. (Ask parents to donate.)

36. Remember, it could always be worse.

37. Always have "Plan B" in mind in case "Plan A" isn't working.

38. Children are going to count on their fingers, and it's OK.

39. If someone is having an impossible day, make arrangements to have him or her visit the teacher next door. This often quiets the child.

40. Laughter is the best medicine. Have everyone laugh for three minutes straight. They won't make it, but they'll have fun trying, and it clears the atmosphere so you can start again.

CLASSROOM MANAGEMENT

Ms. D'Angelo

Classroom Management

Introduction

This is an area that is critical for the well-being of the children and for the success of any kindergarten program. Here, the teacher is the key. Basically, the kindergartener likes a set schedule and thrives on routine, so have consistency in your days. In the beginning, be fair but firm. Be consistent. Follow-through is essential.

Initially, have a list of **Room Rules** and **Consequences** posted, and go over this daily for the first week so that the child understands the behavior that is to be expected.

Do not continue instruction until the children are quiet. If you have to wait . . . wait. Then praise them for being polite and ready.

If a child is out of sorts, don't take it personally. There may have been trouble on the bus, in the home, before the child even got to school. Have a "Time Out" area so that a child can be removed from the group and settle down.

As the teacher, you need to be rested, healthy, and well grounded yourself. Children need to know that you are friendly but as firm as a rock that they can't push. The teacher is in charge here, and that's you! It comes through in your voice, in your posture, in your mannerisms. Practice before a mirror. It's especially important during the first month that you set the tone, act business-like, and let the class know what you expect. This will pay dividends later in the year. You can't be a buddy; you're a teacher now.

*During the first month or two, classroom management **is** what the children are learning.* Later you can concentrate on other areas of teaching and learning.

Instruction and Practice for Success

A kindergarten class does not know automatically how to line up at the door, for example, so devise a method and tell them what it is, and then practice *lining up at the door*. They need to know what is expected of them. Here are other things to practice for success:

- **Washing hands**. Have the students practice washing their hands. Show them how to turn on the water, how to access the soap, how to rinse, how to turn off the water, how to get the paper toweling (and how much), and where to put the used paper toweling. They need to know how to do this, before they can do it successfully on their own, so it calls for instruction and practice. Turn it into a lesson, and let every child do it while the others watch and learn, too.

- **Getting a drink**. Managing the drinking fountain is a challenge for some students and they need practice. If the fountain is inside the classroom, this can be turned into a lesson (or a game) where students are involved in "calling upon" the next person to get a drink. They can do this through the use of a stuffed toy, or a "drink ticket" that one child can give to another, since they won't know names at first. If the fountain is in the hall, have the students line up, get a drink, then go to another line, and quietly wait.

- **Walking in the hall.** Practice walking from the classroom door to the end of the hall, then back again. Do this several times. Students can work on their posture at this time, and pretend that they are members of a marching band—straighten up, shoulders back, eyes straight ahead, hands at sides, ready, go slowly! They can pretend to be fashion models walking down a runway. Make walking down the hallway a pleasurable exercise experience for them.

- Other routines to practice include:

  fire drill procedure—ring bell, go to the door and out the door, down the hall, to the designated area, line up there, take attendance, wait in line, return (no talking—assess the success with the students; do it again).

  going to the office—learn the route; walk quietly

  going to the auditorium—sitting in their designated area, getting back up, lining up at the door, and returning to the room (no talking—assess the success; Did it go well? What do we need to keep in mind for next time?)

  going to the cafeteria—sitting in their designated area, getting back up, cleaning up their space, lining up at the door, no talking in the hall on the return trip (assess the success)

  lining up from outdoor recess to go back into the building

  your "quiet" signal—lights out, ring a bell

Classroom Management Activities

Circle Time Chit-Chat

Many kindergarteners love to talk and have lots to tell each day when they come in the door—news about pets, a trip to the dentist, new skates, a game of ball, a visit from a relative, and so on.

On especially chatty days (Monday is a good one, since students haven't seen each other as a group for a couple of days), arrange to have students "tell it to a neighbor" during Circle Time. Have students count off around the circle (1,2,1,2,1,2). Then, have them pair off, with a Number 1 facing a Number 2, all around the circle. Next, for 5 minutes, it's "chit-chat" time. All of the Number 1's talk for 2-1/2 minutes, while the Number 2's listen, at which time the teacher gives an agreed-upon signal (e.g., ring a bell, strum a chord on a banjo, turn a toy upside down, and so on). Then, all of the Number 2's talk for 2-1/2 minutes, while the Number 1's listen, at which time the signal is given again. This time it means, "Shhh! We're all talked out!" Now we can listen and go on with the day.

Helping Children With AD/HD

During large group instruction it is a good idea to seat students with AD/HD among students who are well-focused. These children also benefit from hearing the directions again on a cassette tape.

For visual tracking, encourage the use of a marker to hold underneath words, objects, or a line of print. Wearing earphones for the express purpose of blocking out noise can be effective with special-needs students during quiet work time, or when they are looking through a picture book.

Privacy Boards

Set up some areas in the room with folding cardboard boards to block distractors during specified times, or when a child prefers to work there. Study carrels in out-of-the-way places are also helpful for some children.

Big Sister/Big Brother

By all means, team up with upper-grade levels so that students from upper grades can help younger students by working with letter–sound recognition cards, counting objects, grouping objects by 2's or 5's, classifying objects by color or by size or by category, and writing down story information that children dictate. If one or two students can be with your group during the morning circle time, they can listen to your directions right along with the children. Then, when another student comes in to relieve them, they can pass the information along to the other student.

The Big Yellow School Bus

Make a large yellow school bus outline from construction paper and post it at the door entrance. Then, place different colored squares on the bus. Label the squares as BUS #_____, and list the names of the children who ride that bus. Then, when it is time to line up at the end of the day, that information is readily available.

Assign children a "bus buddy" from the classroom, so that when they line up to get on the bus, they look out for each other.

Activity Pages

Make sure that the print is dark, so children do not have the added burden of trying to see what is on the page. This is especially important for those who are visually challenged. *Also,* distribute only one page at a time.

Color Coding

Use color whenever possible. Shelves can be color coded with red, yellow, and blue dots, for example. Then the items that belong on each shelf can have a colored dot on them, so students can readily sort and return the items.

Use colored bins, and place colored markers or yarn on items that belong in the bins.

If you have learning centers or stations, these can be color coded with a large balloon. Items can then be color coded that belong at each station.

Areas of the room can be color coded, and if children sit in groups, these may be color coded. Certain colors of rugs on the floor also serve as areas where activities can take place.

The Mystery Apron

Buy an apron that builders wear—one with lots of pockets—or make an apron and sew on a variety of large pockets. Keep a different object in each pocket, and when the class needs a change of pace, pull an object from a pocket and do an activity that refreshes the students for learning. Some examples of items to keep in pockets include:

- a silver bell (ring it, and then listen to music, move to music)

- a tiny book (time to settle down and listen to a story)

- a yellow circle (time to go outdoors to play in the sun)

- a miniature toy (5 minutes extra play time today IF we get our work done quietly)

- a stuffed animal (sleepy time—our friend says "noisy boys and girls are tired boys and girls" so let's take 5 minutes to get all of those wiggles out and then close our eyes and rest

Perkins, the Helpful Puppet

Introduce the students to a hand puppet that only the teacher can "hear." It can be kept high above the classroom perched on a cupboard or a shelf, not only because it likes the view, but because it's a little shy. (Give the puppet a first name.)

At times the teacher can cup her hand to her ear and quite dramatically say, "Perkins! Is that you? (Pause). Yes I know, we are a bit noisy, but we'll quiet down so you can get your rest." Then turn to the students and whisper, "Let's keep the volume turned down so that Perkins can get his sleep. We woke him up, and we don't want him to get cranky."

Perkins Likes to Write Fancy Notes

Sometimes the puppet can even write a note and the teacher, who knows it's there, of course, can call attention to it at just the right moment. Or, sometimes it's sticking out just the right amount to be noticed, and a child brings it to the attention of everyone. What does Perkins have to say to us? The teacher can reach way up and get it and read it to the class. It can say, "I really like the way this class is working today! If I were a cat, I'd pur-r-r!" (This note can be written on a cat shape.) Or, "Your singing was so beautiful, it made my heart sing!" (This note can be written on a heart shape.) Or "Your art work is splendiferous! My very favorite color in the whole world is pur . . ." (Oops, the rest is missing. Perkins ran out of space. What color name begins with 'p-u-r'? This note can be written on purple paper.)

Perkins the Puppet Is Alert

Sometimes the puppet note might say, "It was quite noisy today during playtime and I had to cover up my ears." Or, "I saw two people running indoors and I know they won't do that again. I'm not mentioning any names; it's our secret."

Clap/Clap, Clap/Clap/Clap (AA, BBB Pattern)

To gain the attention of the entire group, begin clapping a rhythm. Have the students clap with you (this engages their hands and turns attention to this activity). Continue the clapping rhythm, and then slow it down. Have a signal for finally ending the clapping (last segment is clapped over the head, teacher turns out lights on the last segment, and so on).

When clapping is finished, students keep hands folded together (so they do not become busy doing something else), and focus attention upon the teacher for the next direction.

Do this clapping exercise deliberately early in the year for practice, so that students catch on to the idea that this is an attention-getting device, and that an important direction will immediately follow.

Naptime Atmosphere

Plan on a mid-session nap time so that students can take a rest. During this time, they can get a pillow that they have brought for this purpose, and go anywhere in the room to nap. Some might wish to bring in a stuffed toy "nap buddy." Play soothing background music, turn out the overhead lights, and turn lamps on for a safe, homey atmosphere. Students can be "awakened" by the playing of a music box; then stretch, put away their pillow or nap buddy, and go to the circle for the next activity direction or a "wake up" story time.

Time-out to Visit the Three Little Pigs . . . Don't Stay Away Too Long

Some days children need a refuge, a place to spend some quiet time alone—you know it and they know it. If a child wants to drop out and visit with the three little pigs, here's how they can do it gracefully.

Secure a tall refrigerator box, and cover three outside surfaces in the following way. It's possible to have children help with this hideaway:

1. Cover one side with brown construction paper, and glue sticks around the edges.
2. Cover a second side with red paper. For a brick look, cut a sponge into a rectangular shape, dip it into black paint, and dab it onto the red paper in rows.
3. Cover a third side with yellow cloth, with straw glued on.
4. The fourth side can be cut out. Place a curtain rod or dowel rod at the top, and make a colorful curtain for privacy. Furnish the inside with a little throw rug, a chair, pillows, and picture books.

Children may be sent to visit the storybook characters, or they may wish to visit on their own. (*Note:* Maria Montessori, early childhood educator, said that when children were misbehaving they should be allowed to have "time out" from the group, and then return when they felt ready to cooperate. She viewed an uncooperative child as an ill child. In her school, when the child chose to rejoin the group, the rest of the children happily greeted him or her and expressed joy that the child was feeling well again. See: *The Montessori Method* by Maria Montessori, NY: Schocken Books, 1964.)

Other Hideaway Areas

Other quiet, private areas can include:

- a beanbag chair tucked in the corner
- a wicker chair
- a rocking chair
- an upholstered chair
- under the teacher's desk with a pillow

- under a specified desk with a pillow
- in the tent (table with a cloth draped over it)

Traffic Control

Sometimes the kindergartener runs inside the classroom out of shear eagerness to share something with a friend or with the teacher. However, running is not to be encouraged indoors because of the safety factor.

Some rules that might help:

- No more than one person up at a time from each group.
- No more than three people moving about the room during _____ time.
- No one moving in FAST GEAR inside the building.
- *Walking* shoes indoors; *Running* shoes outdoors.

Have students pretend they are a cab or a bus or a car, and practice shifting gears. At a given signal, have them shift themselves into neutral gear—waiting. Then, shift into low gear—moving slowly and carefully. Only on the playground can they move into high gear—running, in areas where it is permitted.

Have children "practice walking slowly" from Point A to Point B in the classroom.

Praise students for the way they are walking carefully in the classroom.

Singing Directions

Some teachers choose to sing out their directions, rather than calling them out. The tune can be made up as you go along. Try it!

Lining Up—Traffic Control

Children can continue to learn during the lining-up-at-the-door process, and enjoy this time of day. Have a method for getting children into a line at the door. For example, line up in the following ways:

- eye color ("All those with blue eyes, stand." Then call names to line up.)
- hair color
- shoe design
- clothing colors
- clothing patterns (plaid, polka dots, stripes)
- favorite food (pizza lovers, hot dog lovers, hamburger lovers)
- favorite seasons
- favorite dessert (make up interesting combinations)
- favorite storybook characters

OR use a variety of movement when lining up:

- hop like a bunny
- drag along like an elephant
- skip like a kangaroo
- stalk like a tiger
- walk tall like a giraffe
- glide like a bluejay
- sniff, sniff like a bunny rabbit
- tippy-toe like a quiet mouse

Do you plan to have a girls' line and a boys' line? Do you plan to have partners or a single line? Children need to know this in advance.

The teacher should be the LINE LEADER because you then control the pace of the walk, and can stop the line at any time to enable students to catch up, quiet down, etc.

Keep an Uncluttered Classroom

As the day wears on, keep an eye on the chalkboard and erase information that is no longer needed. This avoids visual confusion, and also helps the child who has difficulty with location skills.

The same can be said for desktops and tabletops—avoid clutter. Build clean-up time into the day's schedule, and have the children help keep the environment clutter-free. Make sure there is adequate storage space for items, and bins and buckets and tubs to help contain items.

Special Help from Clocks

Some children are engaged in special programs during the day, such as Speech class. Use a small paper clock and tape it to the child's desk as a reminder that when the clock on the wall "looks just like this one," then it's time for them to go to the office, or to Room 21, or to see Mr. _____.

Giving Directions

Make sure everyone is quiet. Do not speak until everyone has his or her eyes upon you. Encourage children to put on their "bunny ears," or their "Peter Rabbit ears"—big ears—and be very, very quiet.

Face the students when talking to them—do not turn sideways or speak to their back. Make sure you keep moving your eyes to maintain eye contact at all times. Give directions slowly.

REVIEW: Repeat directions and put them in order. "*First*, we will do this. *Second*, we will do this, . . ." and so on. *Then*, go over it again, and have children tell you what comes first, what comes second, and so on.

Preparing for Transitions

In order to make smooth transitions from one activity to another, make sure children know what is coming next and what is expected of them. Have agreed-upon signals:

- start playing a recording; when it is finished, everyone should have put everything away and be seated on the rug (or circle)
- when lights flick on and off, that means start cleaning up
- use a drum—*five* drumbeats mean start cleaning up . . . then *four* drumbeats mean clean up should be in process . . . *three* drumbeats mean clean-up is almost done . . . and so on

Give directions in advance. For example,

- Say, "After storytime, we will take a nap."
- Say, "When we return from Library, put your book in your bookbag and then go back to your activity."
- Say, "When we go back into the classroom, step on the Magic Carpet by the doorway, and your feet will lead you to the Circle Area. Sit down and show me you're ready."

I'm Listening for Ready Feet

During story time, or whole-group instruction, make sure students are relaxed before you begin. Use the following:

"I'm listening for ready feet." (*keep feet still*)

"I'm looking for folded arms." (*hands off neighbors*)

"I'm looking for those beautiful eyes." (*look at teacher*)

"I'm looking for closed lips." (*no talking*)

"I like the way you're showing that you're ready."

Keeping Tattling to a Minimum

Try ignoring tattling unless it deals with a *safety issue*. A child who is tattling is often looking for attention. Is the complaint major or minor? If a child tells you about someone who put the blue brush in the yellow paint can, just say, "Uh hum, and what are YOU doing now?" This redirects and refocuses the child's attention to his or her task at hand.

If the teacher constantly reacts to tattling, then the child is in the position of being the "manager." Assure the child that you're quite aware of what's going on, and do nothing at that point. Later, when you have Circle Time you may wish to address the matter in question (pushing in line, taking only one piece of paper at a time, etc., in a way that serves as a general reminder to all).

Some General Do's and Some Don'ts Too

- **Follow through.** Think carefully about your words and then carry them out.

- **Discipline in private.** Taking a child aside for a quiet reminder may be all a child needs to get back on task.

- **Be consistent.** This allows children to know their boundaries and limits.

- **Be fair, but firm.** You need to be a leader who has an "air of business" about you. *Fair* means being able to see both sides, make good decisions, weigh consequences. *Firm* means standing your ground.

- **Act like a leader.** If you plan and organize well, you will know where you're headed and won't be thrown off by detours that are sure to come up. *If you're not the leader, then children will follow the one who is* . . . and that may be the loudest child, the bully, the one who is out of control.

- **Have an agreement with another teacher.** Make an arrangement with another teacher so that a disruptive child may be sent to that classroom for time out.

- **Keep calm.** Do not raise your voice and shout. Rather, turn out the lights until everyone settles down, including the teacher.

- **No power struggles.** The kindergartener is not one to get into an argument with; it is inappropriate.

- **Hands-off policy.** Don't use physical punishment.
- **Play period.** Children need to work out their aggression through play, and perhaps after a good run on the playground, a child may be physically ready to cooperate. Don't eliminate it.

Kindergarten Champions

Make "good worker" badges and tape them to the shirt of the children who earn them. Or, stamp the hand of the good workers, or give them a sticker, or let someone carry the "good worker" puppet around with them for the next half hour, or let someone wear the "good worker" hat for the next activity. Make sure they are praised for good work habits and cooperation, and they will continue to exhibit this type of behavior.

Talk Over Potential Discipline Problems

If you've been trying on your own and things aren't getting much better, talk it over with a staff member or the principal in a professional manner. Chances are you will get some good advice and a new technique for dealing with the situation.

Name Your Group

Early in the year, give a name (or vote upon one) for the class. This helps give group members a sense of belonging, and they can learn to take pride in their group. (For example, "The Kindergarten Champs," "The Kindergarten Winners," "The Kindergarten Jets," and so on, are names from which to choose.)

The teacher can refer to the group title often when giving praise or when trying to get the attention of the group. For example:

1. "That's just the kind of thing we expect from a Kindergarten Champ! Thanks, Joey, for picking up that pencil."
2. "Congratulations to Tiffany, a super Kindergarten Winner! She just let Noel in line to get a drink."
3. "Al-l-l-l-right! I'm looking for Kindergarten Jets that are ready to walk down the hall and show everyone what a good group we are! Stand tall, shoulders back, head up, arms at sides, lips locked, ready . . . go."
4. "I'm so proud of the Kindergarten Champs for the way they listened carefully when the loudspeaker was on."

Does Your Room Look Inviting?

This does much to "set the tone" for learning and behavior. Much time is spent by the teacher working in the room to help "create a learning environment" both *before* and *after* the children are in attendance. Although the kindergartener is willing to help clean up, and should be asked to do so, it often means that the teacher has to reclean, reorganize the play area, rewash the chalkboard, reorganize the shelves, etc., after the students leave. Perhaps you can arrange to have an upper-grade "Teacher Helper Club" assist with this.

Put the Storybook Characters in Charge

Does your room reflect "learning going on here" by having a variety of areas and places and things to attract attention? Some teachers use the opaque projector to trace storybook characters (color and cut out) that are placed prominently on display in certain areas.

For example, large cut-outs of favorite picture book characters may be "in charge" of certain centers. Imagine *The Very Hungry Caterpillar* (Eric Carle), cut-out in startling green, over the Science Center; a *Strega Nona* (Tomi dePaola) cut-out, with a real apron, overseeing the easel; a bright yellow *Curious George* (H. A. Rey) cut-out overseeing the Math Center; a big, bright, bold *The Cat in the Hat* (Dr. Seuss) cut-out at the Writing Center, etc. Change your characters periodically, and have the children decide who they will be. Some get attached to the characters and resist the change, so go with the feeling of the group.

Attractive Surroundings Make Us Feel Good

- Are the bulletin boards colorful and attractive? Some teachers give ONE bulletin board to the children to manage, and then they manage the rest.
- Is children's art work on display? (It can be framed by stapling it to a larger sheet of colored paper.) Some teachers turn one wall into the "Art Gallery."
- If your wastebaskets are filled to overflowing, ask for larger ones, or have children periodically stomp down the paper with their foot.
- Cover tables with colorful vinyl tablecloths that can be scrubbed clean.
- Take a colored photo of an area to show what it should look like after cleaned up.

- Some children may not be used to picking up after themselves, and having a "cleaning crew" assigned to each area will help all of the children work together. They can wear a bright orange scarf tied around their waist as a clean-up signal.
- Build "clean up time" into your schedule, rather than rushing to get it done.

A Hand on the Shoulder

For the aggressive child or the one who is having difficulty with behavior management, walk slowly in that child's direction and put a reassuring hand on his or her shoulder. Sometimes you will need to rearrange their work area, move them around in their chair, but try doing it without saying a word to them (other than a direct look). While doing this, don't miss a beat in terms of your conversation or attention to the other children.

Teacher, What Big Eyes You Have (and in the back of your head, too!)

A teacher needs to be aware of what is going on both nearby and in the far corners of the room. Keep circulating, keep looking. Catch someone's eye and give a nonverbal signal.

Above all, look directly into the eyes of students when talking with them. This is powerful for keeping them focused.

Parent Conferencing, Phone Conferencing

Keep in contact with a parent who is concerned, along with you, about the behavior and performance of his or her child, especially if the child is in an "acting out" mode. Perhaps the child has just been put on medication. Invite the parent to school on days when the medication is given and days when it is not, if there is a big difference.

Also, sometimes it's nice to just give parents a call with a friendly message of how well their child did in school today and how proud you are of the child.

Enlist the Aid of the Classmates

Sometimes an extremely disruptive student can sour a lesson or even begin to pull others into unacceptable behavior. If this should happen, you need to have a heart-to-heart talk with the group. Send the disruptive student on an errand to the office (prearranged) with the message to detain her or him for 10 minutes.

Then, talk to the group about their classmate's behavior and what everyone can do to help! Usually, it is getting students to ignore the behavior. The message to convey is to follow the teacher's lead and not that of the child. Suggest to them that they not be "pulled in" by another's behavior. Give them a boost by letting them know you're counting on them to help you, and that you know they can do it. Assure them that the child in question is not "bad" but simply not behaving like a grown-up kindergartener.

Start a Support Group or Discussion Group

See the Home/School Connection section.

OK, How Did We Do Today?

Before children go home, gather them together, so that you can talk about the day and what you did together, what you learned, how things went, what you need to work on, etc. *Always leave them on a positive note*—a puppet can help here. The puppet can give them the "warm fuzzie" they need and deserve, and the puppet can't wait until they come back tomorrow to work on _____ and also on _____.

Teacher Resource Bibliography

Albert, Linda. *A Teacher's Guide to Cooperative Discipline*. Circle Pines, MN: American Guidance Service, 1989.

Bodenhamer, Gregory. *Back in Control*. Englewood Cliffs, NJ: Prentice Hall, 1983.

Chiarelott, Leigh, Leonard Davidman, and Kevin Ryan. *Lenses on Teaching: Developing Perspectives on Classroom Life*. NY: Holt, Rinehart and Winston, Inc., 1990.

Dreikurs, Rudolf and Pearl Cassel. *Discipline Without Tears*. NY: Hawthorne Books, 1972. (recently revised)

Moss, Robert A. *Why Johnny Can't Concentrate: Coping With Attention Deficit Problems*. NY: Bantam Books, 1990.

Classroom Management Survival Tips

Some New, Some Review

1. Make two sets of name tags—one for the child's table space or desk, and one to wear around the neck to special classes.

2. Hang name tags on a hook by the door.

3. Make name labels and tape them over coat hooks and/or cubbies.

4. Have a "Weekly Room Helper's Chart." Put children in charge of jobs such as:

   - straightening the books (Librarian)
   - cleaning the sink (Plumber)
   - answering the knock at the door (Host/Hostess)
   - leading the salute to the flag and the song (Director)
   - taking notes to office or another teacher (Messenger)
   - cleaning up special Center areas (Science Director, Writing Director, Math Director, etc.)
   - helpers with snack time (Health Officers)
   - cleaning up the floor—all children should do this at the end of the session, and two can be the General Directors
   - general teacher's helper (Teacher Assistant)

5. The Clothing/Boots/Hats/Mittens area needs to be straightened daily by two general housekeepers before the day begins so that the room looks presentable. (Explain to students that they want to be proud of their room when visitors come.) This area can look like a cyclone struck it, and it takes just a little extra time to clean it up for a pleasant visual environment.

6. Build "clean up time" into the schedule at the end of the session. Don't close the session *on the run*.

7. Always evaluate the day with the children before they go home, and praise them for a job well done and mention things that we'll work on tomorrow.

8. Establish a routine. Children thrive on a schedule.

9. Don't speak when children aren't listening and ready. Wait.

10. Establish a signal for getting the group's attention:
    * turn off the lights
    * clap a pattern with your hands
    * say "freeze" and everyone halts right where they are, like a statue

11. Practice #10 above, in the beginning, even when children are doing well, just so they get the idea of how to respond to your signals. Then praise them.

12. Establish and discuss room rules and consequences for misbehavior.

13. POST room rules and consequences for misbehavior.

14. Keep a large, clear plastic see-through jug on a table or countertop and when students are being good workers, drop a nut (walnut, chestnut) or little pebble inside with much ceremony and praise. When jug is filled, it's time for a treat (food, extra playtime, extra story, a game). Then empty the jug and begin again.

15. Special food treats work well for behavior modification (cookies, popcorn, small candies).

16. Have children practice walking in the classroom—two at a time while the rest observe. This way, they learn the appropriate speed for indoor walking.

17. The teacher is the line-leader down the hall, and in that way controls the speed of the line and can stop at any time.

18. Practice walking in the hall. Keep stopping and starting until they get the message that this is a quiet activity.

19. Each day the teacher can select a different student to be his or her partner as line leader. Be sure to hold hands.

20. Establish good listening habits for story time. Sometimes we read and listen, and sometimes we read and discuss. But, we always listen.

21. Send a child to a nearby seat (behind the audience) during story time if he or she cannot conform to listening standards. That way, the child is away from the group but can still hear the story.

22. Don't give the child more work as punishment, and don't take away the child's play time as punishment. Work with your rules and consequences instead.

23. A special reward that works for a good citizen is being invited to sit at the teacher's desk during snack time, work time, and so on.

24. At the end of work time, place a stuffed toy at the table that had the best workers. The stuffed toy chose to sit there, of course.

25. Give a bookmark as a special reward for good workers. (See the Classroom Management activity pages.)

26. Give a special certificate for good workers (See the Classroom Management activity pages.)

27. Open up Centers gradually, one by one, until students know what is expected of them there.

28. If Center behavior consistently deteriorates (blocks knocked down deliberately, water splashed, and so on), put a "CLOSED" sign in the area for a few days and talk about desired behaviors.

29. Keep the lights off and heads down for a rest when noise level is too high. Tell them, "Noisy boys and girls are tired boys and girls, and your noise is telling me that you're tired and need a nap. So OK, that's what we'll do."

30. Speak with a soft voice and children will usually respond in kind. However, pretend to take a very loud voice out of your pocket and use it, and then put it back—with a dramatic flair. Children don't like the loud voice, and you can assure them that you don't either, so we want to keep it in the pocket.

31. Use puppets to help with classroom management. Puppets can whisper in the teacher's ear, and they can write messages to the class.

32. "Oh, I like the way Antonio is ready!" will cause everyone to turn to look at the ready student and to get ready also.

33. Use the same standards for everyone—no favorites!

34. It's better to be over-planned than under-planned. (If you find that you have "time on your hands," you will need to work on additional circle time activities, additional learning games, or additional alphabet and number activities.)

35. Have a little broom and dustpan handy for clean-up.

36. Use your eyes—look directly at children when speaking to them. Use the "eyes in the back of your head" to ward off potential problems.

37. Use nonverbal communication to send positive and negative messages to the students (a smile, a wink, a nod, a thumb's up sign, a raising of the eyebrows, a finger to the lips for quiet, and so on).

38. Children follow the leader. That's the role of the teacher. If the teacher does not step forward as a strong leader, the children will follow the one who does—and unfortunately, it can be a noisy child who is engaging in acting-out behavior.

39. Keep kitty litter under the sink, and sprinkle it generously if a child has an upset stomach and gets sick. Call the custodian for clean-up.

40. On an especially hot, sunny day, go outdoors and sit under a shady tree and read poetry and picture books. Then, everyone's ready to go back to work again.

41. Often a child who is acting out may be doing it because she or he does not know the boundaries. Take that child aside and make sure there is a common understanding of the rules. Reassure the child that you know she or he can do well.

42. Find something to like and enjoy about each child, and praise it.

43. Tell children when they're doing well. Tell them when they've done well. Tell them if they're not living up to the expectations set forth in the classroom or building goals.

44. The Magic Touch—touch children, hold their hand, smile at them and enjoy them.

45. Keep in mind that the kindergarteners are "works in progress." They're depending on YOU. Have a kind heart and a firm will. Develop patience. Never hold a grudge! Each day is a new day!

Classroom Management Activity Pages

Perkins the Helpful Puppet (*classroom rules*)

Ren Bear's I.D. (*learning vital information*)

The High-Five Award (*certificate for good listeners*)

The Unicorn "Let's Get Along" Chant
  (*problem solving*)

Mr. and Mrs. Fox Go to School (*classroom rules*)

Pretty Kitty; Faithful Dog (*bookmarks*)

Perkins the Helpful Puppet

Color me and cut
me out.

I'll help you learn
what it's all about.

Perkins can help say three of
our classroom rules.

Ren Bear's I.D.

REN BEAR SAYS: Learn your name, address, and phone number.

You can use a stamp pad for your fingerprints.

My Name _____

phone

house number

LEFT

RIGHT

The High-Five Award

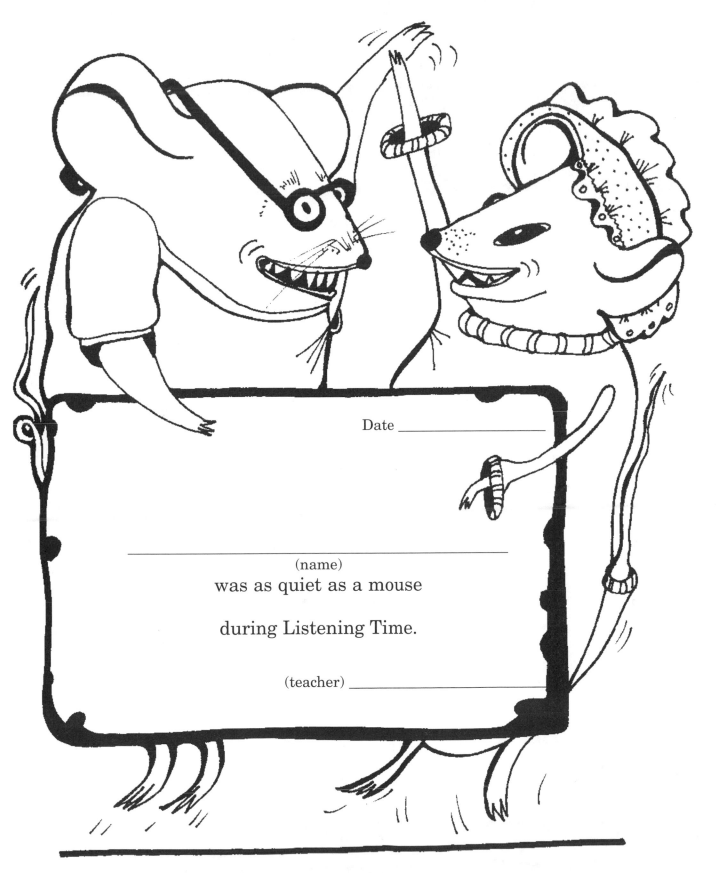

Date _____

_____
(name)

was as quiet as a mouse

during Listening Time.

(teacher) _____

The Unicorn "Let's Get Along" Chant

Learn this chant.
Say it often.

THINK with your head,

FEEL with your heart,

Don't scream and shout,

Let's talk it out.

Name _____

Mr. and Mrs. Fox Go to School

This foxy couple has twins who will both be in kindergarten next year.

They want to know the rules. Can you give them three?

RULES:

1.

2.

3.

Name _____   Name _____

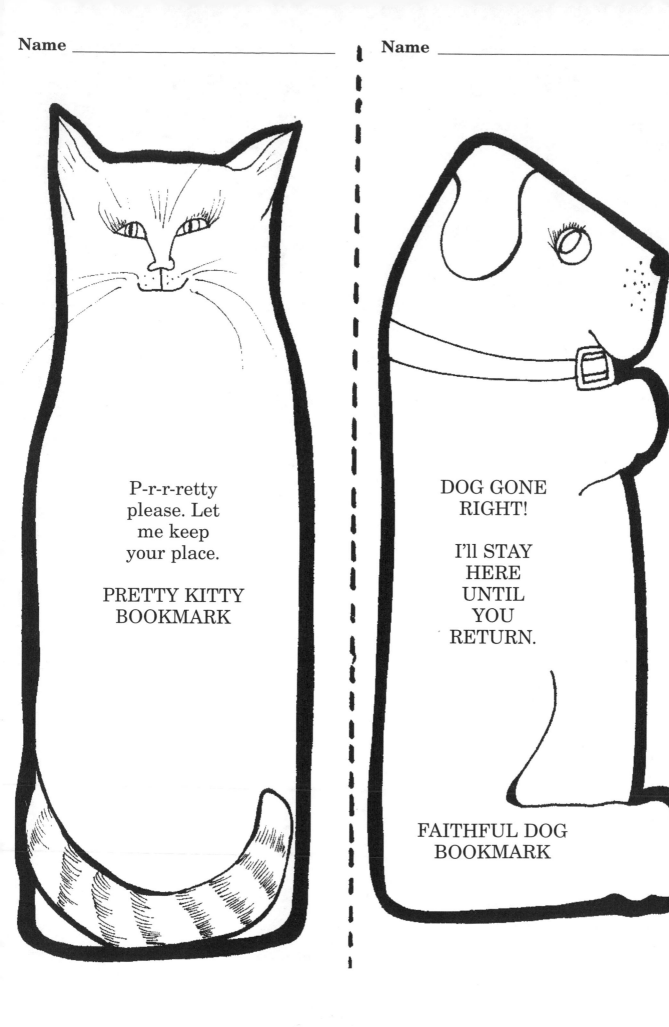

P-r-r-retty
please. Let
me keep
your place.

PRETTY KITTY
BOOKMARK

DOG GONE
RIGHT!

I'll STAY
HERE
UNTIL
YOU
RETURN.

FAITHFUL DOG
BOOKMARK

READING

Mrs. Swingly

Reading

Introduction

In many kindergarten programs, reading is taught in an integrated manner. This means that the four key elements of language arts—reading, writing, speaking, listening—are not divided into components, but, rather, are taught with a *whole language* approach. With this integrated method, you do not always know where one element ends and the other begins. While some of the ideas in this book are integrated, others will be separated so that the *four skill areas* may be emphasized. In addition, *children's literature* will be integrated into the curriculum of study as a way of engaging the imagination of young children and making the reading/writing/speaking/listening and learning connection.

Reading Readiness/Emergent Literacy

What do these two terms mean? *Reading Readiness* is a term that has been around for a long time, and it is applied, literally, to the state of the child's being "ready" to learn to read. That includes such skills as knowing letter–sound relationships, being willing and able to decode new words, and having the ability to make sense from printed symbols. It also implies that a child must achieve a state of physical readiness (e.g., being able to sit still, being able to attend, being able to retain information) before formal instruction can be successful. In other words, formal instruction is made easier once an appropriate level of maturation has been reached.

The term *Emergent Literacy* implies that the child is "already in a state of readiness" for learning, and more informal means need to be used to strengthen a student's growing awareness of the world in terms of language development. Before students enter kindergarten, many have had formal instruction in a preschool setting. Also, during infancy children are surrounded by print in the environment, such as newspapers, magazines, catalogs, billboards, picture books, blinking neon signs, "junque mail" hung on the doorknob, television, cereal box print, soup can labels, and so on. With this abundance of *environmental print*, they have more knowledge about reading and writing than they are given credit for. We need to tap into that knowledge and build upon it. This shifts the emphasis from a deficit approach to one of looking at the child's strengths.

The emergent reader knows what a book is, and how to turn the pages. These children understand what a story is, and can "read" a favorite book from memory, or retell it in their own words.

The beginning reader has already moved to the point of making predictions about story outcomes. They can often identify letters in words, they notice the use of punctuation, and can identify the text and illustrations. They can often fill in missing rhyming words, and know that text is read from left to right and top to bottom.

The process of learning to read is a skill that needs to be developed and rein-forced. It does not magically appear in kindergarten, and we must remember that children are at different stages in their development. So, what works for one, may not work for another. One of the many keys to success is repetition and drill, but that does not automatically mean drudgery. Rather, it means finding many different ways to continually practice the same information. Children are natural mimics and like to memorize letters, numbers, words, and chants. Let's strengthen this skill in kindergarten. Learning to read takes practice, practice, practice.

Kindergarteners need to recognize alphabet letters and say them; they need to "see" letters being written down that form words (an experience chart is an excellent vehicle for this); they need exposure to the world of "words"—poetry can help here, and so can a NEWS OF THE DAY chart that teacher and students do together at the beginning of each day, And they need daily opportunities to listen to stories being read aloud, and enjoyed. They need opportunities to play, to observe and interact with their environment and peers, to create through art, and to talk about what they have experienced. *And they require interaction with an observant, thoughtful, caring, dedicated teacher who is, after all, the key to a successful kindergarten experience.*

What Is a "Print Rich" Environment?

In this setting, there is print everywhere! One glance around the classroom reveals printed material hanging from the ceiling, on the walls, on the door, on charts, in baskets, on posters, on graphs, and so on. Also, there is often a cozy area that has an abundance of colorful picture books, pillows, a big chair or sofa, and a rug. This setting calls out for children to stop by and read.

Also, display colorful picture books on the countertop along the windows, and on a small table so that they are at eye level. When you finish reading a book aloud, add it to this collection so that children can go there and look at it again. Have children select a storybook from this area that they would like to listen to again.

In addition, an area can be set up for writing to take place. This includes paper, felt pens, pencils of different sizes, chalkboards, chalk, and also books that serve as resources. This sends the message to children that print of all kinds is valued and has meaning. Speaking and listening are important in this language-rich environment as well, and will be addressed in detail in those specific sections, but also integrated with the reading section. **It is important that children make the connection between speaking the words, writing the letters that make the words, and then reading the words back again while everyone is listening.**

Reading Activities

Setting Up a Cozy Corner for Reading

Send a message home to parents telling them of your intent to create a cozy corner, a special area for reading, and asking for donations for this area of the classroom. Have them search their basements, garages and storage areas for magazines, a rug, a chair, beanbag chairs, pillows, a table, a lamp, a small clock, a plant—anything that is considered to be of value for this environment. Allow children to go there during free-choice time, so that they can curl up with a good picture book. If you have Big Books available, keep one or two in this area also.

Bring on the Teddy Bears!

Prop up a teddy bear in the Cozy Corner area, along with a book about bears. Invite students to bring in a teddy bear or a stuffed animal for this area. You may want to name your cozy area. Use the opaque projector to make a large cut-out figure of Winnie the Pooh, Paddington Bear, and even other familiar bears, and place them in the corner with a big banner that invites children to read. This cozy spot can also be where the children gather daily on the rug to listen to the teacher read a story or two. Later, a child may be encouraged to snuggle comfortably with a stuffed bear while looking through a book. Invite them to "read" or explain the story to the bear. A rocking chair, along with a number of eye-catching picture books, will help invite children to choose this area during their free time.

Some Favorite Bear Stories

Be sure to include the following books, available from your school or public library:

Where's My Teddy? by Jez Alborough is in rhyme. A boy named Eddie is looking for his teddy in the forest at the same time that a giant-sized real bear is also looking for its teddy. It becomes a delightful turn-about tale when they discover that they have each other's teddy. Children will read this one again and again to any teddy bear that will listen. This is also available as a Big Book.

Blueberries for Sal by Robert McClosky is a good companion book for *Where's My Teddy?* Here we have a similar situation, a parallel plot, with two turn-about tales that delight young children.

This cozy reading area can include several versions of *Goldilocks and the Three Bears*. Along with the whole class, make a comparison chart for the stories, noting similarities and differences in terms of the story and the illustrations. For example, read the traditional tale and then compare it with *Goldilocks and the Three Bears* by James Marshall, a fractured tale. *Deep in the Forest* by Brinton Turkle is another good selection for the bears theme. In this book, a take-off on the three bears tale, the house in which three people live is invaded by a bear. This is a wordless picture book, so children are free to supply their own vocabulary. (See the Writing section.)

The cozy reading area would not be complete without having the teacher read aloud stories from *Winnie-the-Pooh* by A. A. Milne. Perhaps snack time could be referred to as "elevensies" since Pooh always likes to snack, especially if its crackers and honey.

When you invite students to bring in their teddy bears from home, it is because everyone knows that teddy bears enjoy listening to a good story. (Have some extra ones on hand in the classroom.) This can lead to a graphing activity of story books about bears, which may include information about the title, the author, and the illustrator. Also, discuss the following: What is the name of the main character? Where does the story take place (setting)? What does the illustrator show us in one book and not in another? And so on. Write the information with the children, so that they can become familiar with the process of *speaking* the words, *writing* the words, *reading* the words, and *listening* to the words.

The Sign-Up Sheet

Once the Cozy Corner gets under way, post a Sign-up Sheet nearby so that students can sign up to "read" a bear story to a teddy bear, while sitting in a comfortable chair or a rocking chair. Then discuss the books. Ask the children which part of the book *the teddy bear* liked best, which part made *the teddy bear* laugh, which picture *the teddy bear* especially liked. They're really telling us what *they* think and soon the children will be talking naturally about the main idea, the most interesting part of a story, the illustrations, their favorite story and why, and the beginning and the ending.

This can lead to many discussions about the books. Students have been known to say, "When I read *Goldilocks and the Three Bears* to *my* bear, Hollyberry, she liked the part about the broken chair best." Another child may respond by saying, "Well, when I read it to Bradley Bear, he liked it when Goldilocks ran out of the house." Children are learning to talk about information that they acquire from books, and they are talking quite naturally about the main idea of a story, the characters, their favorite part, and so on. Also, they are practicing the art of conversation.

For more bear adventures in picture books, read the fanciful *James Bear and the Goose Gathering* by Jim Latimer, with pictures by Betsy Franco-Feeney; about the bear who cries as he watches a wedding on TV in *The Bear Who Came to Stay* by Allen Woodman and David Kirby, with illustrations by Harvey Stevenson; and *Four Bears in a Box* by Martha Alexander.

Stuffed (But Not Stuffy) Cats, Dogs, and Other Animals

Invite children to bring other stuffed animals into the Cozy Corner for reading. If a student brings in a stuffed cat, for example, it's time to run to the library for *Horace* by Holly Keller, a book about an adopted cat who runs away because he looks different. Also look for *Mrs. Katz and Tush* by Patricia Polacco, an intergenerational, multi-ethnic book about a young African-American boy who suggests to a grieving Jewish widow at holiday time that she needs a companion cat. For a different theme, try *Smoky Night* by Eve Bunting, with illustrations by David Diaz, a book about street riots and a lost cat. Also, *The Three-Legged Cat* by Margaret Mahy, with illustrations by Jonathan Allen First, shows that everyone can fit in someplace. The teacher can read the books aloud to the entire group.

Which Cat Would You Want to Be?

These very different books can lead to meaningful discussions with children about story settings, and which cat they would prefer to be and why. The books could also stimulate children to tell stories about their own pet cats. This can lead to drawing and painting, and an early writing experience where the child dictates a statement about the cat and the teacher writes it down. Or, the child can be encouraged to write the information.

When children share the book with a stuffed animal, they may tell the story, or "read" the pictures, and some may be able to read some of the words.

Going to the Dogs!

Some excellent dog stories that are appreciated by stuffed dogs include: *Dylan's Day Out* by Peter Catalanotto and *The Adventures of Taxi Dog,* a series by Debra and Sal Barracca, with pictures by Mark Buehner. Another favorite is *The Dog Who Had Kittens* by Polly M. Robertus, with illustrations by Janet Stevens.

More Animals!

Some other good animal stories enjoyed by stuffed animals include: *We Hide, You Seek* by Jose Aruego and Ariane Dewey, *Armadillo Rodeo* by Jan Brett, and *A Pocket for Corduroy* by Don Freeman, also available in Spanish, *Un bolsillo para Corduroy*, which can lead to an investigation of what's in everybody's pockets—which can then lead to a discussion of similarities and differences, and to counting, categorizing and graphing information supplied right from our very own pockets. This is a natural integration with mathematics. (See the Bibliography for more animal stories.)

Circle Time Lesson

Make a large monthly calendar and read it every day in terms of the days of the week, the name of the month, and the year. Early in the year, a daily lesson may go something like this:

T: **Who remembers the name of the month?** (Teacher carefully repeats name.) **Let's all say the name of the month together. What letter does it begin with? What sound does that letter make? Who can see something in the room that begins with that same sound? Good.**

T: **Let's read the days of the week on the calendar.** (Point to each name.)

c: **Sunday, Monday, Tuesday, Wednesday,** etc.

T: **Raise your hand if you know what day it is today.** (Establish this.)

T: **If yesterday was the fifth, raise your hand if you know what the date or number is today? What comes after 5?** (Establish this.)

(At this point, the date may be written on the calendar, or it may already be written on a shape, and a child can be asked to identify the numeral six. Then, tack it to the calendar.)

T: **Today is Tuesday, and it begins with the letter T. T sounds like "t,t,t—as in turtle or tooth. Who can think of another word that begins with the "t,t,t" sound?**

Record information daily during Circle Time about the events that will take place during the day. The children benefit from seeing the teacher in the process of writing. The chalkboard may be preferred, or the information can be written on an experience chart. Read it with the class and save the sheets to use as giant worksheets, or for a Big Book record of each week.

A typical day sheet may be as follows:

> Today is Friday. We think it's a cold and windy day.
>
> Elfrida's cat had baby kittens in her closet.
>
> Today we will practice the letter "R."

As the teacher prints this before the group, make comments about the letters. For example:

- **"This letter goes way down into the basement."** (y)
- **"Notice that we have two words alike at the beginning of a sentence."** (Today)
- **"Here's Kyle's favorite letter—he likes 'k.'"**
- **"This word won't fit here, so let's start a new line."**

This helps to keep the attention of the group. At the same time, the teacher is engaged in reading instruction and modeling the writing process.

Classroom Labels

Make labels for items in the classroom, so students will see that print serves a function. Make labels for the door, lights, sink, window, coat rack, cupboard, teacher's desk, rulers, markers, stapler, easel, shelves, plant area, animal area, and so on. Call attention to these labels and to the letters. Occasionally ask children to find a particular letter on the labels (such as an **a** or an **s** when working with special letters). This is a good idea for the child who is having difficulty focusing upon words and letters.

"Follow-Me" Strips

Use blank, horizontal strips made from construction paper and hold them under a line of print when focusing upon material printed on the chalkboard or on the calendar. This helps the children with special needs to focus and attend to the line of print being discussed. Have a supply of "follow-me" strips near the picture book area, so that students can use them for help when focusing upon one line of print at a time.

Name Tags/Name Necklace

Make name tags for the student desks or table area. Also, make a set of name tags with string and store them on a hook by the door. They can be worn as a name necklace when the class goes to special classes such as art, library, and music. A good reading exercise is to hold up each name tag and the person who recognizes his or her name can claim it. This gives practice with name recognition (self and others). It also helps with behavior management, too.

Go on a Ceiling Poetry Walk

Print sentences or phrases of a favorite poem on colorful shapes and hang these from the ceiling. Then, go on a poetry walk around the room, saying (reading) the phrase or the complete poem as you stand or sit under the large shape on which the words are written. Children enjoy the repetition and rhyme of poetry, and silly poems make reading fun. (See the Bibliography for poetry book suggestions.)

Go on an Alphabet Letter Hunt Using Children's Names (and Graph It)

In order for reading to take place, children need a sense of the sound of a letter (letter–sound relationship). Start with the child's name, since many kindergarteners can print or recognize their own name. Make a chart with the alphabet printed along the bottom of the grid. Give each child his or her name printed on oaktag. Take turns having students point to the first letter of their name, and then locate that first letter on the alphabet grid chart. They can place an "X" above the letter with a red crayon. Now we are in the process of creating a graph (numbers) from our reading lesson. When the first letter is completed, examine the chart to determine how many have the letter **A** in their name as the first letter, **B** as the first letter, and so on.

An ABC Bear Book

The picture book *Alphabears* by Kathleen Hague, with illustrations by Michael Hauge, is a helpful teaching aid at this time, since the twenty-six alphabears have a name and a rhyme that tell something about them. Each child can find the name of the bear that begins with his or her own first initial, and get acquainted with that page and that bear. Make bear-shaped name tags and print the name of the alphabear on each. Have students wear them for name tags on a "Teddy Bear Name Day," and call the students by that name (Amanda Bear, Byron Bear, Charles Bear, Devon Bear, etc.). Some children will be ready to learn the rhyme that goes with their letter.

More Activities with Names

- How many students have a name that begins with the same letter? Repeat those names so children can hear the sound. Point to the second letter in their name and have them find that letter on the alphabet chart. Point to the last letter in their name, and have them locate the letter on the chart.

- Have children say their name and find something in the room that begins with that same letter. Say it; write it.

- Have children find the beginning letter of their first name (or last name) in five different places (magazine, room label, book, pamphlet, newspaper, etc.).

- Have children find variations of their first letter—capital, lower case, fancy letter used in advertising, and so on. (You will need magazines, newspapers, "junque" mail.)

- Have all children sit in a circle. The teacher can scatter the student name cards around in the center of the circle. Call upon two or three children at a time to locate their own name, take it back to their spot, and place it on the floor in front of them. The name cards can be collected from the students in alphabetical order.

Be Proud of Your Name

Some children may need to be reminded that a name is special. The book *Chrysanthemum* by Kevin Henkes may be good to read aloud to a class in which there is a variety of unusual names. *A Porcupine Named Fluffy* by Helen Lester is another good read-aloud book about names.

A Great Big Tub for "A Letter a Week"

To emphasize letter–sound relationships, spotlight a "letter of the week." Some good beginning consonant letters are **t, r, b,** and **m.** The following information will help you to set up your letter tub and to provide some potential activities that are meaningful:

- Set up an area for this activity and have a bright plastic tub for the items. A colorful label taped to the side can say, "Rub a dub dub, there are letters in my tub." Then, in a note home to parents, refer to the tub letter of the week and encourage them to send in items that begin with the letter-of-the-week sound. Students can bring in items and deposit them in this tub. This tub may be used during Circle Time on one or two weekdays. Students can handle the items, list them, match them with the written names, and use this tub kit during play time.

  For example: T—toy train, toy truck, towel, tissue

  R—rubber band, ruler, ribbon, raincoat

  B—basket, bowl, bucket, balloon

  M—marble, map, macaroni, mitten

- Select a volunteer each week to paint a large picture at the easel of something that begins with the particular letter. Later, put all the pictures together, label them (laminate, if possible), and bind them to make a giant ABC Book. Students can dictate a sentence for their picture (or print it) and thus become an author as well as an illustrator!

- Bring in newspapers and have students find and circle the letter of the week. Notice its location in the word—beginning, ending, within the word.

"Show-and-Tell Letter Day"

A variation of Show and Tell is to have a "Show-and-Tell Letter Day" when students have to bring in an item to share and name the beginning letter of the item. They should be able to locate the letter in print, or print it on the chalkboard.

Soup's On—Read It and Eat!

Bring in a cooking pot and several cans of the same kind of soup (such as, chicken noodle). Leave the items on the counter for the first half of the week; and encourage children to examine the labels, find letters they know, listen for the sounds. Can they think of other words that begin with those sounds? Later in the week, carefully peel off the labels (save them) and heat the soup and eat it. *Have a conversation about eating all of those good letters and sounds on the label that tell about the soup.* (See Note below.*) Change the soup choice weekly, and discuss the print on the can labels.

When you have done this about five times, make a graph with four different colorful soup labels along the side or bottom. Students can color in the grid space that denotes their very favorite soup. (Some soup favorites are: Vegetable, Chicken with Rice, Chicken Noodle, Alphabet, and Tomato.) This can also be used during a math lesson—counting, addition, more, less, most, more than. Hang the large graph in the room so that children can take a pointer and keep reading the labels, seeing their names, and counting. Children are integrating reading/language arts/math.

Laminate the remaining labels for classifying. Make a storybook about soups.

Yummy—Listen to a Good Soup Story

While children are sipping their soup, there are good soup tales for the teacher to read aloud. Some are as follows: *Stone Soup* by John Warren Stewig, *Tiger Soup: An Anansi Story from Jamaica* by Frances Temple, *Growing Vegetable Soup* by Lois Ehlert, and *Mean Soup* by Betsy Everitt.

***Note:** In Colonial Days at Christmas time, a gingerbread horn was made in the shape of a *horn book,* with the ABC's imprinted on it. The gingerbread was served, and children were encouraged to think of it as "eating the knowledge." We can use this same idea today with soup. (**Source:** Eric Sloan, *ABC Book of Early Americana* [NY: Doubleday, 1963].)

Visual Discrimination with the ABC's

Make a double set of alphabet cards. Line one set up along the chalkboard and *distribute the other set to the students*. Children can match the second set with the first one by following clues given by the teacher.

- Sing the traditional "Alphabet Song." Observe the students and discover who seems to know it well and who will need help learning the song.
- Point to each letter (alphabetical order) and ask, "What is the letter name? What sound does it make? Stand if you have this letter and hold it up for us to see." Then, ask that student to place it in front of the one on the chalkboard. (Later, the order can be mixed.)
- Match cards by verbal clues. (For example: "I'm thinking of the letter that is the *last* letter in the word <u>flag</u>," OR "I'm thinking of the letter that is the *first* letter in the word <u>wink</u>."

Stop, Look and Listen: Visual/Verbal Clues

Make two sets of alphabet cards and place one along the chalkboard. Place the other set underneath it, but not necessarily in order. (For some students, the two sets may need to be in order, however.) For some groups, you may want to use only three letters at a time. Match cards by visual/verbal clues. (For example: "I'm thinking of a letter that is made up of three straight lines, and it flies in the air at the beginning of <u>k</u>ite. The letter is _____.") Next, have the student locate the letter **k** and place the second **k** card in front of the **k** already there. Trace along it with the index finger, while everyone else traces the letter in the air.

The following examples can be used by the teacher with the whole group, using the format "I'm thinking of a letter that has _____. Who am I?" Record it on a cassette tape and students can play this puzzle game during free-choice time. Here are some clues to record and to use with the class in an attempt to add variety, as children identify those mysterious alphabet letters:

- **A** Three straight lines; it flies around in an airplane.
- **B** One straight line and two bumps; it's beautiful like a baby.
- **C** One round line in a half circle; it has claws like a cat.
- **D** One straight line and one round line; it digs in the dirt.
- **E** One straight line top to bottom and three straight lines out to the side like stiff eagle feathers.
- **F** One straight line top to bottom, two straight lines out to the side; it has fins like a fish.

G One curved line and one straight line; it glows like gold.

H Two straight lines from top to bottom and one straight line in the middle; it hikes down the highway.

I One straight line from top to bottom; it's as icy as an icicle.

J One straight line that curves at the bottom; it likes juicy jam.

K One straight line top to bottom and two straight lines that are bent in the middle; it kicks like a kangaroo.

L One straight line top to bottom and one straight line at the bottom; it loves lollipops.

M Four straight lines; two on the ends and a funnel in the middle; it munches on M and M's®.

N Two straight lines from top to bottom and one straight line that connects them at an angle; it's noisy all night.

O One curved line that begins and ends in the same place; it's as round as an orange.

P One straight line and one curved line; it likes to pretend it's a parrot.

Q One curved line that begins and ends in the same place and one straight line that drops out of the bottom; it's as quiet as a quail.

R Two straight lines and a curved line; it likes to run with the rabbits.

S One curvy line that keeps on going; it's as slithery as a snake.

T One straight line top to bottom and one line on top from left to right; it tickles a tiger.

U One curved line that likes to stay under an umbrella.

V Two straight lines that start at the top and meet at the bottom; it has a voice like velvet.

W Four straight lines, like a double V; it is wet like a whale.

X Two straight lines that cross each other; its sound is tricky like a fox. (Sound of "ksss" and "zzzz.")

Y Three straight lines; two join together and one goes straight down; it likes yellow yarn.

Z Three straight zig-zag lines; it makes a sound like a ZAP!

An excellent ABC book that focuses upon the construction and form of each letter is *Ed Emberly's ABC's* by Ed Emberly. This book helps children with the letter formations, as well as the letter–sound relationship. For more help with construction of the letters, you can:

- Use a geoboard and colorful rubber bands so that children can form the letters.

- Use plasticine or playdough so that children can roll out and shape the letters for a hands-on experience.
- Make picture cards for the puzzle game (rebus).

Nibble Your Way Through the Alphabet . . . Like a Mouse

There is nothing quite like food to reinforce learning for the kindergartener. Lois Ehlert's colorful picture book *Eating the Alphabet* will help you to do just that. Make a list of food that could be served for each letter of the alphabet, and then ask for donations from parents, or be on the look-out for sales. Remember, each child does not need to get a whole banana for **b**; a mouse-size sample bite would do, or even a taste of butterscotch pudding made in the classroom with the children. In supermarkets, tiny food samples are often cooked right there and served on the spot. Appeal to the imagination of the children. They will enjoy the alphabet food experience by pretending they are like little mice sampling tiny mouse-size bites, and it won't be costly.

A tiny mousetrap (remove spring) can be set with a morsel of food on ABC food days. And, of course, the mouse is "hooked on the ABC food" that disappears each day . . . perhaps a note is left behind. The mouse always gets the food, learns the letter of the day, but manages not to get caught! To add another dimension to the mysterious ABC mouse, it could leave books to be read aloud to the children. Some good ones to begin with are *Mouse in the House* by Patricia Baehr; *The Mother's Day Mice* by Eve Bunting, with illustrations by Jan Brett; *Whose Mouse Are You?* by Robert Kraus; and *Alexander and the Wind-Up Mouse* by Leo Lionni.

The Alligator Alphabet Tooth Dentist

Make a large green construction paper alligator with a bright red mouth. Cut out 52 triangular teeth shapes. Using a felt-tip marking pen, carefully print each upper-case letter (26) and lower-case letter on a tooth shape. Paste the upper-case letters to the top of the mouth so that they are permanent (flat side of triangle goes up against the gum line). Lower-case letters can be attached to the bottom gum line with Velcro® for easy removal. Students can "take the alli-

gator to the dentist to get his teeth fixed" by matching the upper- and lower-case letters along the gum line. (They are manipulating only the lower-case letters.)

Make a large purple alligator with a bright orange mouth from construction paper. Use the same approach as above, but this time paste the lower-case letters to the bottom of the mouth and use Velcro® for the upper-case gum line. Students can match the teeth by searching for the upper-case letters. (They are manipulating only the upper-case letters.)

Alligator's Toothache, or the Great Alligator Malocclusion

The new vocabulary word, "malocclusion," means improper meeting of the upper and lower teeth, which can result in an underbite or an overbite. Change the alligator teeth so that the upper- and lower-case alphabet letters are deliberately mismatched (an improper meeting). This causes the alligator to have a malocclusion (an opportunity for that new vocabulary word) that results in a bad toothache. It won't go away until the children can take out the mismatched teeth and match them up in the proper order! For a reward from the alli-gator for curing his problem, cut up several apples into small pieces and place them on a serving dish. Both *apple* and *alligator* have the same beginning sound, and the alligator knows that apples make a healthy snack for teeth. A cheerful note from the alligator (written by the teacher) provides a good reading opportunity and a pleasant snack time. The next day, a friendly thank-you note from the Tooth Fairy to the Alligator could mysteriously appear. What does it say? Who can help read it?

Reading While Waiting for the Dentist

Often the dentist's office has magazines and books to be read in the waiting room. Here are some good books about alligators that the alligator would like to hear along with the ABC activities: *Keep Your Mouth Closed, Dear* by Aliki and *Monty* by James Stevenson.

Discovering a Book

The teacher can use a puppet to help children learn how to handle books, and learn which is the front cover and which is the back cover. Children can also learn terms such as "endpapers," "title page," "dedication," and so on. In this case, the hand puppet has discovered a book and doesn't know what it is. The teacher can use the following script to reinforce the information with the students.

PUPPET SCRIPT FOR BOOK DISCOVERY

PUPPET: **Oh, Ms. _____, . . . Ms._____. Look what I found.**

TEACHER: **Do you know what this is?** (Holds up a picture book.)

PUPPET: **Something good to eat?**

TEACHER: **No, it's something good to read. It's called a book.**

PUPPET: **A book? What do you do with it?**

TEACHER: **I'll show you.** (Teacher demonstrates.) **FIRST, you make sure you have clean hands. Check your hands. THEN, you carefully open the cover. THEN, you turn the pages one by one very carefully as you look at the pictures, or read the words on the page.**

PUPPET: **That looks like fun! I can't wait to read a good book.**

(*Note to teacher*: You do not have to be a ventriloquist to use puppets since children usually look at the puppet when it's moving and "talking.")

The Book Poem: A Proper Recipe for Handling a Book

This can be used with the puppet activity. Children can memorize it, learn the finger play, and say it regularly as a reminder of how to handle books. It also serves as a quieting activity for getting ready to read or listen to a story. Try to get a rhythm going, much the same as that in the song "Skip to My Lou."

First you check your clean hands,	
Look, look, look.	(*check hands*)
Then you settle down with a story book.	(*wiggle in seat, hug book*)
Open up the cover carefully.	(*pretend to open the cover*)
Turn the pages slowly—1, 2, 3.	(*pretend to carefully handle pages for 3 turns*)
Now you read the story, are you ready?	(*nod 'yes'*)
Find the very first word.	
Hold the book steady.	(*pretend to grip book firmly*)
Read the printed words from left to right.	(*move head from left to right 3 times*)
You will love to read both day	(*sit cross legged, hands together, ready to listen*)
And night!	

This song can be used at the beginning of storytime to help the children settle down to become good listeners.

Predicting Words

Use the context to help predict words in a sentence. Familiar stories, or sentences like the following where children are given a choice, can be used. You can also use ridiculously "silly words" and regular words.

1. The firefighter ran for a hose and turned on the _____. (**water, umbrella**)
2. "Oh, it's _____. Now I can use my new umbrella." (**raining, snowing**)
3. "Wear your boots so your _____ don't get wet," called Mother. (**fingers, feet**)
4. Check the _____ and see what time it is. (**thermometer, clock**)
5. The iron was too _____ to handle. (**hot, seashells**)

Turn Your Back on the Letters

For a multisensory approach to letter–sound relationships, have children work in pairs. One is the scribe and the other is the book. The scribe uses the index finger to slowly print a letter on the back of the partner. The partner has to guess what the letter is. This is very helpful for children who need extra help with focusing their attention.

Teeth and Claws: Many Clues Mean Accurate Predictions About Words

1. In the following sentence, there can be more than one choice:
   EXAMPLE: Sammy, my cat, has sharp _____. (**teeth, claws**).
2. If we have more information, or clues, our word predictions are more on target. Children need practice with context clues. Here are some helpful ones to get you started. Explain that they are to listen for the "blank" and then see which word makes sense. (**Classroom management hint:** Have them raise index finger if they wish to be called on, rather than having them call out the answer.)
   EXAMPLE: Sammy, my cat, has sharp _____ and scratched Billy with his back paws. (**teeth, claws**)

EXAMPLE: When my cat, Sammy, yawns and opens his mouth wide, you can see his sharp _____. (**teeth, claws**)

Hot/Cold, Shy/Bold

Students need practice with opposites (antonyms). They need to learn simple words with the aid of pictures, and Rebus word cards that they can match. See "Rebus Words" and "Rebus Pictures" reproducible activity pages for cards to reproduce, color, laminate, and cut.

hot	cold
boy	girl
day	night
wet	dry
dark	light
bad	good

Meet Chippy Chipmunk

Draw a picture of a chipmunk on the chalkboard with colored chalk. Print the name Chippy on its T-shirt or hat. In a balloon shape by Chippy, write the letters **ch**. Say the "ch" sound repeatedly with the students, so that they learn it.

Next, start building words in Chippy's balloon bubble that begin with **ch** (chew, chalk, cherry, chocolate).

The word "church" begins and ends with Chippy's sound. (*Teacher note:* "Ch" is a digraph—two letters put together to make a new sound.)

Use picture books to read aloud about chipmunks as you reinforce the *ch* sound. Two good ones are *Chipmunk Song* by Joanne Ryder and *Chipmunk!* by Jessie Haas.

Night Owl Says "Sh" to Chippy

Since Chippy is active during the day and the owl is nocturnal (active at night), the owl is bothered by all of the "ch, ch, ch" sounds, and keeps saying "sh, sh, sh."

Draw a picture of an owl on the board by the chipmunk, and put the letters **sh** in its speech bubble. During playtime, children will enjoy making up stories about these two, and can use the "ch" and "sh" sounds.

Eventually, start looking for words and pictures that begin with the letters "sh" so that the owl can use its sound, and the children can learn the words and letters (for example: shoe, ship, shine, shin, etc.).

The owl may like to have you read aloud some books about owls, such as *Owl Moon* by Jane Yolen and *Good Night, Owl* by Pat Hutchins.

Suzy Wants to Borrow Owl's Shhhhhhhh-ugar

News flash! Did you hear that Suzie borrowed the "sh" sound from the Sugar Owl? Have children be on the alert for this. Make it into a "whisper story," and tell how Susie went to Owl's to borrow some sugar to bake a cake, but Owl was sleeping, so Susie helped herself to the sugar and to the "sh" sound. This can make the word "sugar" tricky. Usually we hear **s** in words like *Suzy, Sunday, silly, six, seven, sand* and *sit*. We hear Owl saying **sh** in words like *shell, shampoo, ship, shine,* and *shore*. (Make a list of words that begin with **sh** and a list that begins with **s**. Then print the word *sugar* off to one side.) Point out to students that we actually say "shuger" even though it looks like "sugar." They will enjoy knowing this little tidbit about Susie and the Sugar Owl, and will learn that the letters are not always consistent in the sounds that they make. **By making the inconsistencies into stories rather than rules, children are more apt to accept them and learn from them.** (Have children be on the alert for any other words that begin with **s** but sound like **sh**.)

Use ABC Picture Books

There is an abundance of beautiful ABC picture books at the library. Borrow enough so that either each child can work with one or that two children can work together. Distribute the ABC books and have the students do the following:

- Say, "Turn to the 'B' page. What is the picture on your page, Margaret? On your page, Brenna? On your page, Zoe?"
- Say, "Turn to the 'S' page. What is the picture on that page?" (Use the same format of calling upon children.)

Children will be successful with this activity because they are locating information that is accurately portrayed on the page, and they have the "right" answer. It gives children an opportunity to hunt through the alphabet, and to determine whether the letter is close to the beginning, the middle, or the ending of the book.

Hunt through the alphabet books periodically for several weeks, making sure that students get a different ABC book each day.

Make an ABC chart for the classroom. Write down the words for the pictures that the students find in the ABC books. Soon there will be a Big Book of ABC's for the classroom. Children can be called upon to do the illustrations for the words. Make bright, beautiful ABC picture books. (See the Bibliography for ABC books.)

Words Are Magnetic!

Have magnetic letters available so that students can use them to create words on the chalkboard. These letters can be used to spell the days of the week. Students can also be helped to notice that "day" is a part of each name (Mon<u>day</u>, Tues<u>day</u>, etc.). Be constantly pointing out patterns to the students.

Chalkboard Artistry

Have a supply of paintbrushes and water cans nearby so that students can practice making their letters on the chalkboard. Dip the brush in water, and practice writing letters or words. This dries quickly and another child can come along and use the brush.

Match a Shape Silhouette

Make a posterboard game by placing common objects on colorful posterboard and tracing their outlines. Use items such as scissors, a computer disk, a pencil, a key, and so on. Place all of the actual items in a ziplock plastic bag. Students can use this as a kit for identifying the shapes, and placing the objects on top of the shapes. This sharpens observation skills needed for distinguishing one letter shape from another.

Matching Items and Using Poetry

Use real items and have children match the things that go together (for example: straw/cup, sock/shoe, stamp/envelope, book/bookmark, pencil/paper). A good rhyming book to use with this activity is *A House Is a House for Me* by Mary Ann Hoberman, illustrated by Betty Fraser. The narrative begins with:

A hill is a house for an ant, an ant
A hive is a house for a bee
A hole is a house for a mole or a mouse
And a house is a house for me.

Soon children get the idea of relationships and start making connections. During playtime especially, they will note that "a box is a house for a teabag" or "a teapot's a house for some tea." During dress-up time, students can be helped to remember that "my coat is a house for my body" and "my hat is a house for my head." The book is a springboard to a discovery of things that go together, or match, and it makes learning fun!

Fun and Learning with Poetry

Be sure to use plenty of poetry in your kindergarten classroom because children enjoy the rhythm and the rhyme. They learn new words that "match" and catch on quickly. *For Laughing Out Loud: Poems to Tickle Your Funnybone* by Jack Prelutsky and *Talking Like the Rain: A First Book of Poems* by Dorothy M. Kennedy and X. J. Kennedy are two good poetry anthologies. Other poetry books include *Fathers, Mothers, Sisters, Brothers: A Collection of Family Poems* by Mary Ann Hoberman; *In for Winter, Out for Spring* by Arnold Adoff; and *One at a Time* by David McCord. Children also enjoy the playful language in *The Cat in the Hat* and *Green Eggs and Ham* by Dr. Suess. (See the Bibliography for more poetry suggestions.)

Stop, Go, Yield

Cut out magazines pictures of highway signs that have messages with print, and some with pictures only (for example: duck crossing showing ducks followed by ducklings). Store these in two sets of envelopes. Children can match the signs that are alike. Use international road signs for this activity, too.

An excellent picture book that will be useful as a teaching tool is *We Read A to Z* by Donald Crews. This book has directional messages, such as "upper right corner" and "bottom," which are very helpful for the beginning reader. (This book is also useful with math concepts and colors.)

Which One Is Different?

Use basic shapes to construct learning boards so that children gain practice selecting the one object in the row that is different (not in compliance).

Use rubber stamps to construct learning boards of items in a row. Children can select the ones that are alike, or the one that doesn't belong. They can use the stamps to make up their own worksheets, too.

Concentration Games

Using a grid, make visual matching games by creating two gameboards that are identical. Then, laminate them both, and cut just one into squares. Store them as a set in a large manila envelope. Children can gain practice matching the items. (Use magazine pictures, rubber stamps, printing.)

Pizza Wheel Word Match

These circular, durable cardboard pieces are handy items for games. Divide one into six or eight sections and print one word in each section. Then, have a set of six or eight clip clothespins with a Rebus symbol printed on it that matches the word. Children can read and clip.

Keep an Author's Journal

Encourage students to write in a journal daily (and illustrate the story or sentence). They can write about their experiences—new baby, new puppy, a funny thing happened on the way to school, new shoes, and so on.

The Book Basket—Emergent Books

Keep a basket filled with books for the emergent readers, for example: *Dear Zoo* by Rod Campbell; *A Very Busy Spider* and *A Very Quiet Cricket* by Eric Carle; *Whose Mouse Are You?* by Robert Kraus, with illustrations by Jose Aruego and Ariane Dewey; *Brown Bear, Brown Bear, What Do You See?* by Bill Martin, Jr., illustrated by Eric Carle; and *Have You Seen My Duckling?* by Nancy Tafuri. (See the Bibliography for more suggestions.)

Who's Here Today?

Make a large Attendance poster from colorful posterboard with each child's name in a row. Hang it by the door. Also, print each child's name on a clip clothespin. When children come into the classroom for the day, they can remember to take their clip clothespin (with their name on it) from a designated spot, and clip it *beside* their name to show that they are present.

For all-day kindergarten, children can place their clip pin on a chart that shows "I brought my lunch," "I'm buying my lunch," or "I'm buying milk only" (or whatever is appropriate for your class).

Hello, What Shape Are You In?

Print a word on the chalkboard and draw an outline around it. Then, call attention to the shape, or *configuration,* of the word. When working with configuration, begin with short words such as *boy* and *girl.* Later, use long names such as *giraffe* and *dinosaur.* This calls attention to the shape of the letters.

Letter Condominiums—Where Do the Letters Live?

Some live on the first floor only, some live on the first floor with a basement, and some live in a condo on the first and second floors.

This information provides essential clues for students—knowing that some letters are lower case (a small box shape) and that they "live on the first floor," (**a, c, e, i, m, n, o, r, s, u, v, w, x, z**). Some letters rent space below the first floor, too, and "have a basement" (**g, j, p, q, y**), and some "live on the first and second floors" (**b, d, f, h, k, l, t**).

Have students categorize the letters by using "basement," "first floor," and "second floor" categories.

Make a chart to show their condos, with the letters inside.

My, What Different Shapes You Have, Grandmother!

Create a game by making two sets of shape words. Print the word on one set, and just make the shape outline of the word on the second set. Students can match the blank shape with the word shape. This game can be placed in a little basket with a red-checkered cloth and called "Red Riding Hood's Basket." It can contain storybook character names such as Red Riding Hood, wolf, grandmother, hunter, basket, ill, forest, bed. Children can retell the popular *Red Riding Hood* story using the story names and shapes. Later, add a set of Rebus pictures or finger puppets of the characters, so that students can match the character with the name.

For a multicultural version of this story, be sure to include the Chinese tale *Lon Po Po* by Ed Young. *Little Red Riding Hood* retold and illustrated by Trina

Schart Hyman is a good European version, and *Red Riding Hood* by James Marshall is a modern version.

Early Reading Story Charts

Children need to practice words repeatedly. A Rebus chart story, resembling the pages of a book, gives them that opportunity. To make one, divide the chart paper into four sections (squares). At the top, print the title "The Birthday Party." Carefully print a sentence from the story in each square (page) and use Rebus picture clues. Using a long pointer, read the story daily. Allow students the opportunity to use this chart and pointer during their free time. Here is the story:

THE BIRTHDAY PARTY

We will have a party with cake.
We will have a party with candles.
We will have a party with ice cream.
We will have a party with presents.
Happy Birthday!

Make a Reading Book

This is a book-making project that can take a week or longer. Use the same story (see previous activity) that was printed on a big chart and used with the entire group. The book will be six pages in length. Use three pieces of 8-1/2" x 11" ditto paper, and draw a line, from right to left, halfway down the page. Print the words so that they will appear *at the bottom* of the half-sheets. Cut them. Give students one page per day and have them draw the accompanying picture. Staple the story pages together when finished. Practice the story together. When children take the book home, they should feel a sense of accomplishment with reading.

More Reading Charts and Reading Books

Students can create their own title for this four-page book, with a folded construction paper cover sheet. Partial drawings can be placed on each page to assist with the illustration, and to serve as a picture clue. (See the reproducible activity pages for an "I Can Read" book in the Writing section.)

TITLE:

By:

I can run.   I can sit.   I can jump.   I can sleep.

The Seven Bears Like Vests

A page of this book can be worked on each day. Students can color the bear's vest (and bear) and trace the color word. Remember, the emphasis is upon the repetition of the words. The color of the bear will serve as a picture clue for the color word when the child "reads" the book. (For variety in illustrations, use a red marker, orange sponge paint, yellow fuzzy material on the yellow bear, construction paper, colored yarn, colored felt, and so on.) (See the reproducible activity pages in the Art section entitled "Teddy Bear Vests, My Book of Colors.")

This bear likes red.
This bear likes orange.
This bear likes yellow.
This bear likes green.
This bear likes blue.
This bear likes purple.

Let's Make Books—Author Corner

Students can be involved in the process of making books by writing, illustrating, and preparing covers. They can use their knowledge of books to create their own. Who is the story about? What experience does the child want to record? Encourage the child to design colorful endpapers to lead up to the story, and have a sample of picture books with colorful endpapers to serve as examples.

Old MacDonald's Pocket Full of Rhymes

Make a farmer figure for the bulletin board at eye-level, and staple an old pair of real dungarees onto it. Or, just hang old MacDonald's jeans to a clothesline strung up in the corner. Cut the inside seam of each pocket and sew a pillowcase inside for a deep, *deep* pocket. Give the two front pockets an exaggerated look on the outside by outlining them with bulky yarn (glue it on). Place three items in the left pocket and three items in the right pocket. Use actual items, or magazine pictures, photographs, or a combination thereof. Make sure that each item in the left pocket has an item in the right pocket with which it rhymes. Students need repeated practice in hunting for words that rhyme. Here are some ideas for items to get you started:

Pocket One	*Pocket Two*
cat (*toy*)	hat (*real*)
pan (*real*)	man (*photo*)
fork (*real*)	cork (*real*)
pen (*real*)	hen (*toy*)
soap (*real*)	rope (*real*)
lamp (*picture*)	stamp (*real*)

For variety with rhyming and repetition, try using phrases written on bright, colorful shapes. You may choose to use Rebus picture clues as well. Here are some to get you started:

See the mitten	See the kitten
Here's the dog	Here's the log
There's the bat	There's the rat

For variety with word order, make two identical flash cards using the same sentence. Have a complete sentence flash card in one pocket. In the second pocket, place the identical sentence that has been cut up into words and phrases. It's there, but students have to find it and match it.

Make a Colorful ABC Sampler

Use a large piece of burlap and print the alphabet letters on it with a black felt-tipped pen. Hang it at eye-level, and let children sew over the black lines.

Use *plastic needles* and colorful yarn. (Observe good rules with the needles, having no more than two students working on the sampler at one time.) Later, hang it up in the room. Children can trace over the letters with their fingertips and compare their letters with ones they find in books. This is a good activity for the kinesthetic learner.

Tips for Putting Zip in Storytelling and Reading Aloud

Storytime is a special time because the teacher and the group are working as a unit—laughing, smiling, nodding, and licking their lips right along with the fox who's after the hen and shuddering with the hen who's afraid of the fox. The teacher needs to enjoy the story as much as the students, and needs to make it come to life for them.

Storytelling can take place with a flannel board and cut-outs, without the aid of the book. Children can retell stories they have heard, using the flannel board. With the wide variety of picture books available today, story time is not only rich with words, but also rich with beautiful art work in a variety of media. Some tips for reading time are:

- Keep the length of the story within the students' attention span.
- If interest begins to lag, shorten the story or finish it another time.
- Read the story. Don't "over-discuss" it the first time around.
- Keep student interruptions to a minimum. It's time for story listening now, and talking about it later.
- Wait until everyone is quiet and ready before beginning.
- Make sure everyone can see the pictures you hold up.
- Know the story, if possible.
- Record yourself on tape so that you can listen later and make adjustments in your pitch, inflection, pronunciation, rate of speed.
- Record the story so that children can enjoy it repeatedly, and "read along" with a copy of the picture book.
- Use eye contact with the children.
- Develop mobile facial expressions that help make the book come to life (a mouth dropped open with surprise, eyes wide with wonder or apprehension, etc.).

A Tisket, a Tasket, a Little Story Basket

For variety, read or tell a story using props. Have a wicker basket with a cover, and appropriate props inside to go along with the story that you decide to read or tell. Then, leave the story basket out for a few days so that students can retell the story. Remove the props from the basket, and prepare another story basket with appropriate props. Soon, students will catch onto the idea that the appearance of the story basket means a pleasant adventure with books.

Dealing with Special Needs

Observe these children closely and capitalize upon their strengths. Perhaps one child has strength in verbal communication, and another with ideas to add to a webbing activity. If so, make sure that the children receive praise and feel good about what they *can* do.

Working in groups can help these children because then an individual contribution is not so noticeable. They are able to pick up important information from other group members.

Strengthening Memory

Give all children, and especially those with this specific need, an opportunity to strengthen their memory span. Give verbal directions that become increasingly complex. For example:

- "Go to the countertop and bring back the blue book."
- "Go to the countertop and get the blue book. Then put it in the Cozy Reading Corner."
- "Go to the second shelf under the window, find the paste, and put it next to the sink."

The Memory Tray

Put five or six items on a tray. Hold the tray so that the children can get a good look at it. Then put a cloth over the tray. How many items can they name?

Again put five or six items on a tray. Have children look at them, and then instruct them to close their eyes and try to visualize them. Then, have them open their eyes again to see the items, then close again, to visualize them. Then name them. With repetition, students get better at doing this, and it increases attention span.

Take one item off the tray and have students name the missing item. As a challenge, take more than one item off the tray. Make sure this activity does not become frustrating for some students.

These memory activities can be done in a small group with two or three students. Gradually increase the number of items on the tray.

Also, leave the Memory Tray out for a few days and let children choose this as a free-choice activity, so they can work on strengthening their memory skills and be "playing a game" at the same time.

Teach It, Learn It

Sometimes children with a short attention span will pay more attention if they have to impart the information to someone else. Pair a special-needs child with a child who can teach a task, but put them both in charge of explaining it to another student.

English as a Second Language

Honor the first language of the child, but recognize that in order for the child to achieve, the second language needs to be mastered. Activities that will help the child include storybooks, poetry, picture–word cards, computer games with pictures and print, and listening to taped directions. Also, this child needs to be included in all activities. Find something in which this child excels and praise the child for all to hear.

Studies indicate that second-language learners benefit from watching television commercials; it's all there—words, pictures, repetition, and sometimes a catchy rhythm or rhyme. This may be useful information for the parent at conference time.

Mary Knows a Letter Sound

This is sung to the tune "Mary Had a Little Lamb." First, the teacher is the singer. As the children become familiar with the activity, then they can sing along.

Mary knows a letter sound,
Letter sound,
Letter sound.
Mary knows a letter sound.
What sound does she hear?

SAY: more   maybe   mouse   (*teacher says the words*)

SAY: more   maybe   mouse   (*children repeat the words*)

SAY: THE LETTER IS _____.   (*children say it*)

Mary hears the letter "m,"
M, M, M,
M, M, M.
Mary hears the letter "m,"
more, maybe, mouse.

(all sing and clap)

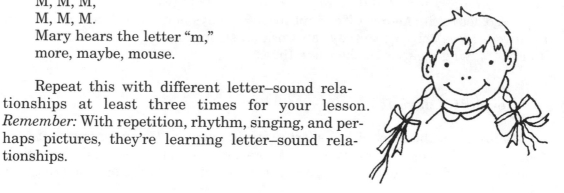

Repeat this with different letter–sound relationships at least three times for your lesson. *Remember:* With repetition, rhythm, singing, and perhaps pictures, they're learning letter–sound relationships.

Reading/Writing/Speaking/Listening Survival Tips

Some New, Some Review

Although these subjects are referred to as Language Arts, in this text they are addressed separately in an effort to focus upon each one. Throughout the book they are often intertwined in the subject matter areas, since they have been referred to as the "glue" that holds the curriculum together.

1. Children need to know the alphabet, and the sound/symbol relationships, or reading will not take place.

2. Practice letter–sound relationships daily. Make a game of it.

3. Children learn television commercials because they are repetitious, short, and often sung. Let's take a cue from this.

4. Read aloud to children every day. You are modeling the language and enriching their vocabulary. Poetry works well for rhyming sounds.

5. Encourage parents to take children to Story Hour at the local library, and to get a library card and books for their child.

6. Have jigsaw puzzles in the classroom for children to use. The experience with shapes helps them to notice curves and straight lines that will be helpful in distinguishing letter shapes.

7. Small motor coordination is just being developed, so it's difficult for children to stay within lines. For variation, they can practice making letters at the chalkboard (with chalk or with a brush and water) or form them with clay.

8. Have rules for listening. Don't speak until everyone is quiet.

9. Have a signal for quiet listening—lights out, clapping a pattern.

10. Give children opportunities to speak to the group. *Show and Tell* is the original oral report.

11. Provide listening opportunities—music, sounds, stories, bells.

12. Don't get caught up in the "Phonics vs. Whole Language" debate. It's simply not an either/or issue. Children need a wide variety of skills.

13. Have many print samples in the classroom—newspapers, magazines, picture books, pamphlets, menus, and so on.

14. Make sure to have paper and pencil available in the Housekeeping Area so that students can use them during role play when talking on the telephone.

15. Show a story video with the sound on mute, and have students talk about the story message. Then listen to it.

16. Remember that wordless picture books invite children to create the story with language in their own words.

17. Engage in partner–reading with picture books. That is, have two students look through a book together and talk about it.

18. Invite children to bring stuffed toys into the classroom and prop them up in your reading area. Children can "read" to them.

19. Have a variety of colored pencils in your writing area.

20. Set up a listening center in the classroom so children can listen to a story and look at the text simultaneously.

21. Record directions on cassette tapes and have children listen to them. This is especially helpful for the child who needs help with listening.

22. "I like the way Muchtar is listening," causes everyone to look his way and imitate his behavior.

23. Communicate with students via puppets—they can whisper in your ear, they can write notes, and they can talk out loud. (Children are usually watching the puppet rather than you.)

24. Collect a basket full of "junque" mail and have students use it. They can circle letters, words, and cut out pictures for letter–sound relationships.

25. Have a Letter-of-the-Week and create activities around it, such as a food treat that begins with that letter, a storybook title that begins with that letter, or a box of items that begin with that letter.

26. Locate another kindergarten classroom in your school district or a neighboring one, where the teacher is willing to correspond with your class. Write letters on experience chart paper.

27. Do not correct a child's speech. For example, if a child says, "I like basketti for lunch," model the word by replying, "Yes, spaghetti is tasty."

28. Write a newsletter to parents at least bi-monthly indicating what you are studying, what areas of focus are coming up, what you need for the classroom. Save space for the "Artist of the Day" to draw something and you can print underneath it (or have the child print) a sentence about it.

29. Have children type their stories on the typewriter or on the computer.

30. Go to the public library frequently on your way home. Bring in several ABC picture books each time, along with other picture books.

31. During outdoor recess, children can bounce a ball while reciting the alphabet to see how far they can go. Also, "jump the alphabet" with a jump rope.

32. Have each child print his or her name at the beginning of each month and save it in their portfolio. You will have a record of their handwriting progress throughout the school year.

33. Children need a sense of story before they can write one.

34. Go slowly. Reading, for some, is a long journey and for others it's a short trip. Either way, make it pleasant.

READING ACTIVITY PAGES

(Some activities may also be used for writing, speaking, or listening.)

Words That Rhyme (*sound identification*)

ABC Tiny Book (*reading; writing*)

    Capital Letters/Lower-Case Letters

    A, B, C, D

    E, F, G, H

    I, J, K, L

    M, N, O, P

    Q, R, S, T

    U, V, W, X

    Y, Z, and Title Page

Long Vowel Flash Cards

Short Vowel Flash Cards

Migrate to a Good Book; Hibernate Here (*bookmarks*)

Rebus Pictures (*making sentences*)

Rebus Words (*flash cards*)

Goldilocks, Snow White, Red Riding Hood (*reading; graphing*)

Which Story Guy Gets Your Vote? (*reading; graphing*)

Words That Rhyme

Look at the item on the left. Say it. Then name each item on the same line. If it rhymes, draw a circle around it. If it does not rhyme, put an X on it.

ABC Tiny Book

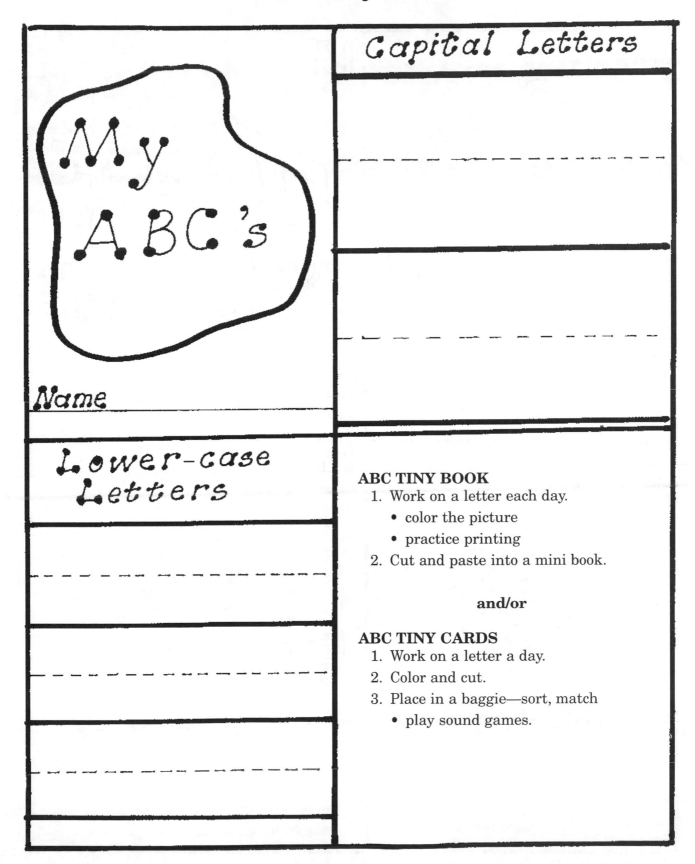

My
A B C 's

Name _____

Capital Letters

Lower-case Letters

ABC TINY BOOK
1. Work on a letter each day.
   - color the picture
   - practice printing
2. Cut and paste into a mini book.

and/or

ABC TINY CARDS
1. Work on a letter a day.
2. Color and cut.
3. Place in a baggie—sort, match
   - play sound games.

ABC Tiny Book

ABC Tiny Book

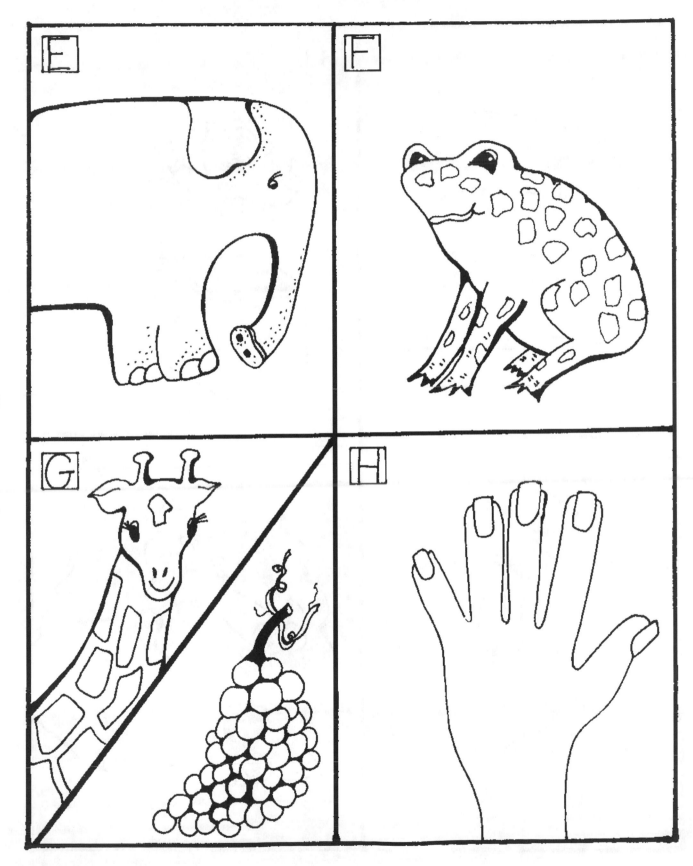

ABC Tiny Book

ABC Tiny Book

ABC Tiny Book

ABC Tiny Book

x-ray

ABC Tiny Book

Y

Z

My
ABC
Book

Name _____

My
ABC
Cards

Name _____

Long Vowel Flash Cards

It's time to practice vowels and their LONG sound. Look at each picture, say what it is, and listen for the beginning sound. Can you hear it? Color the pictures. Cut them into cards. Mix them up, turn them upside down. Turn them over one by one and say the name of the item and the sound. You can do this with a friend, too.

    THIS WILL HELP YOU WITH YOUR BEGINNING READING.

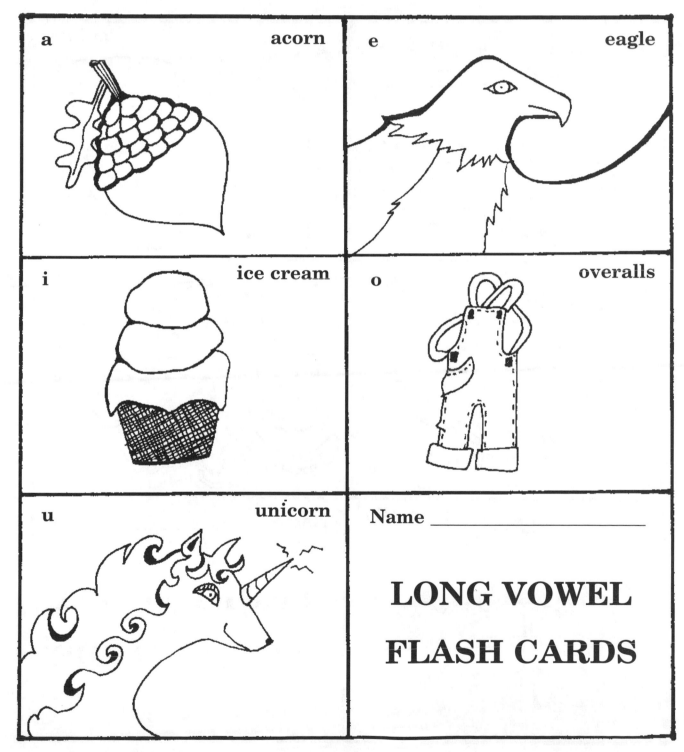

a   acorn

e   eagle

i   ice cream

o   overalls

u   unicorn

Name _____

LONG VOWEL

FLASH CARDS

Short Vowel Flash Cards

Now that you know about vowels and their special sounds, you can practice. Look at each picture, say what it is, and listen for the beginning sound. Can you hear it? Color each picture. Cut them into cards. Turn them upside down. Then, turn them over one by one and say the name of the item and listen for the beginning sound. Say it. You can work with a friend.
YOU CAN USE YOUR LONG AND SHORT VOWEL CARDS FOR A MATCHING GAME.

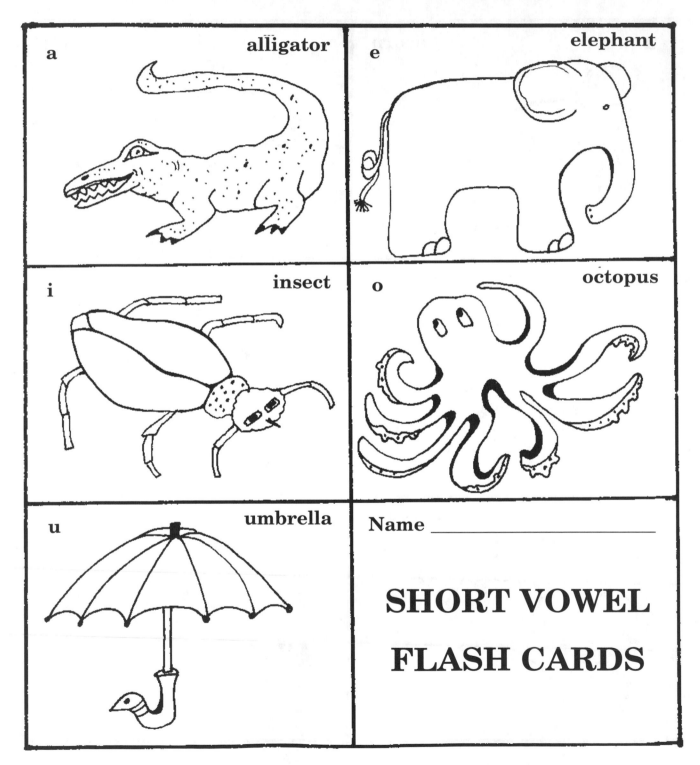

a   alligator

e   elephant

i   insect

o   octopus

u   umbrella

Name _____

SHORT VOWEL FLASH CARDS

My Name _____   My Name _____

cut

Migrate To A Good Book

Hibernate Here

Rebus Pictures

Identify the pictures. Color them. Cut them apart on the black lines. Use them with the Rebus Words to make up sentences. Read the sentence aloud. Can you print it, too?

Work with a partner and read your sentences to each other. Write them together. Keep your pictures and words together in a little envelope with your name on it.

Rebus Words

Rebus sentences contain both words and pictures. The words below can help you. Practice reading them. Cut them apart on the black lines. Use the words and pictures from the Rebus Pictures page to arrange the picture and word cards in a row. Make a sentence, then make more. Can you write them? (You can make nonsense sentences, too.)

the	on	up	down
and	she	he	it
I	to	an	in
boy	girl	me	you

Name _____

Goldilocks, Snow White, Red Riding Hood

Make a folktale graph of your favorite female character. Neatly color the square above your choice. THEN, ask five classmates to do the same. Compare your graphs in class.

SQUARE COLORS: Goldilocks = yellow, Snow White = blue, Red Riding Hood = red

Which Story Guy Gets Your Vote?

Conduct a survey. Ask 7 people to vote for their favorite character. Put an X in the space above the character. YOU CAN VOTE, TOO. Then add up the totals. Compare graphs with other classmates. Can you retell the three stories?

total:	total:	total:

Jack and the Beanstalk   **Beauty and the Beast**   **Cinderella**

WRITING

Mrs. Meulendyke

Writing

Introduction

Reading and writing are bound together. Children *read* what they write, and *write* what they will eventually read.

Many kindergarteners come to school with the capability of printing their name, usually in solid capital letters. Some come having already learned to write the alphabet or to use "invented spelling" . . . some come and enjoy the process of scribbling . . . and some have not had the experience of holding a pencil, crayon, piece of chalk, or a felt-tip pen in their hand. In other words, they are in varied stages of development in terms of being able to grasp an object and to make marks with it on a piece of paper.

Girls are usually more advanced in terms of *small* motor coordination, which gives them the ability to grasp a pencil and crayon with relative ease, and to control the small muscles in their hands when crayoning and using a felt-tipped pen. Many boys are still trying to gain mastery over small muscle coordination.

Therefore, it is not unusual for girls to sit still and work with their hands on activities that involve printing with a pencil or some other object, or stringing beads, or working on a lacing board. Boys normally develop small muscle control later than girls, so grasping a big brush and painting with broad strokes at the easel is easier for them to master than trying to use a pencil and to stay between the lines on writing paper. Boys, however, are often ahead of girls in terms of *gross* motor development (sweeping arm movements, throwing, jumping, running). That is why boys are more apt to select activities that involve physical action of their whole body.

However, there is a need for both quiet activities and action-packed movement, so writing needs to be made into an inviting and ongoing activity in the kindergarten setting.

Writing Activities

Set Up an Inviting Center for Writing

Set aside an area for writing in the kindergarten. Make sure it is in an area of the room that is adjacent to quiet activities, rather than by the noisy building block area. The writing area needs to be made attractive in terms of color and supplies. Materials can be placed in bright plastic containers, little buckets, baskets, pots and pans, or a metal teakettle. Also, materials can be added and taken away at various times throughout the month or year to help maintain student interest.

Some materials to have available include:

- felt-tip markers in a variety of colors
- felt-tip markers in a variety of widths
- crayons, both thick and thin
- colored pencils
- colored chalk
- individual chalkboards
- paper in different sizes, and some plain and some with lines
- paper in different colors
- paper cut into shapes that invite writing (triangle, cat, dog, rabbit)
- paper with different textures
- old envelopes
- lacing boards
- string and beads of different sizes
- ink pads
- stamps for the ink pads
- magazines
- newspapers
- children's picture books
- "junque" mail
- postcards
- activity pages
- rural mailbox
- city mailbox
- playdough (for forming letters)
- alphabet strips
- word cards (key words)
- stationery with colorful borders

Perhaps you can contact local businesses for help in obtaining some of these supplies.

Picture Books Invite Student Writing

Children may be motivated to write especially when they see that characters in picture books send and receive letters. *The Jolly Postman or Other People's Letters* and *The Jolly Christmas Postman* by Janet and Allan Ahlberg are two especially inviting books. Children can open the books and find envelope pages that house a variety of types of letters and envelopes (party invitation, catalog, formal letter, postcard, air mail envelope, and so on). They, too, can write a letter to a fairy tale character.

Another delightful book along this same line is *Letters from Felix, A Little Rabbit on a World Tour* by Annette Langen, with illustrations by Constanza Droop. The pages are done in envelope style that show the front with an address and colorful stamps. Turn the page and reach inside for a letter from Felix from London, England; Paris, France; Rome, Italy; Cairo, Egypt; Kenya, Africa; and New York, USA. The book also includes a suitcase on the last page with a flap that can be opened. Inside are six colorful shaped logos that represent the places Felix visited. The endpapers have a colorful map to "read" so that the route of Felix can be traced. Hmm . . . this may give the class some ideas!

Send Your Own Stuffed Animal on a Real Letter-Writing Adventure

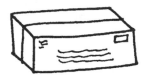

Many teachers have reported success with the following stuffed animal activity, which generates interest in both writing and reading letters, in sending and receiving mail, and in postage stamps. The activity gives purpose to "reading" a map.

Send a stuffed animal (named by the students) with a letter (composed as a total class activity) to someone the teacher or parent knows in another city—someone willing to get the project rolling. In the letter, do the following: (**1**) Tell something about the class (how many boys, how many girls, the name of the school, what the students like to learn about). Also include something special from your city or school—a city map, a logo, a pencil, postcard, and so on. (**2**) Ask that the recipient respond with a letter to the class telling something about themselves, and where their stuffed animal wound up. Ask if they can include some token that represents their particular city (newspaper, flyer, map, photo of a special monument or bridge, postcard, a library bookmark, and so on). Also, find out where they could take the stuffed animal in their fair city (what events are going on—such as the circus, ice show, special sports event, theatre) and what the stuffed animal "saw" while in their city (bridge, statue, commuter train, university). Finally, (**3**) where they sent the stuffed animal on its journey.

> **Note:** *The box should contain a general note from the teacher telling the purpose of this exercise, and asking that the stuffed animal (bear, rabbit, duck, mouse) be returned to the class by a certain date. Glue this to the inside cover, and make sure the return address is in full view.*

If everyone follows through along the way, this can turn out to be an excellent learning experience for the students as "real" letters keep coming into the classroom telling about the adventures of the stuffed animal. Even if two kindergartens (side by side) do this activity, it will be different because the people sending/receiving the letters will not be the same. Imagine the surprise of the students if the stuffed animal does get to fly in an airplane to a foreign country! Now they can learn about air mail with its special envelopes, thinner paper, and foreign stamps. They can look for the special location on a map or globe, too.

It's risky if only one animal is sent on its way, so some classes send at least two, if not three, as a starting point for their writing adventure.

Making Logos

Introduce the term "logo." Teams have a logo, a store has a logo, sporting goods have a logo, and so on. *It is a form of environmental print with which children are familiar and to which they have been exposed since infancy.* A logo communicates information. Go on a logo hunt through mail order catalogs, the newspaper, "junque" mail, and magazines. Children can design and make their own logos.

Writing on Shapes and Textures

Cut up construction paper or unlined paper into shapes such as a rabbit shape, a cat shape, or a duck shape and have students write on the shapes. The shapes invite the student to write *to* a storybook character, or *about* a particular animal, or even a special pet. Some children may scribble, some may invent spelling, some may ask how to form letters or how to spell words. This is an informal time to work with print.

On a rainy day, set out paper that has been cut into an umbrella shape. Prepare in advance for sunny-day paper (large yellow circles), snowy-day paper (snowman shape, or top hat shape, or triangular carrot nose). Cut up rough brown paper grocery bags and have students write on the blank inside space on days when there are mud puddles and muddy shoes.

Write the Ending

Read a picture book to students—right up to the last page. Then, have students draw the ending. Next, have them write (or dictate) the text that would complete the story. Then, compare their endings and listen to the author's ending. This helps children bring closure to their own writing.

Chalk the Talk

Have several kits that include a small chalkboard, chalk, and an eraser, and place them in individual ziplock plastic bags. Students can practice writing by using these materials. They can copy information from labels in the classroom, from storybooks, from word lists, or they can practice writing informally in a variety of ways.

Alphabet Line

Make an ABC line, similar to a number line, and have it prominently displayed at the Writing Area.

Sandpaper Letters

Cut out ABC's from sandpaper and paste them on heavy oaktag. Many students with special needs benefit from running their index finger over the letter to "feel" its shape. Match upper- and lower-case letter cards this way.

Children can work in pairs to "feel a letter shape." With eyes closed, they can trace the shape and guess what the letter is.

Follow the Train Track

Make a variety of line segments (- - - - -) on one 8-1/2" x 11" sheet of paper. Label straight lines as "Track 1," and curvy lines as "Track 2," and so on. Laminate them. Then have students trace over the line with a light colored water-base pen, which can be washed away. Many students need the practice with the left to right motion; this also strengthens their eye-hand coordination.

The teacher can make a variety of these pages from Track 1 through Track 10 for practice. (See "Make a Bee Line for the Honey" and "Marty Mouse Finds a Pencil" reproducible activity pages.)

Lights Out! Flash On!

For students who are having a great deal of difficulty with the concept of moving from left to right, and staying on a line, try the following activity. Draw a wiggly line on the chalkboard from left to right. Turn out the lights. Turn on a flashlight. Have one student at a time "trace" the line with the flashlight, trying to stay on track. Some students will need repeated practice with this activity.

The Chef Is Baking Letters

From a large white sheet of paper, make a cylinder for a chef's hat band and staple the ends together. Then, staple tissue paper in the top for a puffy, bouffant look. Obtain a cookie sheet and a supply of plasticene. Students can wear the chef's hat and roll out letters using coils of dough, plasticene, or play-dough. Then, have them create letters and words with the coils. They can roll out their first name. They can try rolling out their telephone number, too. This is good practice for letter formation, using something other than a pencil or felt-tip pen.

The Chef Is Taking Letter Orders

Some students may be able to create letters and words, and really enjoy playing chef. For these students, a more challenging activity would be to have "customer order cards" available. Each card can have a variety of orders, such as:

Order #1	Order #2
1—A	5—O
2—p	1—R
3—z	4—n

For this activity, have some blank "customer order cards" available, so that students can create the orders (using pencil) and fill the orders (using dough).

Show-and-Tell Draw and Write

Have students write the story that they told today during "Show and Tell." Have them draw an illustration for it.

Name Practice Cards

Write each child's name on writing paper and laminate it. Then, children can find their name paper, and practice writing their name again and again on the lines underneath the sample. Use a water-base pen, and wash it off for another day, another try.

Laminated Newspaper Pages

Laminate pages from the newspaper, and have children use the page by circling all of the letters they know, or all of the words that begin with a certain letter, or end with a certain letter, and so on. Use a water-base pen, and wash off the page for other exercises.

Also, take apart old magazine pages and laminate them so that children can print on them with water-base pens and work the dot-to-dot puzzles, trace large letters or animals or birds, and so on.

Rural Route for Writing

Encourage students to place their envelopes (with hand-drawn stamp, or rubber stamp) in the rural route mailbox that you have made available in the writing station. They can write to make-believe storybook characters, or to puppets in the room—and on some days there may be mail *in* the box for them.

The Post Office

Set up a post office in the classroom. Large milk containers or shoe boxes can be covered with prepasted paper and bound together, or large cylindrical coffee cans can be spray painted and glued together. Each child's name can appear on the front of the opening.

Notices that are to go home can be placed in these boxes and students can be directed to check their mailbox daily for messages and papers that can be sent home.

The Portable Mailbox

Secure an old lunch box (garage sales are good places to find them). Paint it red, white, and blue with stars and stripes. Inside, place paper, two felt pens, three colored pencils, two regular pencils, and a big eraser. This mailbox can go home overnight (or over the weekend) with a student whose name is drawn out of a mail bag by a puppet. The teacher can have a conference with the student who returns the mailbox, and talk about the writing that took place at home, or perhaps it can be shared with all during Circle Time.

What Is a "Sense of Story" and Where Do You Get It?

Children are said to have a "sense of story" when they can recognize there is a beginning, a middle, and an ending to a tale. There are so many lovely picture books available today that children can begin to get a "sense of story" by being read to, again and again. This helps them with their own writing of stories.

A teacher can help children to "get it" by doing some of these reinforcement activities after the book has been enjoyed. Do not do the following steps with every book you read. For some books, you may want to focus upon just the beginning, or just the ending words, or all of the things that happened in the middle. By engaging in conversation *about* the book, you are helping children build a sense of story.

1. When the story is finished, go back to the *beginning* and take another look at the words the author used to begin the story (Once upon a time, One fine day, In a little house in the woods, etc.).

2. Discuss the *ending*. It means the story is finished, over, done. What is the very last sentence. Was it a happy ending? Did students like the ending? Could there have been a different ending?

3. What's in the *middle*? These are the things that happen in a story. Go back over a picture book, page by page, and talk about what happened first, then next, and then next, and then next . . . until you get right up to the ending.

When children have a sense of story, it will be evident in their own writing.

Rope Off a Story

When writing an experience chart story, take brightly colored loopy yarn and tape it all around the edge of the words that form the beginning, and then the ending. Everything else is the middle. This helps the visual learners.

Build the Story Burger

Make a huge burger shape from construction paper for the bulletin board, or place it on a big chart. Have a tan puffy bun shape at the top (beginning), and another tan puffy bun shape at the bottom (ending). Leave a big empty space for the burger (middle) or the part in-between:

- One sentence can be put on a leafy green strip (lettuce).
- Another sentence can be put on a red strip (tomato).
- Another sentence can be put on a yellow strip (cheese).

- Another sentence can be put on a brown strip (burger).

This way, children are "building a story," sequentially, and it will help them when they start to write their own.

Children can make their own individual, colorful burger stories.

My Very Own Journal

Children do not automatically know what a "journal" is, and so it must be explained, modeled, and practiced together before they can be expected to go off on their own and have success with their very own journal.

A journal is a chronicle of events, and that is one place to begin with the kindergarteners rather than telling them to "just write" in their journal, as they stare at the blank page. *Just write what?*

It is helpful to keep a class journal for one week on large chart paper that has been stapled together, or in a Big Book with blank pages. This can be done during Circle Time. Talk about the events that took place yesterday in class and review them. (We had a fire drill. We played on the swings. The principal read to our class. Alfonso's mother brought in a birthday treat, etc.)

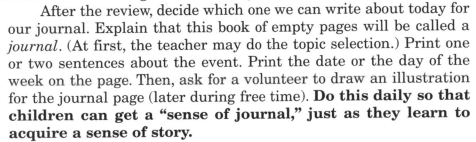

After the review, decide which one we can write about today for our journal. Explain that this book of empty pages will be called a *journal*. (At first, the teacher may do the topic selection.) Print one or two sentences about the event. Print the date or the day of the week on the page. Then, ask for a volunteer to draw an illustration for the journal page (later during free time). **Do this daily so that children can get a "sense of journal," just as they learn to acquire a sense of story.**

Upkeep

Continually refresh the labels in the classroom with varying shapes and colors. (Upper-grade teacher-helpers can assist you with this.) Sometimes a child from the classroom can be asked to "copy" a label and then that can replace the one that has become dog-eared. Also, keep changing the art work, graphs, work on display, bulletin boards, etc., to maintain a high interest level.

Puppets Like to Write and Leave Notes

This idea was referred to in the Reading section. For writing, children can focus upon *how* the puppet wrote the words. If the puppet wrote a message to the class and it just contained one word, what does that mean? Here we get into interpretation of the written message.

Thank-You Notes

Get the class into the habit of writing thank-you notes to those in the school community, or to a classmate, or to a room mother. Depending upon the level of the writing development, sometimes the class may dictate a message to the teacher who prints it, and then the students can all print their names at the end.

This models for them the position of information on the page, such as the date, the greeting, the body of the message, the ending, and the signatures.

Sometimes it is fun to write the thank-you note on a large sheet of chart paper and send it in a 9" x 12" envelope. (Fire stations, police stations, and grocery stores have even been known to display these on the wall.) This makes students proud of their writing and illustrations that accompany the printed words.

WRITING ACTIVITY PAGES

(Some activities may also be used with reading, speaking, and listening.)

A Wolf in Sheep's Clothing (*letter identification*)

Ricky Raccoon's Treasure Chest (*lower-case letters*)

The Snails Write Slowly

An "I Can Read" Book (A)

An "I Can Read" Book (B)

Make a Beeline for the Honey (*straight lines*)

Marty Mouse Finds a Pencil (*curved lines*)

Teddy Bear Writing Paper

A Wolf in Sheep's Clothing

Mrs. Sheep made Baby Wolf a pair of ABC overalls. He wants to learn the letters. You can help. Trace the ABC's.

Color the A's red.
Color the B's blue.
Color the C's green.

Name _____

Ricky Raccoon's Treasure Chest

Ricky found a treasure but he does not know what to do with it. YOU can take your pencil and help him. Thank you.

Name _____

The Snails Write Slowly

The snails want you to practice these five letters slowly with your pencil.

Ready, Get set, SLOW!

An "I Can Read" Book
(Read, write, draw)

MY

BOOK

Words I Can Say

I
can
sit
jump
sleep

Words To Write

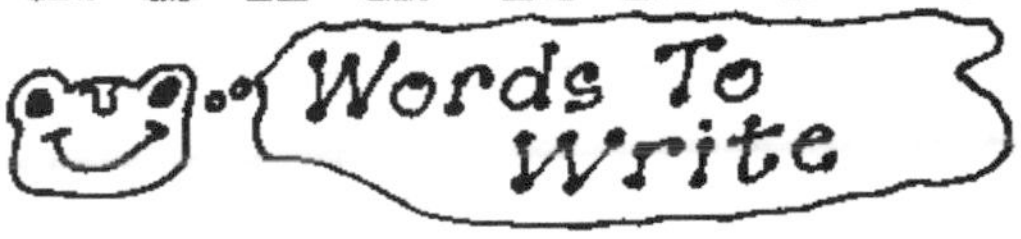

I

can

sit

jump

sleep

book

cut

Illustrate each page.

I can run.

I can sit.

cut

I can jump.

I can sleep.

Make a Beeline for the Honey

This bee is flying in straight lines today. Use a thick crayon, follow the path, and lead the bee to the honey.

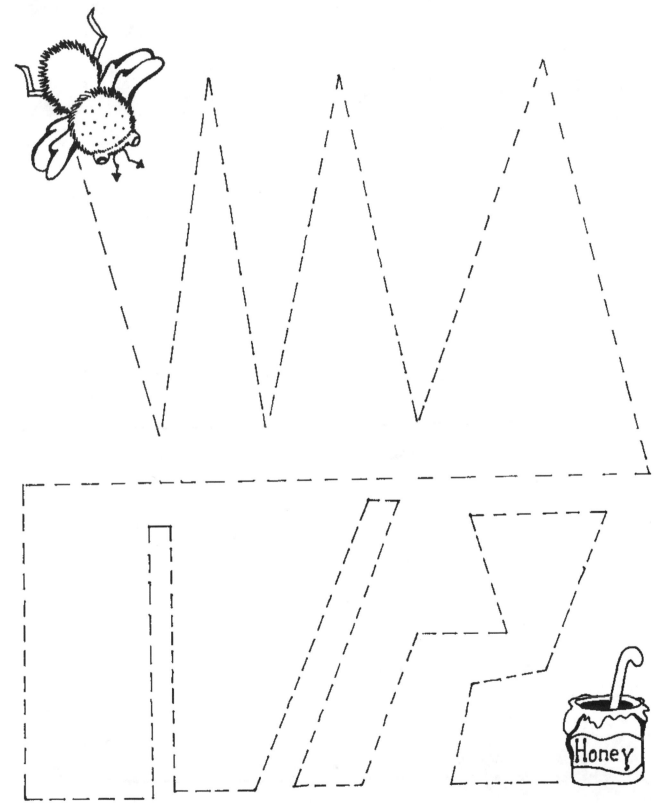

Marty Mouse Finds a Pencil

Marty is a poet. He's got his pencil and now he needs the paper. You can help. Use your pencil to guide him along the path to the paper. Then he can write his poem. Thank you!

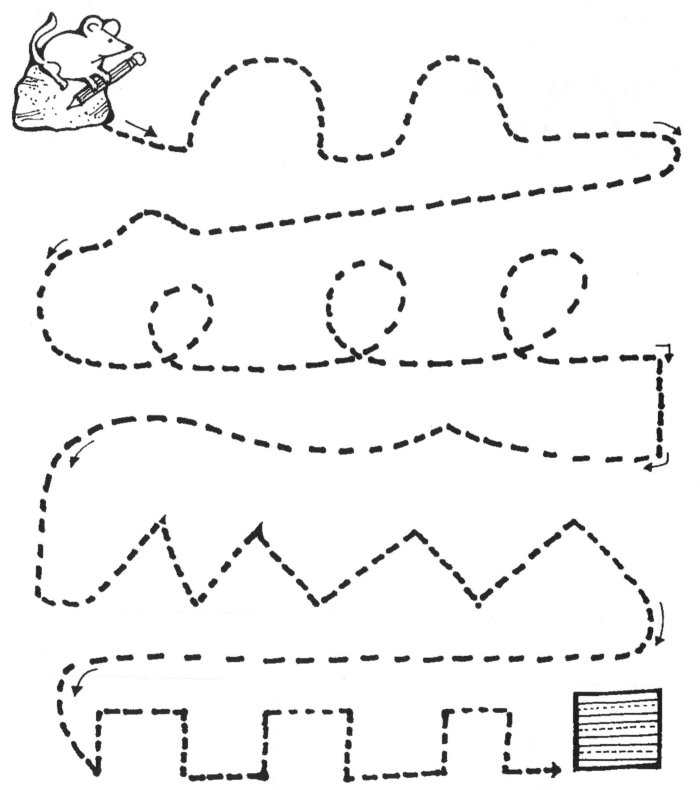

Name ——————————————— **Teddy Bear Writing Paper**

SPEAKING

Ms. Ruane

Speaking

Introduction

Infants the world over begin their speech by babbling. Soon babies are imitating the speech sounds of the people speaking in their own immediate environment, and thus, speaking is closely linked to listening and hearing specific sounds. Recent studies indicate that children can become fluent in a number of languages at an early age. A foreign language is much more difficult to learn when students are older—the mechanisms and circuits in the brain for language learning make the kindergartener "ripe" for learning a second language.

Because children come to school from a variety of socio-economic backgrounds, some kindergarteners need to be encouraged in their speech development, while some display a verbal fluency and a willingness to chatter. Putting speech to body rhythm is an activity that most children enjoy, and they benefit from having the opportunity to exercise their tongue muscles by making repetitious sounds.

Teachers serve as *role models* during this important phase of language development, and thus need to speak slowly and distinctly, and to give clear directions.

At this stage, it is not necessary to correct a child's speech but, rather, to repeat the information accurately. For example, if a child tells you that he likes "basketti" for lunch, make a point of saying that "spaghetti" is tasty, rather than correcting the word itself. Some kindergarteners who are fluent with language will automatically correct their peers—you can often find this happening in the housekeeping corner. (For example, a child may say, "I will tell it to the telephone," and a peer might answer, "You don't talk *to* the telephone, you talk *on* the telephone"). As the teacher, keep a sharp eye and a sharp ear open for children's reactions to peer correction. In many cases, it is best to not make an issue of it.

Speaking Activities

Circle Time Review

flag

Each morning, have students sit cross-legged on the floor in a circle, or in a series of semi-circles. This is a good time to review key words by pointing to a word and having a student say the word. Then have everyone say it. You can review labels hanging around the room (flag, clock, door, sink) by giving a willing student the pointer, and asking him or her to point to the word you say. Or, have the student point to a word label and have everyone say it together. Ask students to repeat the word aloud. You can review the name of the month (have students say it in unison) and review the days of the week (have students say them in unison). Choral speaking is helpful for the reluctant speaker.

Puppets Make the Day a Joy!

Hand puppets, marionettes, finger puppets, etc., are enjoyed by most children, and they are helpful for the shy child. Have a variety of puppets on hand for giving directions, for retelling of favorite stories, and for helping to teach particular concepts or subjects. There can be Marty the Math Puppet, Arty the Art Puppet, Sammy the Science Puppet, and so on. Oven mitts make good puppets, and some are ready-made in the shape of animals. Check your local variety stores, or department stores, or cook stores.

Puppets are magic! They have information that children want to know. Some teachers use a puppet at the beginning of the day's session to ask what the schedule of the day is. The puppet whispers the information in the teacher's ear, and the teacher relays that information to the students. It is a way of unifying the group early in the day's session, so that they can get focused.

Children Like to Make Puppets

Have children make puppets for their own use. The shy child is apt to hold the puppet in front of his or her face and speak from behind the puppet with ease. Puppets foster speaking, listening, singing, and storytelling. (See the Art section of this book.)

Children can enjoy a discussion of how cloth puppets are made. We need three things to get started and they are (1) thread, (2) a needle, and (3) material such as cotton, felt, burlap. Children may benefit from talking about hand-made items vs. machine-made items. Some books to include are: *Baba Yaga and the Little Girl* by Katya Arnold. The girl is sent to fetch a sewing needle from Baba Yaga and ends up winning out in the end because she is helpful. Also, an African-American tale, *The Patchwork Quilt* by Valerie Flournoy, with illustrations by Jerry Pinkney, shows another way to use scraps of materials—along with a lovely lesson in cooperation on this project.

Your Hand Is a Puppet Show!

Take an ordinary pair of white cotton garden gloves and turn them into a story puppet show by adding features to each finger (yarn for hair, felt pieces for faces, and so on). You can re-enact *The Three Little Pigs* by having pigs on three fingers, the wolf on another, and Mother Pig on another. A retelling of *Cinderella* calls for the five characters of Cinderella, the two sisters, the fairy godmother, and the prince. Nursery rhyme characters can be sewn or glued on to one glove and then you can recite five different rhymes.

And Now for Two Hands!

Snow White and the Seven Dwarfs calls for two gloves. One child can use the gloves on each hand, or two children can pair together for a retelling of the story. The characters are the seven dwarfs, Snow White, the wicked stepmother, and the prince. Clip all of the storytelling gloves on a little clothesline, and soon students will select them as a choice during free time. The teacher can also continue to use the puppets with different versions of the tales and various picture books.

Turning Stuffed Toys into Puppets

Old and inexpensive stuffed toys can be made into puppets. Sew a pocket (upside down) on the back of a stuffed toy, or use Velcro to make a cloth hand-holder. These puppet toys can be used to help children get "into role" and speak like the animal or bird or character doll.

Who Digs?

Read the revised children's book *The Diggers* by Margaret Wise Brown, with illustrations by Daniel Kirk. Then have a conversation about the *diggers* in the story. Children can be encouraged to talk about the digging that goes on right in their own backyard. For example:

- squirrels dig a hole and bury nuts
- dogs dig a hole and bury a bone
- cats dig in the flower bed
- people dig and plant flower seeds and bulbs

Let's dig! At the sand table that day, encourage students to dig, burrow, bury items, and then find them. This activity encourages children to speak about what they hid, and what they found. They can take turns doing this.

This might be a good time to bring in flower pots, seeds, and dirt, and do some digging and planting. This facilitates a great deal of opportunity for speaking. For some students, planting may be a new experience and an opportunity to learn some new vocabulary words such as *seed, dirt, plant, dig, grow.* Be sure to make a language experience chart with the class for a record of the procedure.

ABC Choral Speaking Rhyme/Movement

For each exercise, the teacher is both the reader and participant as students gain practice speaking aloud with accompanying body motions and movements. Speaking together gives all students a "voice" whether they know the material or not. Repeatedly using the chants and rhymes helps the students to learn them by heart, helps the leaders to carry the rhythm, and helps the shy child to join the group. Do this daily. Print it on a chart and use illustrations to help the students.

LETTER BUDDIES

A is for AIR that's in the sky — (*wave hands high*)
B is for BIRD who's flying high — (*flap arms at side*)

C is for CAT with long sharp claws — (*curl fingers*)
D is for DOG with great big paws — (*cup hands*)

E is for ELEPHANT swinging its trunk — (*clasp hands, swing arms*)
F is for FROG who jumps . . . KERplunk! — (*jump in place*)

G is for GORILLA climbing a tree — (*hand over hand*)
H is for HAIR on him and on me — (*touch hair*)

I is for ICE CREAM in a big dish — (*pretend to eat*)
J is for JELLO that makes a squish — (*teeth together, let air out*)

K is for KISS between mom and me — (*pucker lips, smack*)
L is for LIPSTICK for all to see — (*touch cheek*)

M is for MAILMAN who brings a letter — (*hand outstretched*)
N is for NEWS that grandma feels better — (*pretend to read*)

O is for the OTTER who likes to float — (*arms at sides, freeze*)
P is for PARROT riding by on a boat — (*wave to parrot*)

Q is for the fairy QUEEN — (*strut*)
R is for her RING of green — (*extend hand*)

S is for SUNSHINE all around (*make circle with arms*)
T is for TULIP, warm in the ground (*bend and sniff*)

U is for UMBRELLA, and if you forget (*hold hand high*)
V is for VELVET gloves that get wet (*wring hands*)

W is for WRITING (*pretend to write
Letters X Y and Z x, y, and z [in air]*)

I know my letter buddies (*shake hands with 3 others*)
Say, aren't you proud of me?

At the end students can shake hands with a buddy and say, "I'm proud of you
_____."
(name of student)

Twitch, Stomp, Toot!

Teacher is the reader and the leader, and keeps the rhythm going. Students speak all together, and do the accompanying motions. (When first learning this, the teacher says it once and children listen and watch. Then, they say it together one verse at a time.) Once they learn it, children will ask to do this activity again and again. They are gaining practice by repeatedly sounding out letter combinations (*tw, ch, st, ng,* and so on).

The rabbit likes to twitch, twitch
twitch, twitch
twitch, twitch
The rabbit likes to twitch, twitch
TWITCH, TWITCH, TWITCH! (*twitch nose*)

The donkey likes to stomp, stomp
stomp, stomp
stomp, stomp
The donkey likes to stomp, stomp
STOMP, STOMP, STOMP! (*stomp feet*)

The bugle likes to toot, toot
toot, toot
toot, toot
The bugle likes to toot, toot
TOOT, TOOT, TOOT! (*make 3 toots through hands
shaped to form bugle*)

The mailman likes to ring, ring
ring, ring
ring, ring
The mailman likes to ring, ring
RING, RING, RING!   *(pretend to ring bell)*

The cuckoo clock goes tick tock
tick tock
tick tock
The cuckoo clock goes tick tock
TICK, TICK, TOCK!   *(swing hands like a pendulum)*

The traffic cop goes   left, right
left, right
left, right
The traffic cop goes   left, right
LEFT, RIGHT, LEFT!   *(move upper body left / right / left)*

TWITCH, TWITCH!   *(make all of these movements as the*
STOMP, STOMP!   *words are said)*
TOOT, TOOT!
RING, RING!
TICK, TOCK!
LEFT, RIGHT!
BYE, BYE!   *(wave)*

The Chin Chuck

The Chin Chuck is performed to the same rhythm as the previous choral-speaking exercise. Children gain practice with speech as an enjoyable group experience.

My kitty likes a chin chuck   *(move fingers under chin)*
chin chuck
chin chuck
My kitty likes a chin chuck
And she says "PURR-R-R-R."   *(low gurgle sound in throat)*

My doggie likes a head scratch   *(scratch head gently)*
head scratch
head scratch
My doggie likes a head scratch
And he says, "WOOF."   *(purse lips, blow air out)*

My baby likes a rock-a-bye   *(cradle arms and swing)*
              rock-a-bye
              rock-a-bye
My baby likes a rock-a-bye
And she says, "GOO!"   *(high gurgle sound in throat)*

My toes like to tippety tap   *(tap toes on floor)*
             tippety tap
             tippety tap
My toes like to tippety tap
TAP, TAP, TAP!   *(three final taps)*

My heels like to clickety clack   *(click heels together)*
              clickety clack
              clickety clack
My heels like to clickety clack
CLICK, CLICK, CLACK!   *(three final clicks)*

My motor likes a tune up   *(twist wrists)*
              tune up
              tune up
My motor likes a tune up
And it says, "HMMMMM."   *(lips together, hum)*

My hands like to open shut   *(open and shut hands)*
              open shut
              open shut
My hands like to open shut
It's time to wave good-bye.   *(wave, then hands at sides)*

(See "The Chin Chuck" reproducible activity pages.)

Picture Stick Story—Fill in the Missing Word

The teacher reads the following short story and children can
fill in the missing words. How will they know which word is missing? *The teacher gives the clue by holding up a picture on a stick.* Where
do you get the pictures? Cut out glossy pictures from magazines, laminate them,
and tape them to a popsicle stick (available at craft shops).

"The Dog, the Cat, and the Mouse"

(You will need picture sticks of a dog, cat, and mouse. Read the story aloud, and
everytime you come to a blank, hold up the appropriate picture and have the students say the word in unison. This strengthens listening and speaking skills.)

Once upon a time, there was a _____(dog) named Chuckles and a _____(cat) named Fancy, who lived together in the same house. Chuckles the _____(dog) and Fancy the _____(cat) were good friends and got along well together. Fancy the _____(cat) and Chuckles the _____(dog) would even curl up together in the afternoon for a snooze. Now one very cold day, a little _____(mouse) got into the house. It was warm and comfortable inside, so the _____(mouse) curled right up on a soft pillow. The pillow was big and brown and fluffy, just like Chuckles, the_____(dog), and yellow and soft, just like the _____(cat) named Fancy. What the _____(mouse) didn't know was that the pillow was a **real** _____(dog) and a **real** _____(cat) taking a nap.

The _____(mouse) stretched and yawned and the _____(dog) said to the _____(cat), "You're tickling me!"

The _____(mouse) scratched its ear, and Fancy the _____(cat) said, "Meow! Now you're tickling me!" to Chuckles the _____(dog).

"Oh, oh!" said the _____(mouse). "I'd better get out of here!" So while the _____(dog) and the _____(cat) continued to nap, the _____(mouse) slowly and quietly tip-toed off the big brown fluffy cushion that was really Chuckles, the _____(dog), and the soft yellow cushion that was really Fancy, the _____(cat).

"Woof!" growled the _____(dog).

"Meow!" answered the _____(cat).

"Lucky me!" thought the _____(mouse) as it quietly tip-toed out the door.

When children are familiar with this story, distribute copies to them of the dog, cat, and mouse. Then, they can hold up the characters at the appropriate time. (See reproducible activity pages for "Stick Puppets for the Dog, Cat, and Mouse.")

The Tongue Trough

Encourage children to open their mouth, stick out their tongue, and make a trough with their tongue by curling up the sides. Some can do this with no effort, while others have difficulty, but with practice they can eventually strengthen the tongue muscles and succeed. Have a large mirror on the wall so that students can observe their tongue, and resist the tendency to touch their tongue with their fingers during this practical exercise.

The Original Oral Report

Take time for "Show and Tell"—it is the original oral report. During this time, children are encouraged to speak out to an audience, to stand before a group of peers and to talk about something of interest to them, or something that happened to them, or to describe something that they are holding in their hands. *They are reporting!* This experience is beneficial to the speaker, as well as to the audience. Perhaps Sharing Time only happens three days per week, with five people sharing during that time, but it is better than not taking the time to allow children to gain practice speaking before an audience.

Some Picture Books Invite Speech

RHYMING: Some books have repetitive phrases, and this invites the children to join in. One such book is *Millions of Cats* by Wanda Gag. Children will join in the refrain, *"hundreds of cats, thousands of cats, millions and billions and trillions of cats,"* and even sway back and forth in the process.

Many fairy tales have refrains that invite speech, such as *The Three Little Pigs* ("then I'll huff, and I'll puff, and I'll blow your house down!") and *Snow White and the Seven Dwarfs* ("mirror, mirror on the wall, who is fairest of them all?").

WORDLESS PICTURE BOOKS: Another type of book that invites speaking and writing is in the category of *wordless picture books.* Some of these include *Tuesday* by David Wiesner, *Pancakes for Breakfast* by Tomi dePaola, *Picnic* by Emily Arnold McCully, *Topsy-Turvies—Pictures to Stretch the Imagination* by Mitsumasa Anno, and *Good Dog Carl* and *Carl's Christmas* by Alexandra Day.

CUMULATIVE TALES: Repetition of various lines invites practice with speaking. Some fine books for this include: *The Rooster Who*

Went to His Uncle's Wedding: A Latin American Folktale by Alma Flor Ada, with illustrations by Kathleen Kuchera. Children can join in the refrain, "No I won't. Why should I?" Also, *The Old Woman and Her Pig,* retold by Paul Galdone, invites the listeners to speak out.

And Let's Include the Poetry Books

There are an abundance of fine poetry books on the market for young children. They are amusing, exaggerated, beautifully illustrated, and promote listening and speaking by appealing to the five senses and to the child's innate sense of rhythm. Children can be encouraged to learn many of these by heart. *A Hippopotamusn't* by J. Patrick Lewis, with illustrations by Victoria Chess, has many short verses that children enjoy hearing again and again, and soon they begin to learn them and join right in. Other books by J. Patrick Lewis include *Ridicholas Nicholas* and *Two-Legged, Four-Legged, No-Legged Rhymes.*

For more poetry books, browse through the Poetry Area in the Children's Section of your public library. Be on the lookout for *A Gopher in the Garden and Other Animal Poems* by Jack Prelutsky; along with John Ciardi's *You Read to Me, I'll Read to You*; Aileen Fisher's *Feathered Ones and Furry*; Shel Silverstein's classic *Where the Sidewalk Ends*; and X. J. Kennedy's anthology *Knock at a Star: A Child's Introduction to Poetry.*

Enjoy Your Voice!

Encourage children to enjoy the range of sounds they can make by having an "Enjoy Your Voice" time. These can get you started:

- say "hummmmm" (like you're wondering about something)
- growl like a tiger
- chirp like a bird
- sing high like a soprano voice
- sing low like a bass voice
- make cooing sounds for the baby
- clear your throat
- say "please" in a hushed tone
- say "thank you" in a voice filled with surprise

Enjoy Your Voice

Some Storybook Assistance for the Shy Child

The shy speaker in the group may be made to feel more comfortable by listening to enjoyable stories that address shyness. These may help: *Chatterbox Jamie* by Nancy Evans Cooney, *Shy Vi* by Wendy Cheyette Lewison, and *Speak Up, Blanche!* by Emily Arnold McCully.

Some speaking assistance for all children may come from this resource: *Eye Winker, Tom Tinker, Chin Chopper: Fifty Musical Fingerplays* by Tom Glazer.

SPEAKING ACTIVITY PAGES

(Some activities may also be used with reading, writing, and listening.)

Dog Puppet (*stick puppet story*)

Cat Puppet (*stick puppet story*)

Mouse Puppet (*stick puppet story*)

The Chin Chuck (*sound story*)

The Chin Chuck (*Rebus sound story*)

Red Riding Hood Concentration Game (*storytelling*)

The Three Pigs (*story cards; storytelling*)

Stick Puppet—Dog

Color and cut out the dog, cat, and mouse to accompany the Picture Stick Puppet Story in the Speaking section.

stick puppets

Stick Puppet—Cat

Stick Puppet—Mouse

The Chin Chuck

My kitty likes a chin chuck
    chin chuck
    chin chuck
My kitty likes a chin chuck
And she says, "PURR -R-R-R."

My doggie likes a head scratch
    head scratch
    head scratch
My doggie likes a head scratch
And he says, "WOOF."

My baby likes a rock-a-bye
    rock-a-bye
    rock-a-bye
My baby likes a rock-a-bye
And she says, "GOO."

My toes like to tippety tap
    tippety tap
    tippety tap
My toes like to tippety tap
TAP! TAP! TAP!

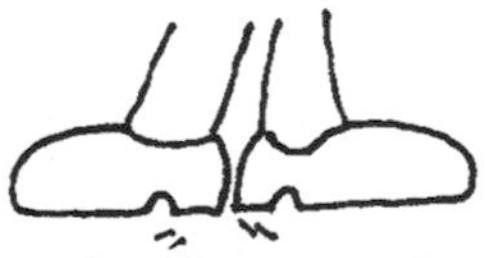

My heels like to clickety clack
    clickety clack
    clickety clack
My heels like to clickety clack
CLICK. CLICK. CLACK.

My motor likes a tune up
    tune up
    tune up
My motor likes a tune up
And it says, "HMMMMMMMM."

My hands like to open shut
    open shut
    open shut
My hands like to open shut
It's time to wave good-bye.

Name _____

The Chin Chuck

Memorize and chant this sound story. These pictures will help to remind you of what comes next. Ready? Go!

The Chin Chuck

1 purr-r

2 woof

3 goo

4 tap

5 click

6 hmm-m

7 open shut

8 Good-bye

Red Riding Hood Concentration Game

Color, laminate, cut. Lay out the squares in three rows of three. Turn the squares over, one at a time, for a match. If they match, keep them. If not, put them back (remember where). Play with a partner, or alone. The one with more cards that match, wins. Shuffle and try again. (The hunter is a *wild card* and is a match with the wolf.)

The Three Pigs—Story Cards

Color, laminate, cut. Match each pig with his house. Now you can retell the story, using these story cards.

LISTENING

Ms. McManus

Listening

(*Note:* The subject of listening is also addressed in the Music/Movement section.)

Introduction

Listening is one of the first language arts skills to be developed. Each child has been engaged in the listening process long before entering kindergarten. This is an essential skill for success, and needs to be worked on within the context of the kindergarten program.

If a child is having difficulty following directions or speaking clearly, it may be that his or her ears need to be checked. In many schools, a hearing test is given prior to entering kindergarten or during the first month of the school year to detect any problems. If hearing problems are suspected, call this to the attention of the school nurse or the principal. Parents should also be notified so that the child can be assessed for hearing loss.

Setting the Conditions for Group Listening

Practice this with the students before reading a storybook, or to set the scene for "Show and Tell" or "Sharing Time." It can be printed on a chart with appropriate Rebus pictures, as a reminder.

I Am a Good Listener

I am sitting down
My legs are crossed.
My hands are together.
My lips are closed.
My eyes are on the speaker.

In an effort to help children learn to listen in a group setting, the teacher needs to show patience and respect for the child. Having the above chart available is helpful, because the teacher can draw attention to the message. Also, during group time when someone forgets good listening habits, the teacher can "catch the eye" of a student and point to one of the directions. Do not begin or continue a lesson if children are talking about something else—this is off-task behavior.

Listening Activities

"I Like the Way Sidney Is Ready"

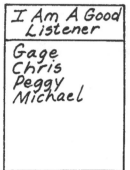

Positive reinforcement works wonders with this age group. Find someone who is ready, praise them, and most children will follow suit. When assembling for group work, the teacher can recognize individuals by saying, in a reassuring voice, "Ramondo is ready." "Now Chris is ready." "And Gage is almost ready . . . , and now Angela is showing us that she's ready to listen." "Thank you, Carlos, for helping Floria put away the blocks" and so on. Children will beam as the teacher recognizes them by calling their name.

Children want to please, and it's simply a matter of training. Children have come from homes with different parenting styles. Some children need more instruction as to *how* to listen and *why* they need to listen. It takes patience on the part of the teacher.

The Teacher's Voice

This is a tool that needs to be cultivated. If the teacher is talking in a LOUD voice, the children will talk in a LOUD voice. If the teacher speaks in measured, soft tones, many of the children will follow suit and it will make the job easier.

Appeal to the kindergartener's imagination. Try *whispering* directions "so that we don't wake up the tiger." (Because if we wake up the tiger he'll run after the puppet.) Also, enjoy a "Whispering Day" occasionally.

Use the analogy of doors opening and closing by telling the children that when their mouth door is open, their ear doors swing shut. So, we want the ear doors to open and the mouth door to close.

Good Listener Headbands

Cut a strip of paper and staple two long construction paper rabbit ears to it. Measure the strip around the head of the child, and staple together the two ends of the strip. Students can wear these headbands as a special reward, or they can all wear them during certain times. Wearing the headbands with over-sized ears serves as a reminder to focus upon the skill of listening in a way that appeals to the imagination.

Close Your Eyes and Listen for the Cat

Have students be "quiet as a mouse" and close their eyes and listen to the sounds in the classroom. Pretend they are helping the mouse, who has to be quiet and listen for the cat. After a minute, have them open their eyes and tell what the mouse could hear (clock ticking, rain on the windowpane, someone breathing, someone walking down the hall, etc.).

A Quiet Whispering Rhyme

Use the following rhyme at any time of day when the class is getting too loud. Start chanting it and students will pick up the rhythm, and quiet down. Repeat it as often as necessary.

I'm quiet as a mouse
I'm alone in the house
That is, except for the c–a–t.   (*spell "cat"; pretend to stroke whiskers*)

I'm quiet as a mouse
I'm alone in the house
The cat is looking for
m–e . . . me.   (*first spell, then say "me"; point to chest with finger*)

Sh! Sh! Sh!
Sh! Sh! Sh!
The cat is looking for
m–e . . . me.   (*lips together*)

Once you have the attention of the group, you can give the necessary directions or reminders.

Let's Go on a Listening Walk

Have students line up, each with a partner, and go through the school on a "Listening Walk." This would be a good time to wear the rabbit ears. When you return to the classroom, have children tell what sounds they heard in the office (phone ringing, computer keys tapping, etc.), in the hall, in the cafeteria, and so on.

Let's Go on an Outdoor Listening Walk

Have students line up for outdoor playtime a bit early one day so that they can listen for outdoor sounds while walking around the playground. Stop and listen to a bird chirping in a tree. Listen to the cars stop and go, stop and go at the corner sign. Can you hear the sound of the brakes? Can you hear an airplane overhead? Can you hear children's voices? Can you perhaps hear music on a radio as a car passes by? Can you hear a dog barking? Tell children you want to know what they heard, when you return to the classroom.

A Sample Experience Chart Story

Come back into the classroom after playtime and talk about the sounds you heard outdoors. On large chart paper, write the listening experience that the group has just had. The lesson may go something like this:

T: "Today we went for a listening walk. How shall we say that?" (*Listen to suggestions, then write.*)

We went for a Listening Walk today.

T: "What did we hear?" (*Listen to suggestions, then write.*)

Ramli heard an airplane in the sky.

Wayan heard the swings creaking and

Furaidah heard a bee buzzing.

T: "We have a wonderful story. How shall we end it?" (*Listen to suggestions, then write.*)

We enjoyed the Listening Walk.

Let's listen for more outdoor sounds.

T: "We need a title. What shall we call our story?" (*Listen to suggestions, then write it at the top.*)

NOTE: The important thing here is that *all* children were engaged in the same experience. They *talk* about it and *see* the words being written down. The teacher can listen to what is being said, and *paraphrase* it in written form. It is not necessary to write down every single word each child says. After it is read, the teacher can point to the capital letter at the beginning of each sentence, and the period at the end that means stop. Children can go back to this again and again and read it. The teacher may ask for illustrators—someone to make the airplane, the swing, the bee, and so on.

Storytime Creates a Bond

Each day, and sometimes twice a day, children should be read to, just for sheer pleasure. There are many beautiful picture books, multicultural picture books, holiday books, poetry books, etc., for children's enjoyment. This is a delightful time of day! It is a special time for the group to bond and for the teacher to bond with the group. It's a time to laugh together, and to be surprised together, and to wonder together. Children see the teacher as a warm person during story time, and that is important for them to experience, since kindergarten is filled with so many new and sometimes frightening challenges. (See the Bibliography for picture books.)

Quiet Reading Time

Encourage children to bring in a comfortable pillow. During this time, children can take their pillow, select a book from the myriad array of library books that are on display in the classroom, and quietly explore a picture book for five minutes. Have each one select one book, and stay with that book. That's important. It is not a time for wandering around the room; it is a time for reading. Soft background music may help set the mood. (If you are working with a group that is extremely restless and having difficulty settling down, follow this period by a snack and let students know that first we read and then we snack.)

Library Visits

Part of the kindergarten teacher's role is to provide picture books of outstanding quality for children. This may mean going to the public library regularly for a good selection of picture books for the classroom, if there is not an abundance of books in the school library. It is well worth the trip! Make friends with the children's librarian and have that person set aside good books for you. Perhaps a visit to the library can be arranged, and each child can secure a library card. (Refer to this in a note home to parents. If they begin to take their children to the library as a result of your effort, it will have been well worth the time spent.)

The Hearing Impaired Child

Some children come to kindergarten and have already been identified as having special needs in the category of "hearing." Be sure this child is seated near the speaker; look directly at this child when giving specific directions; and be sure to listen to the child. It may be necessary for the teacher to wear sound equipment to amplify his or her voice when speaking to a child with special needs. It may be a good idea to team this child with another child who is courteous and helpful, and one who has volunteered to assist. You may want to change the assistant on a regular basis.

Listening on Tape

Record a story on a cassette tape as you are reading it to the class. Then, later, students can relive this experience, including the class comments and conversations. This also works very well for the hearing impaired child who is reassured by hearing the story again.

Listening to Directions on Tape

Instead of repeating directions over and over again for the children who aren't catching on to the routines, or for those who don't hear the directions the first or second time around, record your directions on tape, and have them available at the listening center.

Some children may be specifically directed to this listening area and asked to listen to the tape; then they can tell you and others what the expectations are. You may have a variety of tapes with directions. Use a Rebus symbol to help children identify them. Here are some direction tapes you can record and label:

- record fire drill directions on tape
- record tornado/hurricane/earthquake drill directions on tape
- record reminders for good behavior in the hall, in class, when lining up, in the lunchroom, on the bus
- record classroom information such as
  —where the extra pencils are located
  —where the wastebasket is located
  —where the extra crayons are stored

"Good Day! Welcome to Kindergarten!"

Use the following tape recording as a model for making your own, and direct children to listen to it occasionally. It is good for the child who has an attention deficit disorder, and also serves as a good review and reminder for *all* students.

(SAMPLE TAPE)

"Greetings! You are now in Kindergarten, Room No. _____, and I am your teacher, _____. You are at _____ School, and the name of the principal is _____. Let's listen to this again. Your room number is _____. Your teacher's name is _____. The name of your school is _____. And your principal is _____.

"Settle back and listen carefully while I take you on a tour of the classroom.

"Look at the windows and notice the shelves underneath them. On those shelves you will find the _____.

"Turn so that you are looking at the door. To the left of the door is the sink and the bathroom. That is where the drinking fountain is, too. You can get a drink there during small-group time. When we are all together in the large group, do not leave to get a drink and do not leave to go to the bathroom—unless you cannot wait. Always remember to wash your hands after you use the bathroom.

"Do you see the housekeeping area? (*Wait time*.) You can use that area during free-play time. Do you see the big block area? (*Wait time*.) You can use that area during free-play time. Do you see the easel? (*Wait time*.) You can sign up to use the easel and use it during Choice Time. Do you see . . . (*Record as many areas as you feel are necessary*.)

"Turn so that you are facing the bulletin board. To the right of the board is the Science Table. That is an area you can go to during Work Time. Look at the bulletin board again. To the left of the board is the Writing Area. That is an area you can go to during Work Time.

"Do you see the tissue box next to the sink? You can take one at a time, and remember to cover your mouth when you cough or sneeze. A used tissue can go in your pocket, or it may need to go into the wastebasket by the door. You decide.

"That completes our tour of the classroom. It's good to have YOU in here. Now you know where everything is. Come back again to tour the room.

"At the sound of the bell, press the STOP button. Then press the REWIND button. Thank you." (*Ring a bell for stopping*.)

We're Going to Have a Fire Drill. Are You Ready?

Make a recording of this procedure (in a firm but friendly voice). It will be especially helpful for the fearful child.

Also, practice having a fire drill regularly during the first month of school so that when it actually happens, the students will be prepared and it will go smoothly.

Work and Play Together. These Are Our Rules

Make a recording of your classroom rules and what they mean; tell about the consequences for not following the rules. Also mention the polite way to line up at the door, and to walk down the hall, to get ready for an assembly program, and so on. You may need to assign this tape several times as a "Listening Activity" for children who are having behavior problems.

Circle-Time Recordings

You may enjoy getting into the habit of recording "Circle Time" activities as you begin each day. This is helpful for the child who needs to hear the information again. It is also helpful for the child who has been absent and who has missed a day or two of school.

If You Give a Bear a Cupcake, If You Give a Fish a Flower

How well does the class listen? Can they remember a story they just heard, and predict what will happen when you read the story again? Two books that are extremely helpful in this regard are *If You Give a Mouse a Cookie* and *If You Give a Moose a Muffin,* both by Laura Joffe Numeroff, with illustrations by Felicia Bond. These delightful books seem to charm the children—and before long, they are laughing and chiming right in. They promote good listening skills.

Listen to Letters

Some books for reading aloud provide good information about letter writing, in addition to being good stories. Some of these include: *Love from*  *Uncle Clyde* by Nancy Winslow Parker; *Love, Your Bear Pete* by Dyan Sheldon; and *Anna's Secret Friend* by Yoriko Tsutsui. This experience links listening to reading and writing, and enriches the language arts program.

LISTENING ACTIVITY PAGES

(Some activities may also be used with reading, writing, and speaking.)

An Outdoor Listening Walk

An Indoor Listening Walk

Who Listens?

Listening for Directions (*tape recorder*)

What Do Teddy Bears Like for Story Time?

An Outdoor Listening Walk

Go on an outdoor listening walk on the playground. Then, discuss it. In the spaces below, draw four things you heard.

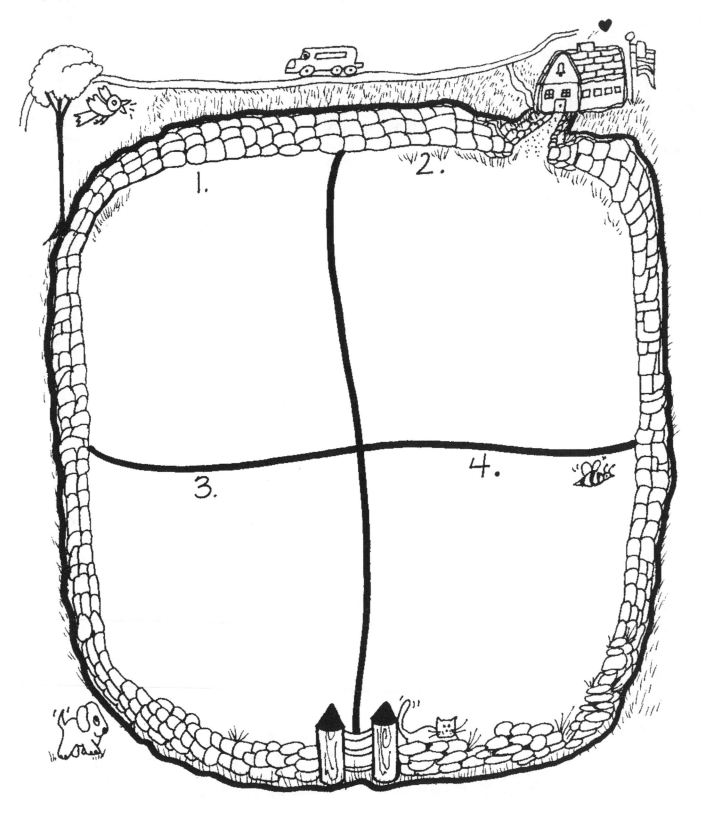

An Indoor Listening Walk

Put on your listening ears and go on an indoor walk. When you return to class, talk about what you heard in each place. Draw one picture in each space below of what you heard.

office

hall

gym

lunchroom

library

other _____

Who Listens?

Sounds are bursting out all over! What sounds could be happening in each flower petal? Talk it over. Then color the flower center, stem, and leaves.

Listening for Directions

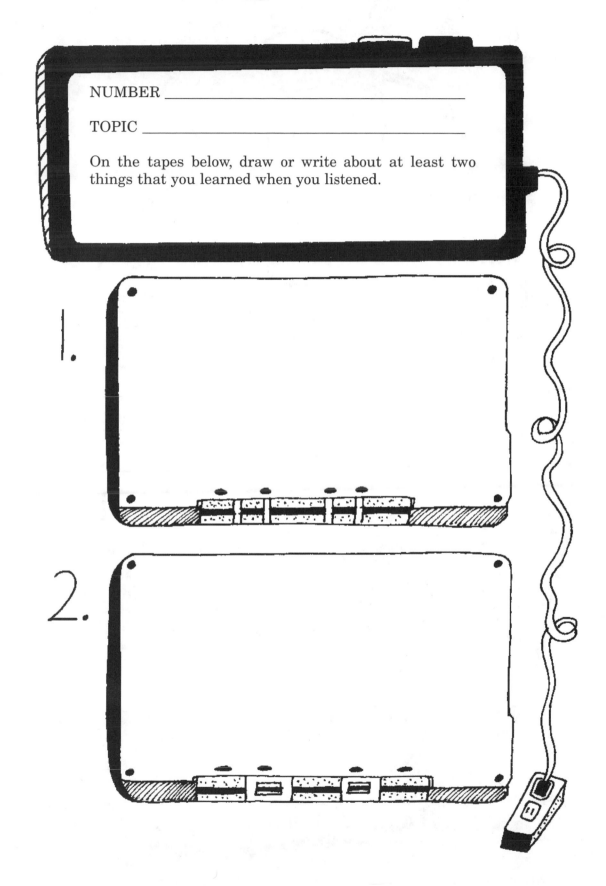

NUMBER _____

TOPIC _____

On the tapes below, draw or write about at least two things that you learned when you listened.

1.

2.

What Do Teddy Bears Like for Story Time?

They like Mother Goose.
How many rhymes do YOU know?

MATHEMATICS

Mrs. Kolwicz

Mathematics

Introduction

Many children come to school knowing how to count by rote memory from one to ten, or even one to fifty or a hundred. This is quite different from having an understanding of the numbers and what they represent.

Children progress through intellectual developmental stages and this is reflected in their ability to process math concepts. At the kindergarten level, most children are in the preoperational stage, according to Piaget, the Swiss psychologist. In this stage, children need *manipulatives* (hands-on) experiences in mathematics. They need to work with *real* items, rather than abstract figures.

Mathematics Standards

During the 1980s, *The National Council of Teachers of Mathematics* (NCTM) set forth a set of standards designed to establish a broad framework for mathematics in our schools. The broad topics for kindergarten and primary grades include the following: problem solving, communication, reasoning, making connections in our daily life, estimation, number sense and numeration, concepts of whole number operations, computation, geometry and spatial sense, measurement, statistics and probability, fractions and decimals, and patterns and relationships.

Standard #1: Problem Solving

This topic is not limited to the field of mathematics, since we solve problems every day in our environment. For example, if the sky looks threatening and we think it may rain, do we take our umbrella?

One way we can apply problem solving directly to mathematics in the kindergarten is to work with setting a table. In the housekeeping corner, put four stuffed animals on chairs and pull them up to the table. Then have children set the table for their company. The focus is on *how* this can be carried out. Do we use placemats or a table cloth? What are we serving? Is this a snack or a full-course dinner? Do we need forks, knives, and spoons or just spoons? Does the beverage call for cups or glasses? Where does the napkin go? Do all of the napkins have to look alike? During this process, children will be counting and working with *how many,* but the focus remains on the problem-solving aspect.

Snack Time Math

Select children to work in pairs to help get ready for snack time. If individual containers of milk are delivered to the classroom, for example, then how many straws will we need? Have two children line up the cartons and then get the package of straws. They can set one straw by each milk carton, and, thus, gain experience with counting and also with *one-to-one correspondence.* Do this daily, with different children.

Standard #2: The Language of Mathematics

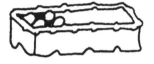

Encourage children to talk about math as they are solving problems. Collect empty egg cartons and small objects of different colors to place inside them (buttons, beads, marbles, flat discs, and so on).

At the Math Center they can work with one egg carton and a container of objects. Put one object in each of the twelve sections. Do they have enough? Do they have *more than* they need? Do they have *less than* they need? How many more do they need? Conversation can be encouraged as children seek to find and agree upon some of the following combinations of materials to put into the container:

- select all objects of one color
- select all objects that are round
- select all objects that are flat
- select all objects that are smooth; rough

At the Math Center, set up "Ren Bear's Bake Shop." You will need a toy telephone, pencil, paper, cookie cutters, and plasticene. Students can work in the shop, answer the phone, take an order over the phone, write it down, and tell how many cookies are needed. Then, roll out the dough, cut it (how many), bake the cookies (time/temperature), package them (spatial), and have them ready for the customer who comes to purchase them (money exchange).

Standard #3: Reasoning with Mathematics

Children need to discover that mathematics *makes sense,* and they can begin to think critically about problem solving. For example, if Goldilocks visits the three bears for lunch, how many apples should Mrs. Bear buy if each one is to have a whole apple? (Use flannel board cut-outs and red circles to represent apples if you do not have real ones or plastic ones available.) Help children to determine that she will need four apples.

Now suppose that Goldilocks visits the Three Little Pigs for lunch. How many apples should the pigs buy if each one is to have a whole apple? Give students the experience of talking this through, again using the flannel board with cut-outs of the characters, so that students will see that the same number is represented.

Then have Goldilocks visit the home of Snow White and the Seven Dwarfs and determine how many apples should be bought if each one is to have a whole apple. By the third example, some children may be able to make a reasonable estimate of the number of apples needed. (Some may say seven apples, but what about Snow White?)

Standard #4: Mathematical Connections

Children need to observe that math is an integral part of their everyday life. When we count out paper for the group, we use math. When we form a circle (a math shape), we're using math. When we buy clothing we buy it by size, even if it's small, medium, and large. Often we are awakened by an alarm clock in the morning (numbers) and can look out at the thermometer hanging outdoors (numbers) or phone the time/temperature service to learn what the temperature is. (We need to know which numerals to dial or punch.)

"I'm a Math Nut"

Have a see-through "Math Nut Jar" in the room. Every time we "catch ourselves using math" in some way (time, temperature, counting, lining up, collecting money, signing up for lunch, giving the plants 1/4 cup of water, feeding the fish 1/2 teaspoon of dry food, and so on), we can put a nut (walnut, buckeye, pecan, chestnut) into the jar. Children will be surprised at how fast it fills up! When it's full, plan a math treat—a square cake that has to be cut into pieces so that everyone gets a piece. Plan it on paper, using a square and long, thin strips of paper to represent cuts.

Make "I'm a Math Nut" badges (see "I'm Nuts About Math" reproducible activity award), and have students wear them and be able to explain at least two ways that they "used" math today.

More Math Connections

Encourage the use of math in the play corner when students set up a store, work with prices, and make change. Have newspaper ads available in the housekeeping section so that students can "read" the food ads to note the specials-of-the-week and how much they cost. Have them notice how important numbers are in their family life:

- how many family members
- what is their phone number
- what is their house number or apartment number
- what is their age; the age of siblings
- how many grandparents they have
- how many rooms in their homes

Standard #5: Estimation

When we estimate, some vocabulary that we use includes words like *almost, nearly, about, between* and *more* or *less*.

Children can start with themselves and their body size. Who is nearly as tall as Jamie? If Jamie and Caroline are nearly the same size, have them stand next to each other with a space in the middle. Who can fit between them who is quite a bit shorter? Taller? Almost the same height?

How Long Is the Table?

Use inter-locking cubes to make a row of ten. This can be used as a base number. Then have students estimate how many cubes it will take to make a line along the entire table. Then do it. How close is their estimate?

The Wings of a Bird

Draw a large bird on the chalkboard with wings extended. Estimate how many students could line up and "fit under" the wings. Then try it. Were they close?

Seed Estimation

Scoop the seeds out of a pumpkin or gourd. Have students estimate the number of seeds, after they have been washed and dried and set in a container for them to sift through. Record their estimation. Then count the seeds—making piles of fives or tens so they gain practice with skip counting.

Is Today Colder or Warmer than Yesterday?

Have a large thermometer available outside your classroom window at children's eye-level and keep recording the temperature on a large chart. Notice the line of mercury and whether it is higher than or lower than yesterday. If we have had five days in a row that are almost the same, what do children predict for tomorrow? Then check to see if they are close.

Standard #6: Number Sense and Numeration

Children need to use manipulatives to develop a sense of number. How much does "seven" of something *look like*, as opposed to "two," for example? And what does seven *feel* like, as opposed to two? Children need to count out materials, add one more, take two away, and determine how many they have altogether. They also need to determine the *magnitude of numbers* and be able to *see* at a glance that thirty-three is more than five, for example.

Tweetie's Kitchen

Make a construction paper cut-out of a large black crow with a big yellow beak, and name it "Tweetie." This bird is in charge of Tweetie's Kitchen Center that students can use to gain a "sense of number." You will need the following:

- a variety of seeds and beans (lentils, navy beans, sunflower seeds)
- kettle or pot for "cooking"
- plastic bowls
- plastic measuring spoons (teaspoons, tablespoons)
- measuring cups
- wooden spoons
- funnels (large and small)
- timer
- assorted pan sizes
- chef's hat and apron (optional)

The only rule is that seeds should be kept separate, unless you wish to have one jar of "mixed" seeds for those that do get mixed together. Allow students to count, pour, mix, and measure so that they gain a sense of numeration.

Soon children can measure their beans by the 1/2 cup, by the 3/4 measuring spoon, and so on. Through experience they will learn that a tablespoon holds more seeds or beans than a teaspoon, and so on. *Guided exploration* with manipulatives is the aim.

Later, add "recipe" cards, such as:

Tweetie's Favorite Navy Bean Cookie Mix

Add together in a *round* bowl:
1 tablespoon navy beans
2 cups navy beans (add through *triangular* funnel)
4 single navy beans

Stir around and around with wooden spoon 10 times to the *right,* then 5
    times to the *left.*
Pour into *rectangle*-shaped pan.
Bake for 3 minutes. (Watch the second hand of the clock.)
Good! Return the beans to their container and clean up.

The Counting Counter

Have a counter or shelf or table set aside for counting objects, putting objects together, and taking them apart. You can buy circular plastic chips by the hundreds. Some commercial products include Centicube®, Unifix® Blocks, Cuisenaire® rods, and base blocks.

Objects gathered and donated can include bottle caps, buttons, clothespins, paper clips, jar lids, rubber bands, and so on.

Standard #7: Concepts of Whole Number Operations

By *operations* we mean addition, subtraction, multiplication, and division. Children need to physically move themselves or manipulate objects to gain a better understanding of operations. They will not understand it from listening to someone tell them about the process—they need to do it, to experience it.

The Field Trip

Make a cut-out figure for each student in the class (or a set number) and cut out seven car shapes. If there are four students per car, how many cars will we need for the trip?

Have students physically place four cut-outs of students in (or on top of) each car. Do this repeatedly until all of the student figures are in cars. Now count the cars. How many cars will we need to take us on our trip?

Do the field trip experience repeatedly, using different destinations and different numbers of students allowed in each car (or mini-van) to determine how many vehicles will be needed.

Making Jello

This is an excellent math/science activity, and a tasty one, too. Students are working with measurement, time, temperature, and change of state from dry to liquid to solid.

Once the jello is set, fractional parts can be experienced. How many students are there? (Count them.) How many pieces will we get if we cut it this way, or that way? This is a good opportunity to use problem-solving with the students.

Half for You, Half for Me

Some items can be cut in half (bread, muffins) and some can be counted (candy, gum drops, carrot sticks). For counting, if two students are given 6 carrot sticks, how can they each get an equal amount, or half? What if they are given 7 carrot sticks? How can two students get an equal amount? Let them work it out, and talk about it.

Standard #8: Whole Number Computation

Before children work with pencil-and-paper computation, they need to have a great deal of practice with the "sense" of numbers. This is where manipulatives (concrete materials) are important.

Flannel Board Math Story

Tell children that today you are going to invite the three bears for lunch. Have cut-outs of three teddy bears in graduated sizes for papa, mama, and baby.

Place the first bear on the flannel board and say, "One."
Place the second bear on the flannel board and say, "Two."
Place the third bear on the flannel board and say, "Three."
Then point to each bear in turn and say, "one, two, three."

This is giving meaning to the concept of three of something, or "three-ness."

Have flannel cut-outs of three bowls and three berries and do the same methodical counting as you place them on the board.

If One Bowl Broke . . . How Many Would We Have?

Use the three bowls mentioned above. This can be worked out on the flannel board, thus giving the children a sense of two of something. Actually, one bowl has been subtracted or taken away, but these terms do not need to be used with the beginner if we are going to build developmentally appropriate concepts of whole numbers. (Use real teddy bears and real bowls, too.)

The Button Basket

Have a container of all types of buttons (large, small, colorful, plain). Remove one from the basket, place it on the table and say "one." Keep going until you have five, for example, so that children have a sense of "five-ness."

Ordering the Buttons

The pace from one mathematical concept to another should be slow, and not all children will be able to grasp the following at the same point.

If you line the five buttons in a row, you can have children point to them and count, "1,2,3,4,5." Then ask, "How many?" (*five*). Another concept to introduce and work on is that of *order*.

Button 1 is first.
Button 2 is second.
Button 3 is third.
Button 4 is fourth.
Button 5 is fifth.

Lining Up at the Drinking Fountain

Ask, "Who wants to be first?" "Who wants to be second?" Keep doing this until you get to "Who wants to be tenth?" Then ask children to count out the number of people in line, "1,2,3,4,5,6,7,8,9,10." The number they stop with in their counting is *always* the number of the group they have counted; that is, of course, if they have matched a number name to each item or person in the group.

Making Digits from Sandpaper

Cut out numerals from sandpaper so that students can trace the digits and "feel" the numeral shape. This will make it easier for them when they use pencil and paper to actually form the numerals.

We Know Lots About Math in the Environment

Ask children where they have seen numerals written at home, at the mall, when traveling by car or bus, etc. Begin to collect magazine pictures that show *environmental math.* Some examples include:

shoe sizes	bus number
gas pump (gallons, cost)	room number
grocery store	telephone number
stamps	calendar
billboards	house number

Where Do We See People Write Numerals?

Ask children this question and list the responses. Some may include:

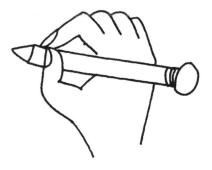

- when asking a person's phone number
- when writing a phone number down after looking it up in the phone book
- when a sales clerk writes up a sale
- when the waiter gives you a check
- when addressing an envelope
- when writing a ZIP Code
- when writing a check or balancing a checkbook
- when ordering sizes from a catalog

The Concept of Zero

zero

Zero is the number of the empty set, and a difficult concept to develop. It may be the "number" given to toys of a particular type, if there are none in the room. For example, how many wagons do we have (3), how many balls (4), how many rocking horses (zero).

Caution—Math Concept Development Under Construction (in big orange letters)

When we see orange construction signs along the highway, we slow down. We need to remember this when developing math concepts in kindergarten. Too often, we put children into workbooks with pencil-and-paper computations when they have no idea what the symbols mean. Remember, *first the math manipulatives* and the talk about and experience with math concepts. Then, numeral writing can be introduced in relation to number recognition. This is the beginning of the *connection* among concrete (realia), semi-abstract (pictorial), and abstract (symbolic) levels.

Standard #9: Geometry and Spatial Sense

Children need opportunities to explore with every-day objects, so that they feel the shape of a sphere, rectangle, triangle, and so on. Also, they need to learn how much space they take up, and gain experience with estimating how large a container they will need for a certain number of objects. If a kindergartener is continually bumping into things or people, he or she may not know, literally, just how much space they take up.

Geoboard Shapes

Show students, using different colored rubber bands, how to make a square and a triangle and a rectangle on the geoboard. Give them ample opportunity to experiment with shapes. (See the "Basic Shapes in Color" reproducible activity page.)

What Shape Is It?

Convert a large box into a "Shape Box" by cutting two round holes in opposite sides. Cover the outside of the box with colorful prepasted paper. Place objects inside the box, and have students feel them and try to guess what shape they are holding. One day, place all spheres in the box (tennis ball, golf ball, basketball, beach ball, marble). At other times use a mixture of shapes.

The Shape of a Rectangle

This game is played with Cuisenaire® rods. Have students put their hands behind their backs and then place a rod in one hand. Have them feel it over and over, using both hands. Next, place three different rods on the table in front of them, and have them name the rod they are holding—Is it #1, #2, or #3? (They are determining length of the rectangle.) When students gain practice with this, put two rods in their hands and have them distinguish between the two while they are looking at a staircase of rods in front of them. They can determine them by color. Two students can work together on this. Also, encourage building with the rods during independent free-choice time.

Let's Pack Our Suitcase

Bring in an old suitcase, and have students pack and unpack the case with items in the classroom, so that they can see first-hand just how much a suitcase will hold. Try this with a duffle bag, with a backpack, with an overnight case, and with a large overseas suitcase.

Make comparisons in terms of space in a suitcase and in a large shoulder bag. Pack and unpack them. Which holds more?

Suppose we're going on a real trip! Have students sit in a circle, and give each one of them an item. This can be clothing (folded shirt, a shoe, socks, hat, gloves, etc.), an item for personal hygiene (toothbrush, toothpaste, soap, washcloth, etc.), or an item for play (huge toy, deck of cards, small puzzle, giant teddy bear and small teddy bear, etc.). Determine what is *essential* because *this needs to go into the suitcase first.* Make a pile of the essential items. Then, determine what items are for pleasure. Make a pile of these items. Can they all fit? This is where we need to use our problem-solving and decision-making skills. Children learn they can't always take everything they would like to pack in an overnight bag or in a suitcase. Often parents appreciate this and will tell you. Also, children learn there is "space" inside a pair of boots and items can be stuffed there.

Hoola Hoop Spaceship

Place a hoola hoop on the floor and have one person step inside, then another, then another, and so on. How many students can fit inside comfortably for take-off? How many can *squeeze* into the space? Encourage students to talk about their personal experiences in an elevator, or on a crowded bus with standing-room only, and so on. For how long can people stay this crowded in a small space? Discuss.

Standard #10: Measurement

Classroom experience with measurement needs to be *concrete*. Children need to have a variety of experiences measuring length and width. They also need to gain experience with how tall something is in comparison with another item, and how heavy an item is by comparison with another item.

How Many Sticks Long Is the Table?

On the playground, go on a stick or twig hunt. Bring in a variety from your own backyard, and store them on end in an empty coffee can. (If sticks and twigs are not available, different lengths of bulky yarn can be used.) Give each student a twig (or piece of yarn) and have them measure the table. Ask, "How many sticks long is the table, Jeri?" Then record that number. Ask, "How many sticks long is the table, Floria?" Then record that number. Do this systematically until everyone has had an opportunity to measure. Have students note that the numbers are all different, or "don't agree." How will we ever know how long the table is? This is the opportunity to introduce the *concept* of standard measure, and to give students the opportunity to use the ruler, which gives the same answer for each student.

How Much Does the Basket Weigh?

Have a bathroom scale available so that children can weigh themselves and each other informally. After they have had experience with this, have them hold a two-pound box of sugar and then step on the scale. Does the actual weight vary by two digits? It should. Children will want to experience this, and add on two digits to their weight. Next, have students hold their objects and see if their weight varies. Then weigh the object itself to see how much it weighs.

Weighing a Pet Rabbit

If you have a classroom pet, it is difficult to get the animal to stay still long enough on the scale surface in order for it to be weighed. One alternative to weighing the pet directly is to have a student hold the pet, settle it down, and then step on the scale and hold still. What is the difference between that weight and the weight when the child gets on the scale alone? Try this with several children to determine the approximate weight of the pet. Children can do this at home with their pet cat or dog to determine the weight of the animal, and will enjoy this new learning experience.

Standard #11: Statistics and Probability

Students need experiences with collecting, organizing, and describing information (data). This can be done with items in their own environment, and through the use of graphs.

Graphs of Ten

A kindergarten classroom can have large graphs displayed on several walls, so that children can refer to the information again and again. For example, work with the numeral "ten" and have students bring in ten of "something." (A note home to parents explaining your intention to create a graph will be helpful.) On a large piece of butcher paper, create a grid. In colorful, bold letters at the top, print a catchy title such as: "TEN—COUNT THEM," or "THE STORY OF TEN." Along the left side list the name of each student. Then, when they bring in their ten items, have them count them, handle them, and eventually paste them (or use clips, pins, glue, tape) to the grid. In this way, they will see continual groupings of ten, as well as the ten objects that each person brought. There will be a variety, such as ten buttons, ten envelopes, ten paper clips, ten pennies, ten ribbons, and ten pieces of candy.

Graph: What Color Are You Wearing Today?

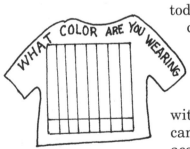

Help students decide the main color they are wearing today. If they're wearing blue jeans and a plaid shirt, the color is blue. Create a color graph by having students select their color from among construction paper squares that have been cut out. Paste them on the color graph. You can also talk about colors in terms of mood, such as feeling blue with sadness, feeling red with anger, or feeling green with envy, and so on. Students can match their mood color to their clothing color—is it an accurate match?

What's Your Favorite Pizza?

Give students 6-inch red circle shapes and felt pens and have them "create" their own pizza with brown circles for pepperoni, green stripes for peppers, yellow for cheese, and so on. (Or, this can be coordinated with gadget printing and tempera paint for an art experience.) Then have a conversation about the pizzas so that students can begin to compare theirs and help categorize them (pepperoni and cheese; pepperoni, cheese, mushrooms; etc.). You may have as many as

seven or eight categories. Print the titles along the bottom of
a giant grid, and have each student come up to the grid
and show where his or her pizza will be attached.

Create a different pizza treat with half a bagel and a
variety of jams and jellies. For morning snack, children
can help make their own strawberry pizza, peach pizza, or
blueberry pizza. They can give them special names, too.

Graphs, Graphs, Graphs

The kindergarten classroom can be alive with colorful graphs with all types
of information. Here are some possibilities to get you started:

- the weather
- color of eyes
- color of shoes
- favorite storybook (from three possibilities)
- favorite season
- favorite food
- favorite soup

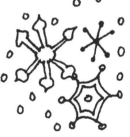

What Is the Probability That It Will Snow Tomorrow?

If this question is asked in the middle of May, the probability may well be zero, depending upon the area of the country
and depending upon the weather pattern of the previous week.

Weather is one area where children can make predictions for the following
day (based upon the past week) and become fairly good predictors. They will
enjoy this experience. Use weather symbols for the charts: cloudy (cotton balls),
rain (umbrella shape), sun (glossy yellow circles), and wind (lengths of wavy
yarn).

Standard #12: Fractions and Decimals

The approach to fractions at this level should be heavily weighted in oral language and in manipulatives.

Students should not be introduced to pencil-and-paper activities until long
after the skills have been mastered, unless it is incidental or unless they ask to
know how a fraction is represented.

One Half Is a Good Place to Begin

For this, you will need two teddy bears and eight pencils. Each teddy bear is to get half of the pencils. How can this be done? By counting out one pencil for the first bear, and placing it in front of the bear. Then, one pencil for the second bear, and placing it in front of the second bear. Follow this procedure until each bear has an equal amount. This is one half of the total number. Repeat this with pencils, crayons, erasers, and so on.

When students help with snack time, have each of the two helpers distribute half of the paper napkins. How do they determine half? By counting out "one for you, one for me, one for you, one for me" until they are distributed equally.

This same procedure can be used with buttons, beads, counting blocks, and so on.

The Concept of "One Half as Equal"

In order to help children gain an understanding of this concept, it is helpful to use food. If you have a rectangular graham cracker with a dividing line through the middle, gently break it in half so that students get equal amounts. This makes the concept quite clear.

The Lion and the Mouse

Make cut-outs of a lion and a mouse for the flannel board. Pretend they are invited to a birthday party where each animal is to get one half of a small pie. Use circular cut-outs to show how the lion cuts one half (not in the middle, but with one very large and one very small piece). Then, the mouse complains that he did not get an equal share. The lion, wanting to be "fair," decides to cut again, and this time it is still not in the middle of the circular cut-out. *Finally,* have the mouse suggest folding the paper in half and cutting on the line. Do this as a demonstration, then cut, and place one piece on top of the other.

On this day, have many pre-cut circular paper pieces in the Math Center so that children can re-enact the story and fold and cut, and fold and cut again, so that the mouse and the lion can get equal pieces of the pie.

Standard #13: Patterns and Relationships

There are patterns everywhere we look—up, down, all around. We wear patterns, too.

Exploring Patterns

Use the flannel board and cut-outs of red tulips and yellow daffodil flower shapes. Put the flowers in rows, and have students "guess" what flower is next.

Daffodil, Tulip, Daffodil, Tulip, _____ (*AB, AB, AB*)

Daffodil, Daffodil, Tulip, Daffodil, Daffodil _____ (*AAB, AAB*)

Lining Up by Eye Color Pattern

How far can we go? Line up at the door by eye color (brown eyes, blue eyes, brown eyes, blue eyes).

Color Pattern Strips

Use three colors of circles and squares (red, yellow, blue). Have students line up the circles in patterns such as red, yellow, blue, red yellow blue (*ABC, ABC*). Then make pattern lines using the squares. **Challenge:** Integrate the circles and squares within the pattern line.

Picture the Sound Pattern

Have cut-outs of dogs and cats and have students place them along a pattern strip, or on a flannel board. How can we say dog/cat, dog/cat, dog/cat, using sounds? ("Grr-r-r/Meow")

What would be the sound pattern of a lion/bee? (R-r-roar/Buz-z-z)

Have children think up and sound out other animal patterns. The class can listen carefully and guess the animals in the pattern.

Stringing Beads

Have two sets of beads and two strings. Make a pattern on one set, and have students string the pattern on the second set. They can then become the pattern maker.

Chalkboard Ledge Patterns

Set up a picture book pattern along the chalkboard. One can be sideways, one upright, one upside down. The next is sideways, so what comes next?

(upright) and what comes next? (upside down). This is an ABC, ABC pattern. Set up another picture book pattern and begin again.

Patterns, Patterns, Patterns

Children can create patterns with concrete items such as seashells, leaves, assorted nuts, assorted keys, assorted silverware (plasticware), and so on.

Dogs and Bones Relationship

Have a pile of cut-out shapes for the flannel board such as dogs, bones, mice, and cheese. Which ones go together? (dogs/bones, mice/cheese)

What's Up? What's Down?

Divide the flannel board in half and call the upper half "sky" and the lower half "ground." Have cut-outs of items that would be obvious for belonging to one area or the other (stars, clouds, rocks, flowers).

Then, have some cut-outs that could be in either place, such as an airplane or a bird. What else can children come up with that might be found in both places? This makes good "math talk."

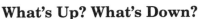

More General Mathematics Activities

The Shape of Things

Children need to feel objects that are round with smooth ends and objects that are square or rectangular with four sides and pointed corners. Collect a variety of round and square (or rectangular) items for your Math Exploration Table, and encourage students to classify them by putting all of the round items in one pile and all of the square (or rectangular) items in another. Read the African tale *The Village of Round & Square Houses* by Ann Grifalconi as a link to the shapes.

Shapes Are Everywhere!

Look around the classroom for round and square shapes. Each classroom is different, but this may help to get you started:

round—clock face, magnifying glass, wastebasket, pencil, crayon, felt pen, stickers

square and rectangular—ruler, door, windows, overhead lights, light switch, posters, tile squares

We Can Make Shapes

Have children work in groups and use their body to make a circle shape and then to make a square shape. Read the storybook *Shapes and Things* by Tana Hoban, and carefully examine the contents.

Walk a Shape

Use masking tape to create large shape outlines on the floor that students can walk around on tip-toe, walk around on their heels, and walk around by placing one foot in front of the other so that the heel and toe are touching. Through this activity, they are grooving the shape concept into their brain kinesthetically.

Who Makes a Good Square?

Some children are tall, some are short. To make a square you will need four students who are similar in height. Have them work together to discover which four make a good square shape when they lie down on the rug. (Does having four students standing in a row help the others to predict whether or not this particular foursome will make a good square shape when lying down? Help children to see that it does.)

Guess a Shape

Have children put their hands behind their backs. Place a round or square (or rectangular) object into their hand and then have them tell you what shape it is.

Three to five children at a time can go to a designated area of the room and close their eyes. Other children can place a round or square object in their hands.

Directions can be given: "All those with round objects, stand on your left foot." "All those with square objects, go to the block area."

A Triangle Focus

Today is "Triangle Day." What's the difference between a triangle and a square? (The triangle has three corners and the square has four corners.) Children can:

- make a triangle shape with hands (two thumbs, two index fingers)
- make a triangle shape on the floor (three children)
- find the triangle shapes in the block area
- find triangular shapes in the classroom
- sort and classify shapes by triangle, circle, square, rectangle

It's Time to Meet Mr. Rectangle

Children need to have a variety of rectangular and square objects to work with, and need to know the similarities and differences between a rectangle and a square. (They both have *four* sides, but the square has four **equal** sides and the rectangle has two long sides and two short sides.)

Introduce Cuisenaire® rods so that students can gain experience with rectangles, length, and building and constructing. It is through this manipulation of the rods that children come to grasp the concept of "rectangle" as well as length. When they are building structures, they also become more familiar with the concept of "balance."

These rods, as well as building blocks, should be an option for students during their free-choice time.

Shapes and Sizes

Have a variety of circles, squares, rectangles, and triangles in different sizes. They can be made of wood, plastic, or cardboard. Mix the objects all together and have children put them in groups that are alike in some way. They may put all round objects in one group and all objects with edges in another.

Then, have them group them in another way. For example, all circles in one pile, all squares in another pile, all rectangles in another, and so on.

Then have them make more discrete groupings with all *large* circles in one group and all *small* circles in another group. Do the same with the other shapes.

Button, Button, Who's Got the Button?

Start a collection of buttons so that students can go to the Button Jar and work with classification of buttons by size, shape, color, number of holes, and other properties. Have this available as an option during free-choice time. The addition of new buttons will add to the challenge of the task. Have students work in pairs so that they can learn from each other.

Everybody Counts All Over the World

The Numerals Are Everywhere!

What do children know about counting in a foreign language? Perhaps some children have ancestors who originally came from places in a different part of the world and they can ask them about counting to ten in a foreign language and then report the information to the class. Set up items that are representative of the country and have children experience counting from one to ten. Visit a large supermarket for foods representative of the country. For example, with Italy, you can use a variety of pasta for counting, categorizing, and patterning.

Become familiar with the *Count Your Way* books by Jim Haskins, with a variety of illustrators. With these picture books you can count your way through Africa, China, Japan, Russia, and so on, and learn a great deal about the country as well.

Counting in Italian

On the chart below, the first column contains the numeral that all children can recognize. The second column contains the name of that numeral, and the third column serves as a phonetic pronunciation key to the names.

1	uno	(OO'no)
2	due	(DO'ay)
3	tre	(tray)
4	quattro	(KWAHT'troh)
5	cinque	(CHEEN'kway)
6	sei	(say)

7	sette	(SEHT'tay)
8	otto	(OHT'to)
9	nove	(NO'vay)
10	dieci	(DYAY'chee)

Ten Little Italian Indians   Try singing this to the tune of "Ten Little Indians." Have children hold up their fingers as they say the numerals. (We are going from the familiar to the unfamiliar. Recent research on the brain and learning shows that this age is the very best time for young children to learn a foreign language.)

OO'no
DOO'ay
TRAY little Indians.
KWAHT'troh
CHEEN'kway
SAY little Indians.
SEHT'tay
OHT'to
NO'vay Indians.
DYAY'chee Indian boys.

Counting in German

Teach children to say the numerals in German, and to sing the song using the German number name.

1	eins	(eyns)
2	zwei	(tsvy)
3	drei	(dry)
4	vier	(feer)
5	funf	(fuenf)
6	sechs	(zekhs)
7	sieben	(ZEE'ben)
8	acht	(ahkht)
9	neun	(noyn)
10	zehn	(tsehn)

Ten Little German Indians   Children will learn this readily if it is sung repeatedly.

EYNS little

TSVY little

DRY little Indians

FEER little

FUENF little

ZEKHS little Indians.

ZEE'ben little

AHKHT little

NOYN little Indians.

TSEHN little Indian boys!

Counting in Spanish

Teach children to say the numerals in Spanish, and learn the song using the Spanish number name.

1	uno	(OO'no)
2	dos	(DOSE)
3	tres	(TRAYS)
4	cuatro	(KAWH'tro)
5	cinco	(SEEN'ko)
6	seis	(SEH'ees)
7	seite	(SYEH'teh)
8	ocho	(OH'cho)
9	nueve	(NWEH'yeh)
10	diez	(DYEHS)

Ten Little SPANISH Indians   Children will learn this readily if it is sung repeatedly.

OO'no little

DOSE little

TRAYS little Indians.

KAWH'tro little

SEEN'ko little

SEH'ees little Indians.

SYEH'teh little

OH'cho little

NWEH'veh little Indians.

DYEHS little Indian boys.

Indonesian Number Names

In Bali, there are three important castes, or groups, of people. They are the Brahmana, the Satria, and the Waisa. Two of the castes use number names for their children. Most Balinese families have four offspring.

Number	Brahmana	Waisa
1	Putu	Wayan
2	Madw	Made
3	Nyoman	Nyoman
4	Ketut	Ketut

If you were to meet Wayan, for example, you would know that he or she is the first-born in the family. To a foreigner, it may not be so easy to determine the caste, but the birth-order number name gives us no problem.

If twins are born, the baby born first would be Wayan, and the baby born second would be Made. Since four children would be the norm in a family, if a fifth should be born, the numbering process would begin again with the name Wayan.

This can lead to a discussion of birth order in our own families, and to the number names we would be given. For an exercise, determine who is named "First," who is named "Second," who is named "Third," and who is named "Fourth." Then, is anyone named "First" again in the family?

In the USA, a boy could be named after his father and the title of Jr. (junior) would follow the name, thus denoting that this person is the *second* one in that family with the same name. Some families use Roman numerals, such as George James Cook III, which means the *third* one in that family with the same name. (This form of name/numbering is usually applicable to males, since a family traditionally has taken the last name of the father, although today that varies.) Do we have any "juniors" in our kindergarten classroom?

First   Second   Third

Some Math Picture Books for Kindergarteners

During the last decade, an abundance of delightful math picture books for children have become available on the market. See the Bibliography for some excellent choices, as well as those listed below.

Counting Books:
  Dinner at the Panda Palace,. Stephanie Calmenson
  Fish Eyes: A Book You Can Count On, Lois Ehlert
  This Old Man, Carol Jones
  Ten Potatoes in a Pot and Other Counting Rhymes, Michael Jay Katz
  How Many? How Many? How Many?, Rick Walton
Measurement Books:
  Inch by Inch, Leo Lionni
  How Big Were the Dinosaurs?, Bernard Most
  The Line Up Book, Marisabine Russo
Shape Books:
  What Am I? Looking Through Shapes at Apples and Grapes, N. N. Charles
  'Round and Around, James Skofield
  The Wing on a Flea, Ed Emberly
  Sea Shapes, Suse MacDonald
Subtraction Books:
  Six Sleepy Sheep, Jeffie Ross Gordon
  Moon Jump, a Countdown . . . , Paula Brown
Books About Time:
  It's About Time! (poetry), Lee Bennett Hopkins
  The Grouchy Ladybug, Eric Carle
  Mary Alice, Operator Number Nine, Jeffrey Allen

Singing About Pennies

The following is a well-known traditional American song:

Pop Goes the Weasel

A penny for a spoon of thread,
A penny for a needle,
That's the way the money goes,
Pop! Goes the weasel.

Activities for this song:

1. Examine pennies. Who's picture is on the front? Can you find the date? What does "one cent" mean? (It's another way of saying a penny.) What's the penny made from? What else do you notice about your penny?

2. Use a purse with a snap for closing, or a change purse. While singing the song, take out a penny for the thread, a penny for the needle, and put it on the counter. When singing, "Pop! Goes the Weasel," *snap* the purse shut with a flair in time to the last line.

3. Have ten pennies in the purse. Give five children a chance to use the purse while singing the song. Then count the pennies from one to ten. Then count from *one cent* to *ten cents*.

4. How many pennies equal a nickel? Count out five and have a nickel available. Teach this concept. Make a chart for the room.

5. How many pennies equal a dime? Count out ten and have a dime available. Teach this concept. Make a chart for the room.

6. Some children may be able to work with the concept of combinations of coins that equal ten cents:

   - ten pennies
   - five pennies and one nickel
   - two nickels
   - one dime

Numbers Make Me Sing—"This Old Man"

The following is an English counting song that children enjoy singing and memorizing. Accompanying motions include:

- holding up appropriate number of fingers for the verse
- knocking knuckles together twice for "nick-nack"
- slapping knees with palms of hands twice for "paddy whack"
- extending hand to "give a dog a bone"
- circling one hand around the other for "this old man came rolling home"

1. This old man, he played one. He played nick-nack on my drum. *With a nick-nack, paddy whack, give a dog a bone. This old man came rolling home.*

2. This old man, he played two. He played nick-nack on my shoe. (*repeat italicized lines*)

3. This old man, he played three. He played nick-nack on my tree. (*repeat italicized lines*)

4. This old man, he played four. He played nick-nack at my door. (*repeat italicized lines*)

5. This old man, he played five. He played nick-nack on my hive. (*repeat italicized lines*)

6. This old man, he played six. He played nick-nack on my sticks. (*repeat italicized lines*)

7. This old man, he played seven. He played nick-nack up in heaven. (*repeat italicized lines*)

8. This old man, he played eight. He played nick-nack on my plate. (*repeat italicized lines*)

9. This old man, he played nine. He played nick-nack on my line. (*repeat italicized lines*)

10. This old man, he played ten. He played nick-nack on my pen. (*repeat italicized lines*)

Counting with Mother Math Goose

Children enjoy the repetition and the rhyme and learn to count by rote with this familiar rhyme.

One, two, buckle my shoe.
Three, four, shut the door.
Five, six, pick up sticks.
Seven, eight, it's getting late.
Nine, ten, a big fat hen.
1, 2, 3, 4, 5, 6, 7, 8, 9, 10.

Then backwards:

Nine, ten, a big fat hen.
Seven, eight, it's getting late.
Five, six, pick up sticks.
Three, four, open the door.
One, two, buckle my shoe.
10, 9, 8, 7, 6, 5, 4, 3, 2, 1.

More Fun with Mother Math Goose

One Two Three

One, two, three, four, five,
Once I caught a fish alive.
Six, seven, eight, nine, ten,
But I let it go again.

Why did you let it go?
Because it bit my finger so.
Which finger did it bite?
The little one upon the right.

Listen for the Numbers in the Rhyme

Read more *Mother Goose* rhymes. When the children *hear* a number, have them stand (and be able to say what it was at the end).

The Dove and the Wren (*two and ten*)

The dove says, "Coo, coo, what shall I do?
I can scarce maintain two."
"Pooh, pooh!" says the wren. "I've got ten
And keep them all like gentlemen."

Sing, Sing (*two*)

Sing, sing, what shall I sing?
Cat's run away with the ball of
   string!
Do, do, what shall I do?
The cat has bittin' it right in two.

Pease Porridge (*nine*)

Pease porridge hot,
   Pease porridge cold,
Pease porridge in the pot,
   Nine days old.

Call upon someone who is standing to say the number name. Have them all sit back down and listen for the number in the second verse. Stand at the end if they know it.

Some like it hot,
   Some like it cold,
Some like it in the pot,
   Nine days old.

Baa, Baa, Black Sheep (*three*)

Baa, baa, black sheep,
   Have you any wool?
Yes sir, yes sir,
   three bags full.

Call upon one student who is standing, at the end, to say the number. Then have them all sit back down. For verse two, listen for this: "How many times is one mentioned?" Then add: 1 plus 1 plus 1 equals 3—so the answer is 3. This can be pantomimed with beanbags.

One for my master,
　One for my dame,
And one for the little boy
　Who lives down the lane.

The Black Hen *(ten)*

For this rhyme, the numbers in lines 5 and 6 can be changed as children chant aloud, but line 7 is always "ten" to rhyme with "hen."

Hickety, pickety, my black hen
She lays eggs for gentlemen;
Gentlemen come every day
To see what my black hen did lay.

Was it _____? (No, no, no, no)
Was it _____? (No, no, no, no)
Was it ten? (Yes, yes, yes, yes)
Ten big eggs from my black hen.

(one child can ask a number while all chant the response)

Variation: Distribute number cards (except for ten) to students, and point to one to hold up the card so others can see and then say the number. This is good for number recognition. Those who do know the number names carry the others along until they learn them.

Wee Willie Winkie *(eight)*

Wee Willie Winkie runs through the town,
　Upstairs and downstairs, in his nightgown;
Rapping at the window, crying through the lock,
　"Are the children in their beds? It's now EIGHT o'clock."

Distribute cardboard clocks to several children, and have them put the hands in the appropriate places to show "eight o'clock." OR, call upon a child to change a large model clock in the room. Also, the verse can be changed to "six o'clock, nine o'clock" for practice with time.

A Word About Computers

Computers in the Classroom

Children will come to school in various states of readiness to work with computers. Some children have had experience with computers in their home, have observed an adult working with the computer, and may have their own programs and a facility for working with the computer. Pair these children with those who have little or no computer experience, and let them become the peer-tutor.

Working with a Partner

Working in pairs seems to be effective at this level. Children engage in conversation about the program, the action they can take, how to do something, and they learn from each other. In addition, language development is promoted when children are verbally interacting.

Movement with a Purpose

In addition to learning from the program, many children benefit from making an object move left/right, up/down, over/under, and thus engage in concept development.

Computers Promote Problem Solving

Good software programs offer children many opportunities for making choices and decisions. Some programs include:

- *Freddie Fish and the Case of the Missing Kelp Seeds* (K–2). Mac/Win 3.1 CD. This adventure game for the nonreader involves higher-level problem-solving skills.
- *Math Keys* (K–6). Houghton-Mifflin and MECC (800-685-MECC). The Mac disk sets allow students to practice probability concepts and data analysis with mystery machines and number cubes.
- *Putt-Putt Saves the Zoo* (PreK–1). Mac/Win 3.1 CD. A little cartoon car needs help saving baby animals by solving simple problems.

Computers Empower Children

Children can do many things on the computer that make them feel good. For one thing, they can change their mind and undo a mistake without having to erase and leave a messy look. One touch of the "delete" key and the highlighted area is gone. Some children think of this as magic, whereas the computer is only following their directions. Soon the child realizes that he or she is giving the directions, and the computer is carrying them out. This gives the child a sense of power and control over writing, artwork, and even some of the program material.

Feedback Is Instant

Children do not have to wait for a busy adult to give her or him feedback. The computer gives feedback almost immediately at the touch of a finger. For this reason, many kindergarteners (even adults) enjoy working with computer programs.

A Computer Will Wait

Again, children feel empowered because they can take time to think something through before clicking on a command or a key. A computer has the capacity to wait for long periods of time before a command is given. This helps the young child who needs time to think—and it depends upon the software program being used as well. On some programs when a certain amount of time has lapsed, computers provide children with answers to reduce frustration/anxiety levels.

At Least One per Classroom

National teacher associations advocate that computer instruction begin no later than kindergarten and that there should be at least one in every kindergarten classroom—more if possible. If your school district is lagging in this area, enlist the support of your local PTA.

Computer Programs

Journals such as *Early Childhood Today* and *Teaching Children Mathematics* (published by the National Council of Teachers of Mathematics) review computer software in each issue. These journals give readers bibliographic and price information along with brief descriptions. Check with your school librarian to see if these journals can be ordered for the use of primary-grade teachers.

Computers Meet You at Your Level

Many computer programs are designated for children from ages 2–6 or ages 3–6, thus giving an age and ability range for children in this group. Again, some children may be proficient with some of these programs, and some kindergarteners may just be getting an introduction. Start with the easier programs and then vary them according to ability levels.

Computers and Books

Some children's books are available in software versions. Children are able to click on to various areas of the screen that open windows and doors so they can see beyond the picture, and they can click on to hear the conversation. While this does not replace the experience of having a teacher read aloud a picture book with much enjoyment and conversation, it can give certain books another dimension for children to experience. It can also prolong the pleasure of a book after the teacher has read it.

The Teacher's Computer

Some teachers at this level enjoy bringing in their personal laptop computer so that they can introduce children to outside sources such as the Internet, set up e-mail pals, and link on to the programs that are available with this resource. This usually depends upon the expertise and interest level of the teacher. It can enrich your units of study.

Districtwide Computer Committee

If you have an opportunity to serve on this committee, you will gain an abundance of knowledge and information about resources that are readily available. By all means, be in the forefront when it comes to computers because the students and parents will benefit from your knowledge and input.

Program Choices

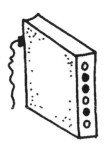

There is a wide variety of material available for this age group. Computer programs come in all subjects. Here are just three examples: *JumpStart Preschool* (Knowledge Adventure, Mac, Windows, 800-622-1244, ages 3–5) deals with colors, shapes and puzzles, and children drag items into place; *James Discovers Math* (Broderbund, Mac, Windows, 800-521-6263, ages 3–6) enables children to play some early math games; and *Bailey's Book House* (Edmark, Mac, Windows, 800-362-2890, ages 2–6) is a beginning language program dealing with rhyming words, letters, and making greeting cards.

Teacher Resources

Journals

Monthly teacher journals such as *Instructor, Teaching K–8, Teaching Children Mathematics, Early Childhood Today,* to name but a few, are available.

Books

Borman, Jamie Lynne. *Computer Dictionary for Kids . . . and Their Parents,* with illustrations by Yvette Santiago Banek. Hauppauge, NY: Barron's Educational Series, Inc., 1995.

Frazier, Deneen, Barbara Kurshan, and Sara Armstrong. *Internet for Kids.* San Francisco, CA: Sybex, 1995.

The Multimedia Home Companion. Rebecca Buffum Taylor, ed. NY: Warner Books, Inc., 1995. (Reviews of titles in edutainment, games, kids' corner, choosing an online service, and so on.)

Mathematics Survival Tips

Some New, Some Review

1. Use concrete objects (manipulatives) that children can handle for counting, adding, and subtracting.
2. Collect a wide variety of objects such as pebbles, buttons, acorns, tiny pinecones, bottle caps, etc., to use as manipulatives.
3. Color-code your shelves (red, yellow, blue). Then, color-code math games and manipulatives with red (those that go on the red shelf), blue (those that go on the blue shelf), and yellow (those that go on the yellow shelf). This makes clean-up time go more smoothly.
4. Keep all rulers in a container (coffee can) on the countertop.
5. Cut numerals out of sandpaper so that children can trace them and learn how to form them (kinesthetic learning).

6. Use play or donated telephones so children can learn to dial and to press their home phone number, an emergency number (911), a relative's number. Explain the redial function.

7. Ask children to name their "favorite number" and why. They're using language skills and enjoying math information.

8. Demonstrate specifically how to use measuring tape, and how to "read it" before giving it to children to use. Demonstrate how to measure a child from shoulder to wrist, around the waist, around the head, from knee to ankle. Now, have them work in pairs to do the same thing for a hands-on measurement experience.

9. When in doubt, make a graph. Graphs are an "instant picture" of information.

10. Children gain experience with counting and one-to-one correspondence when they count out straws and napkins for snack time.

11. Look everywhere in the classroom for patterns—stripes on the flag, tiles on the floor, windowpanes, overhead lights, radiator, register covers, and so on.

12. Check clothing for patterns—stripes, polka dots, circles, squares, triangles. Is it a repeat pattern—*AB, AB* or *ABC, ABC*?

13. Sort and categorize, sort and categorize repeatedly. (Use different clothespins, potatoes, buttons, seashells, pencils, etc.) Have children explain how they categorized—size, color, shape, function.

14. Use two hula hoops and put them on the floor so that they intersect and make a Venn Diagram. Now sort and categorize items according to properties and see how many have both. Example: Sort *large* and *small* buttons— two piles, all colors. Then, to demonstrate the function of the Venn Diagram, hunt for all of the buttons that have four holes and put them in the middle section. Now we have a section for large, a section for small, and a mixed section for large and small but all with four holes.

15. Sort teddy bears by large, medium, small. Then put them all together again and sort by color. This helps get across the concept of sorting and categorizing.

16. To cut down on noise when working with manipulatives, use a piece of felt on the work top.

17. When using an upright felt board, make sure it slants (like an easel); otherwise, the pieces will be apt to fall off.

18. Use Rebus signs on outside of containers so children will know what *and* how many go inside of them.

19. It's okay to count on your fingers.

20. Practice, practice, practice the things you want children to learn.

21. Repetition is especially effective if it is accompanied by an action of some sort—finger plays, *This Little Piggy Went to Market*.

22. Verbal repetition and body action help to reinforce concepts—"The Hokey Pokey" (right foot, left foot, turn about).

23. Children learn the concept of "one half" quickly when dividing food.

24. Children learn numbers quickly when something is personal for them—"Our cat had four kittens," "I have two sisters," "Daddy comes home at five o'clock," "Six people sit at our table."

25. Everybody sit still for one whole minute—time it! Children will learn how long a minute is. This has a quieting effect on the group also.

Mathematics Activity Pages

Basic Shapes in Color (*triangle, circle, square*)

Become a Number Book Designer (*1–10*)

Polly Loves Crackers with Jam (*shape identification*)

Ready, Set, Jump (*measuring inches*)

Fishy Math (*counting*)

Complete the Pattern (*patterning*)

Pattern Beads (*creating a color pattern*)

Granny's Socks (*creating a pattern, then duplicating it*)

Button, Button, Who's Got the Most Buttons? (*graphing*)

Hamburger, Pizza, or Hot Dog? (*survey, graphing*)

Let's Juggle Some Math (*tracing numerals*)

I'm Nuts About Math (*math award*)

One Potato, Two Potato Math Rhyme (*movement, rhyme*)

Wooden Soldier Measuring Chart (*body measurement*)

Working with Weight (*more than, less than*)

Celebrate 100 (*100 days of school math ideas*)

The Fraction Cookie Jar (*one-half*)

Clown Number Hats (*matching objects with number names*)

Good Breakfast Math (*subtraction*)

All Aboard (*Counting 1–10*)

D. J. Dog Bone Company (*counting by tens*)

Calendar

Basic Shapes in Color

Color the triangles GREEN. Color the circles PURPLE. Color the squares ORANGE.

Become a Number Book Designer

Gage M. Bunny plans to make a Number Book. You can make one, too, from 1 to 10.

Polly Loves Crackers with Jam

On each line put an X on the one that does not belong. Then, use your crayons or markers to spread jam on the other crackers. Polly likes strawberry, blueberry, grape, and peach jam.

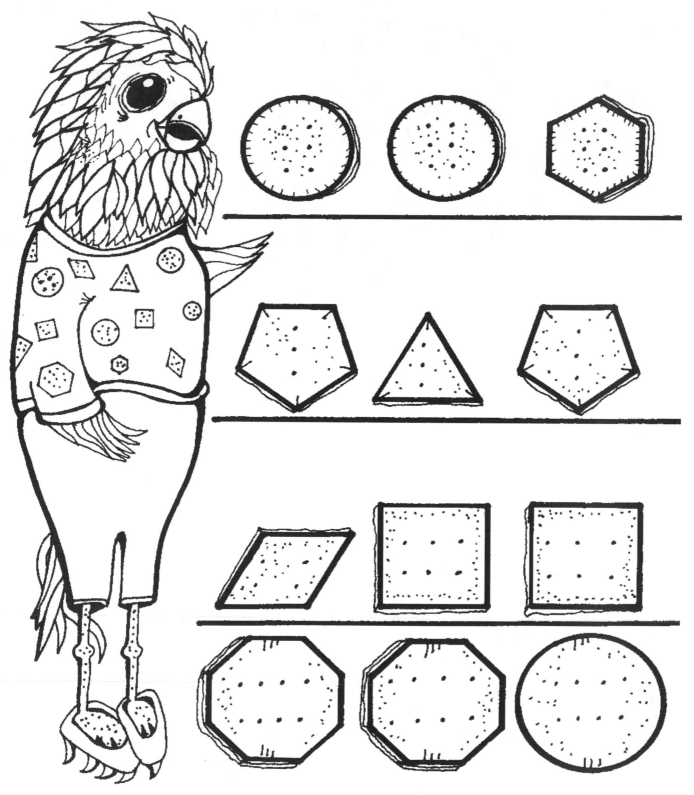

Name _____

Ready, Set, Jump

Use your ruler. Start at the X. Draw a line to show how many inches the rabbit will jump. Color the rabbit that makes the longest jump PINK. Color the rabbit that makes the shortest jump YELLOW.

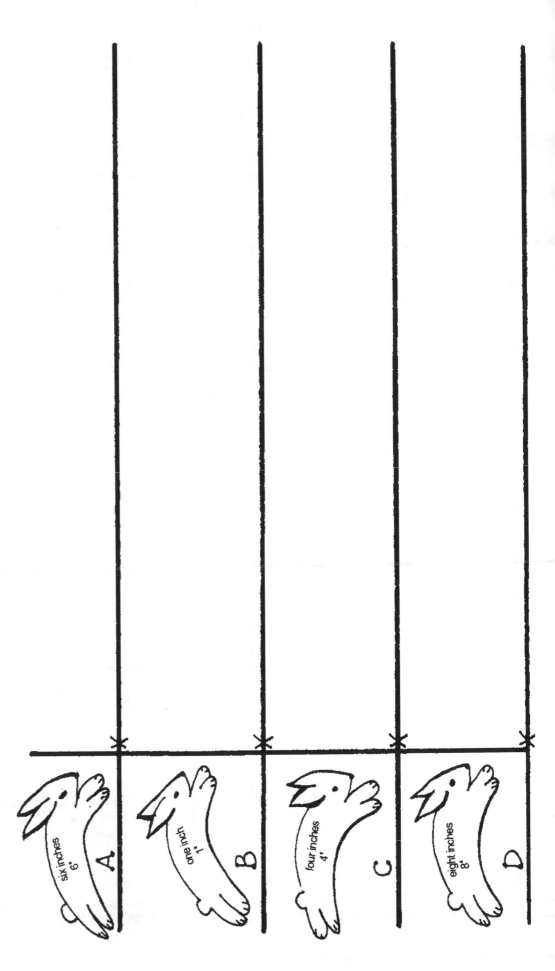

Name _____

Fishy Math

Count the fish in each square. Print that numeral in the circle. Use your magic crayons to make these fish look just beautiful!

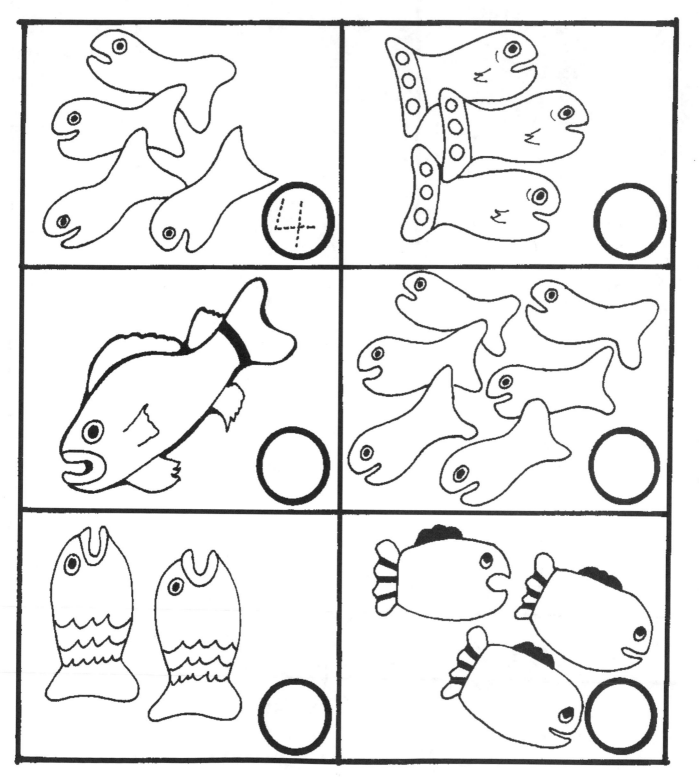

Name _____

Complete the Pattern

Do the sample sun/moon pattern together. Identify the items on each row and complete the pattern. Then, color the objects in each row with alternating colors.

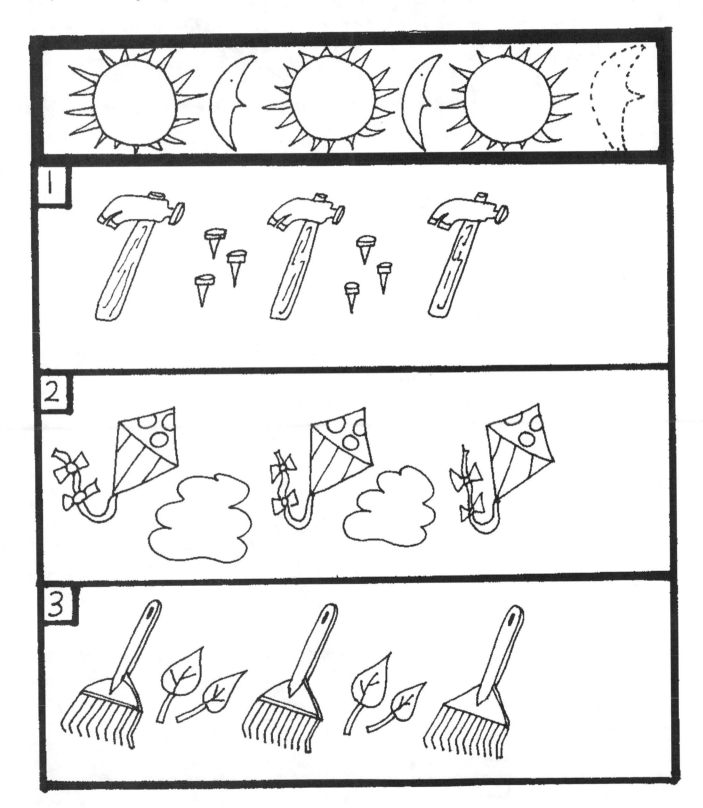

Name _____

Pattern Beads

Color ALL of the beads on String A, using different colors. THEN, color the beads on String B in exactly the same way.

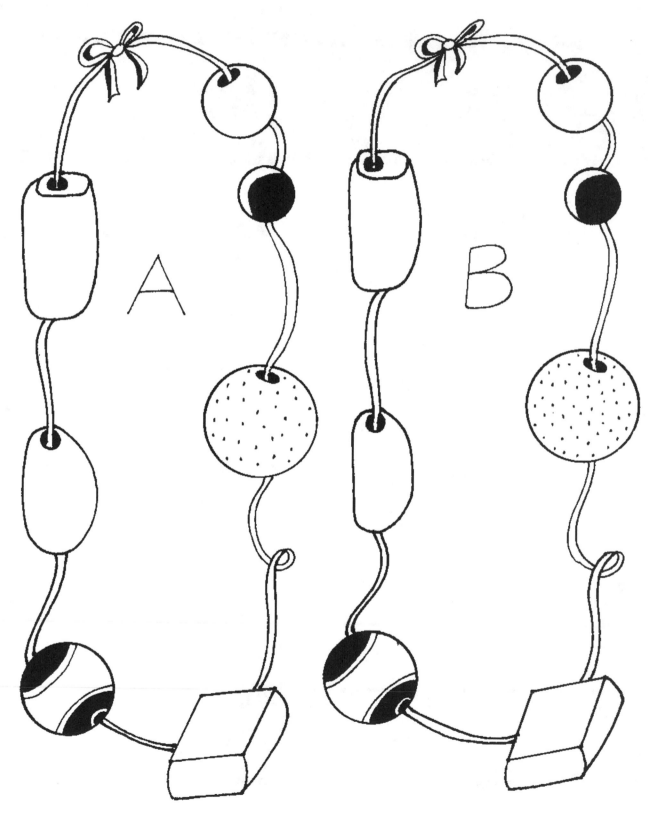

Name

Granny's Socks

Granny likes to knit and you can help her. Color the first sock (A) with different colors. Then, make the second sock (B) look just like it!

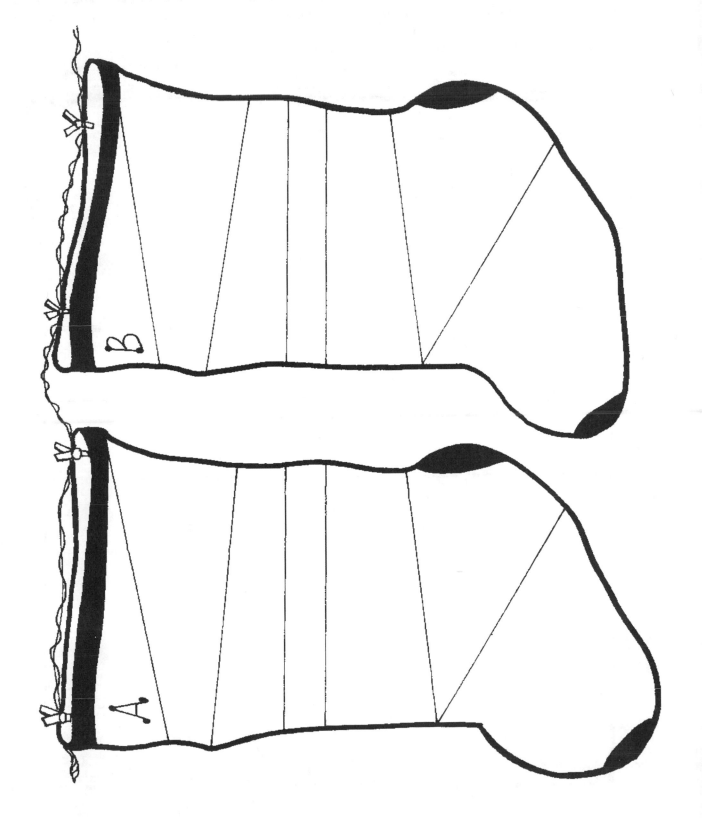

Name _____

Button, Button,
Who's Got the Most Buttons?

Below are four different types of buttons along the bottom. Color each one a different color. Now go on a search in the button jar for the buttons. (If you colored the first button red, color the same ones in the jar red.) Do this for each button. When you finish, make your graph by coloring in the correct number of boxes above each button. (Color the squares red if the button is red.)

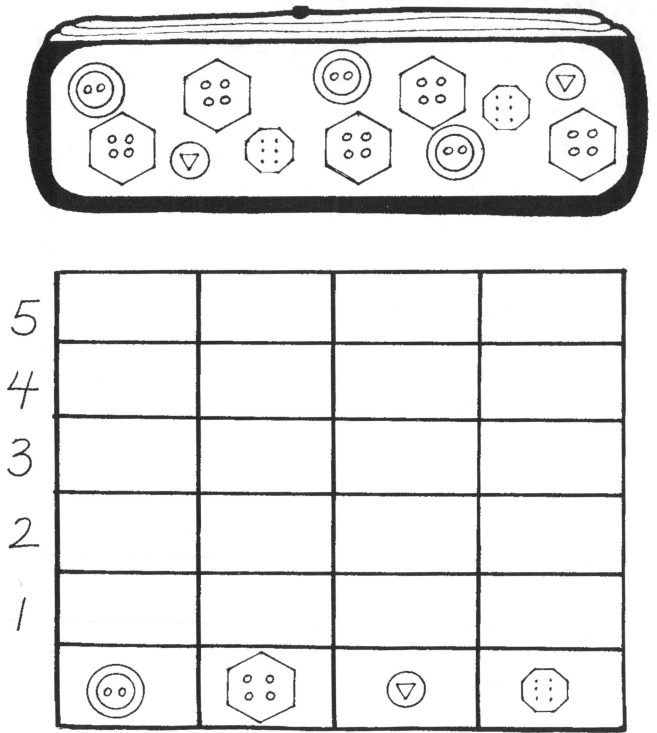

Hamburger, Pizza, or Hot Dog?

Ask ten classmates to select their favorite food. Place an X in the proper column. Count them. Write the TOTAL at the top. Compare your graph with classmates' graphs.

total:	total:	total:
hamburger	pizza	hot dog

Let's Juggle Some Math

E. J. Elephant likes to practice. You can, too, by tracing these numerals. Then color E. J. with happy colors.

I'm Nuts About Math

Trace the numbers on the acorns. Use a different color for each.

Name_____

One plus one is
TWO

Two plus two is
FOUR

Every time that we
do MATH

I seem to like it
MORE

I Am A
Math Nut

Name _____

One Potato, Two Potato Math Rhyme

One potato
Two potato
Three potato
Four

Five potato
Six potato
Seven potato
More

Eight potato
Nine potato
Then there's Ten

Count 1 to 10
And back again.

1 2 3 4 5 6 7 8 9 10

10 9 8 7 6 5 4 3 2 1

Wooden Soldier Measuring Chart

Toy wooden soldiers like to measure and to make comparisons. Let's try it. Work with a partner. Get a piece of string and a yardstick. FIRST, measure the body part with string and stretch it out on the yardstick starting at zero. SECOND, record the nearest inch on the line. Then, like the wooden soldiers, you can make classmate comparisons.

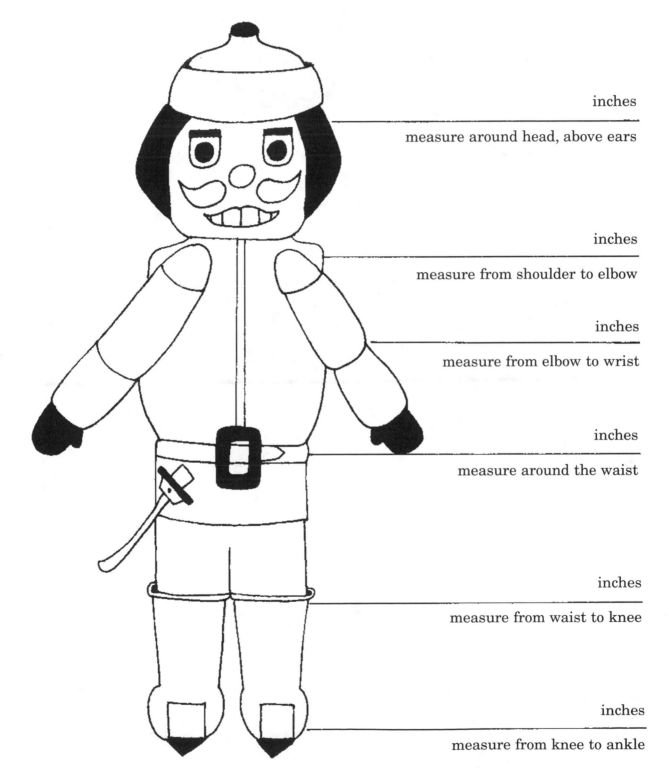

_____ inches

measure around head, above ears

_____ inches

measure from shoulder to elbow

_____ inches

measure from elbow to wrist

_____ inches

measure around the waist

_____ inches

measure from waist to knee

_____ inches

measure from knee to ankle

Name _____

Working with Weight

Put a shoe, or boot, on a scale. How much does it weigh? Record that numeral. Then find three items in the room that weigh LESS THAN that and three items that weigh MORE THAN that. Use your crayons to draw them in the boxes below. (Discuss your findings with classmates.)

Celebrate 100

The 100th day of school usually falls within February. Let's have a 100 MATH DAY!

The Fraction Cookie Jar

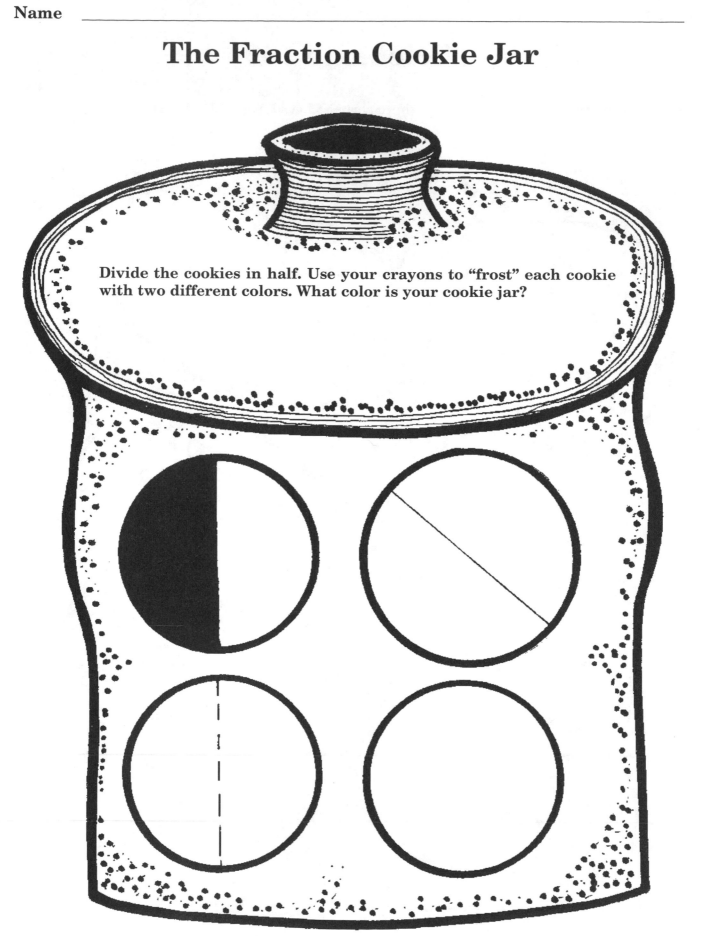

Divide the cookies in half. Use your crayons to "frost" each cookie with two different colors. What color is your cookie jar?

Name _____

Clown Number Hats

Each box has a clown hat with dots on it. Look at each box and count the number of dots on the hat. Then find the matching number word and draw a line to it. Color the fancy hats.

_____

Good Breakfast Math

Practice subtracting with good breakfast food. Each box has a number sentence beneath it. The FIRST numeral tells how many items are in the box. The SECOND numeral tells you how many to "eat" (put on X on it). Write the numeral that tells how many are left. Use your crayons to make the food look healthy.

2 − 1 =

3 − 2 =

1 − 0 =

5 − 1 =

4 − 2 =

3 − 1 =

Name _____

ALL ABOARD

Rusty Bear is getting the Teddy Train ready to roll, but there's still work to do.
You can help by doing the following:

1. Put the numerals on the cars from 1 to 10.
2. Trace the numerals from 1 to 10 at the bottom of the page.
3. Color the train cars.

Thank you!

D. J. Dog Bone Company

D. J. has to count out 100 bones for each sack. You can help him. Count by tens to 100 and write the numerals on the bones. Then color D. J. Thank you.

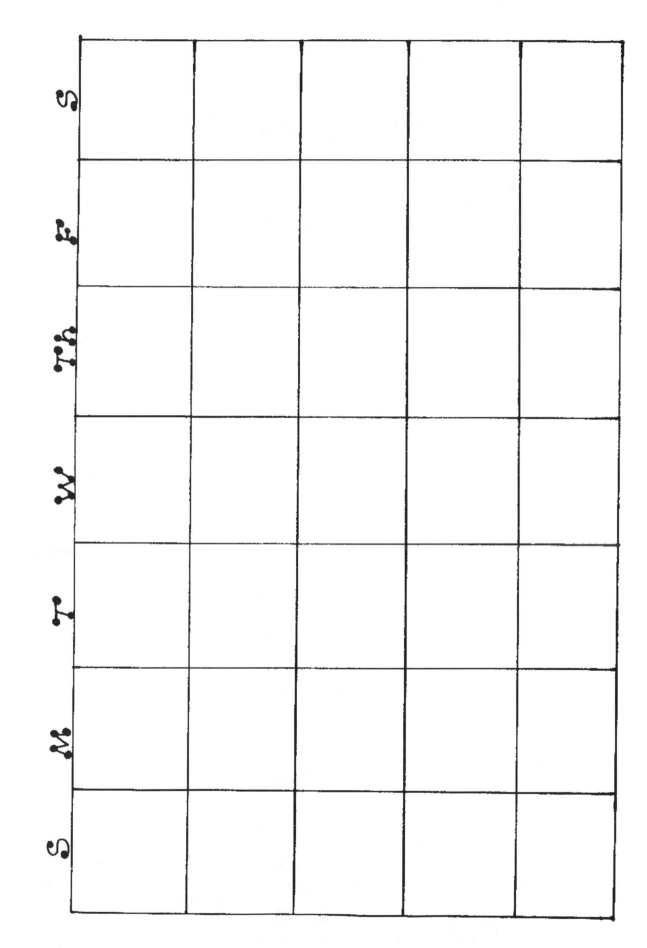

Calendar for the Month of _____

S	M	T	W	Th	F	S

SOCIAL STUDIES

Mr. deZafra

Social Studies

Introduction

Historically, the kindergarten experience was one that "socialized" the child on the road to becoming a group member who contributed to society. This included, among other things, (1) helping the child to gain a knowledge about self and others, and how to get along together, (2) stimulating the child's interest in knowledge about the immediate environment and the physical and natural world, (3) placing value on democratic principles of fair play and majority rule, and (4) linking the child to the larger community through participation in special holidays and festivals.

In today's kindergarten, we have added two components: learning about and accepting cultural diversity, and gaining a greater awareness and acceptance of students who are physically, mentally, and emotionally challenged.

Kindergarten Social Environment

Kindergarten children are engaging in social interaction with peers, learning rules and boundaries, learning about and asking questions about their surroundings—all of which are components of the social studies program. But this program has been expanded because of the access to a wide variety of information available on TV, on the Internet, on CD-ROM materials linked to computers, and through community programs offered by the local library, the zoo, community centers, and arts and science centers.

Developmentally, nothing has changed, of course. Children at this age are naturally self-centered, so we can begin with their world which is composed of families, pets, food, clothing, stores, transportation, communication, a changing society, and all of the other factors they are exposed to in their environment. We can build upon what they already know through conversation (sharing information), picture books, reading aloud, field trips, guest speakers, and by strengthening first-hand observation opportunities in the classroom by allowing children to observe and interact with items from the environment and with their peers.

The kindergarten environment itself needs to be structured, safe, and secure for the children. The pace needs to be unhurried. Give the children time, and peace and quiet for thinking and doing.

It is not so much a question of learning social studies content and memorizing facts at this age, as it is of exposing children to activities that foster an understanding of the complex and changing and often confusing world in which they live.

Social Studies Activities

Meet the Family

Take a photo of the classroom family and hang it up at eye-level so students can see themselves and point to and learn the names of their classmates. Using the copy machine, make a photocopy for each child to take home, along with a list of names of classmates and the room mothers. Have extras available during Open House Night early in the year so that parents can get to know who is in their child's classroom, and begin to refer to them by name.

My Own Family

Write a letter home and ask for a snapshot of the family for a classroom display. Make a colorful bulletin board "Family Tree" using green construction paper for the leaves, and brown construction paper for a huge trunk that goes all the way down to the floor. (First, have students use the brown construction paper and dark brown or black crayon to make bark rubbings from a real tree on the playground, so that it looks more like an actual tree trunk.) By way of the family tree, each child can introduce his or her family to the class. If a photo is not available, have the student(s) draw their family members, and be sure to place that on the tree.

Definition of Family

One definition of family is "a loving group of people who live together and who help each other." Accept the child's family members. Some children may come from a traditional family household while others will not. Some students like to include their pet as a part of their family. Children can learn to readily accept the differences in each family.

Meet Our School Family

Take color prints and/or make a videotape of the school family, including the principal, vice principal, secretary, custodian, nurse, and other team members. On colorful posterboard, make a display of the color prints and print the names of the school family members underneath their picture so students can learn to identify them by name and photo.

The First Family

Introduce the children to the first family of the country—the president's family name, family members, family pet, and the location of the White House in Washington, D.C. on a map or globe. On the World Wide Web is a web site that enables children to take a visit through the White House. Bring in news magazines and newspapers with colored photos to enable the children to identify the faces of the first family members.

There are many picture books that introduce children to presidents and their families. *A Picture Book of Abraham Lincoln* and *A Picture Book of George Washington,* two in a series by David A. Adler, with illustrations by John and Alexandra Wallner, are fine examples.

Make Photo I.D.'s

Take a photograph of each child individually. Find out if the school has a camera and money for film and processing. If not, perhaps a parent who is interested in photography can help. Some teachers, on the other hand, do this on their own.

Take a photo of the child, and make a photo I.D. of that child that includes: name, address, phone number, parent or caregiver's name and phone number. On the other side, you can have categories such as: Favorite Color, Pet's Name, Favorite Food, etc. You may want to include pertinent health information (and medication information) on these photo I.D.'s. Also, use a stamp pad for fingerprints. Laminate the identification card. Let the parents know that you are doing this—many of them are most appreciative and will offer to help with this project.

Make two, one for the child to take home and one to keep in school. Use these I.D.'s when going on a field trip.

We Like to Construct Maps

Children have been exposed to maps many times on television weather channels and on the evening news. Many have seen the span of the entire United States and of the world represented by maps in newspapers, so most have at least an acquaintanceship with maps in their environment. If they have been on family car trips, use of a road map no doubt played a part. Before introducing maps, ask children what they already know about maps.

Encourage children to build with blocks so that they see that maps are "smaller versions" of something real. A tall skyscraper can be three blocks piled high. Homes can be built, as well as stores and gas stations, roads, etc.

For one week, use a rectangular table and have children build a city using blocks, cans, and boxes. Make people from clay figures. They can bring in their miniature toy cars and trucks to travel the "city streets" with their stop signs and traffic signals.

Create a Map of the Classroom

Put a large sheet of kraft paper on the floor. Move it close to one edge of the room and discuss what objects are located along that edge (e.g., windows, shelves, easel, and so on). Then, using chalk, have them draw in those items. Now move the kraft paper to another wall, and talk about what is closest to that side of the paper (e.g., sink, drinking fountain, cozy reading chair, and so on). Follow the same procedure for the four corners of the room. Then, have them use felt pens to trace over the chalk lines. Last, put items on the map that are "in the middle" of the room.

Some children come to understand maps when they are flat on the floor. As soon as the map is hung vertically on the bulletin board, you may lose some of the children who cannot make this transition. But, if you have constructed it together, the transition may not be so difficult.

Point to the Window, Point to the Window on the Map

Since a map represents something that is real, have two children help everyone play a game with the classroom map while seated in the circle. You will need two pointers, one for each child. Have one child go to the real sink and point to it. Have the partner find the sink on the map and point to it. What is to the left of the sink? Point to it. What is to the right of the sink? Point to it. Each of the two children must agree. If one of the children is having difficulty, ask someone to assist, or have the child ask for a friend to come and help.

Then, each of the two students who have been using the pointer can choose a replacement, and take that student's place on the circle. Repeat the process of having one child pointing to something in the room, and the other child locating it on the map. Later, the process can be reversed. First, find it on the map and then find the actual item in the room. Keep doing this, and encourage children to work on this activity during their free-choice time.

Timeline—The Year in Review

At eye-level, or underneath the chalkboard, start with a sheet of construction paper to represent the first month of the school year. Using pictorial representations (Rebus), record important events that happen during September. Then, change to another sheet of paper and another color for October. Keep doing this throughout the year and you will have a meaningful timeline of events (include birthdays, holidays, field trips, special events at school). Keep referring to the timeline as a record of what has been going on in the classroom. Add holidays and birthdays, too. A timeline is another type of "journal," which is a chronicle of events.

Sharing Special Holiday Family Customs

Children from diverse backgrounds have a wealth of information to share about traditions and family customs. When the situations arise, invite students to talk about how holidays are celebrated in their homes. Also, invite parents or relatives from different cultures to share information, 35mm slides and/or photos, and artifacts from their country. Cooking with the students or bringing in food prepared in advance for a mini-tasting experience is also enjoyable and provides a meaningful learning experience for all. It helps to build tolerance for diversity.

At Work and at Play

Have a camera handy at all times, and take photographs of children on the playground and also at work in the classroom. Make a colorful display of these photographs and keep rotating them.

In your newsletter to parents, these photographs can be reproduced and included with the information about the classroom. Also, for Open House, they make an effective bulletin board display and create a great deal of interest.

I'm a Transportation Machine!

First, have students gather on their large circle and ask individuals to demonstrate a special way they can move. Then have students move in that way around the circle. Some suggestions are: walking, skipping, trotting, running (in place), gliding, jumping, and hopping. After reading aloud the picture book *Mirette on a High Wire* by Emily Arnold McCully, secure a piece of rope on the floor; children can enjoy pretending to walk on a tightrope way up high, from one building to another. This is a good balancing activity, and many children need to practice.

We Can't Fly, but Airplanes Can!

How many students have been in an airplane? Let them talk about their experiences. Find magazine pictures of different types of airplanes from piper cubs to jets. Cut them out and make a photo montage for the classroom.

Faster than Turtles, Slower than Trucks

Have children think of all the ways we can be helped to move, and write them down. Some examples include: wheelchairs, crutches, walkers, in-line skates, ice skates, flippers (for swimming), and so on.

Encourage children to think about how fast and how slowly we move in comparison to other animals or objects.

"We move faster than _____ but slower than _____" can be printed on a sentence strip. Have students fill in the blanks first through conversation, and later by completing the strip with an illustration, Rebus style. Later, the strips can be put together on the chalkboard to form a storytrain.

What Do We Ride On, What Do We Ride In?

Work here with the concepts of "on" and "in." Bring in a wealth of picture/information books from the public library on transportation. After the children have had an opportunity to look through them for a few days, along with colorful magazines, talk about the variety of ways that we can go from one place to another. List them, and have children draw the illustrations.

On the circle once again, children can pretend to be driving a car, peddling a bicycle, gliding in a hot air balloon, riding in a train or in an airplane, sailing in a boat, riding on a horse, riding on a camel, riding in an elevator, riding on an escalator, and so on.

Much of this movement will show up in the children's Play Corner, so make room at this time. Encourage children to do some of this movement on the playground as well.

Let's Find Some Good Books About Moving Around

Some good picture books for browsing time or for reading aloud include *Truck* by Donald Crews (excellent perspective), as well as *Big Mama* (train ride) and *Bicycle Race* by Donald Crews. *The Relatives Came* by Cynthia Rylant (automobile), *Hot Air Henry* by Mary Calhoun, with illustrations by Erick Ingraham, and *The Adventures of Taxi Dog* by Debra and Sal Barracca, with pictures by Mark Buehner, also make for satisfying read-aloud adventures that have a focus upon methods of transportation.

The Bicycle Man by Allen Say takes place in Japan. In addition to being a good story, complete with bicycle tricks, two of the main characters are soldiers from the U.S.A. One soldier is black and the other is a white man with a shock of bright red hair, both of whom look totally foreign to the Japanese children. This is a good multi-ethnic experience from everyone's point of view.

The Big Yellow School Bus

Most of the students will be familiar with the big yellow bus. This is an excellent time to invite the bus driver for a visit to discuss safety rules that students must follow when riding on the bus.

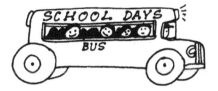

Why Do We Have Rules?

Children need to learn the importance of having rules for everyone to follow, or else we would have chaos and people would get injured. A good format for discussion of rules is the "WHAT/IF" technique. For example, "What if we didn't have traffic lights at the street corner?" Have children discuss the implications of this. Other helpful discussion starters include:

- What if we didn't obey stop signs and kept on going?
- What if we decided to cross the street on the red signal?
- What if everyone threw their trash out of the car window?
- What if fire engine trucks didn't have sirens?

RULES

Children can think of more "WHAT/IF" situations, so that they begin to get the idea that rules are *for* them and *not against* them. Learn this rule song (to the tune of "*Twinkle, Twinkle, Little Star*").

The Rule Song

Here's a little rule for you
It will tell you what to do.
Look both ways to cross the street.
It sends a message to your feet.
Here's a little secret, too.
Rules protect both me and you!

There Are Many Ways to Get to School

An excellent read-aloud picture book is *This Is the Way We Go to School, A Book About Children Around the World* by Edith Baer, with illustrations by Steve Bjorkman. It takes the reader around the world and shows how various children arrive at school. It's a book to go back to again and again. List the various transportation methods, and find the locations of the countries on a globe. They're shown on a map at the back of the book.

Then, use this book to have children pretend to be moving in a variety of vehicles suggested by the book. Children can sing and demonstrate movement to the tune, "This Is the Way We Wash Our Clothes."

This is the way we SKI to school,
SKI to school, SKI to school.
This is the way we SKI to school
So early Monday morning.

We ride in a BOAT to school,
BOAT to school, BOAT to school.
We ride in a BOAT to school
So early Tuesday morning.

This is the way we HIKE to school,
HIKE to school, HIKE to school.
This is the way we HIKE to school
So early Wednesday morning.

This is the way we FLY to school,
FLY to school, FLY to school.
This is the way we FLY to school
So early Thursday morning.

We ride on a BUS to school,
BUS to school, BUS to school.
We ride on a BUS to school
So early Friday morning.

I Speak, You Listen. You Speak, I Listen

Social studies involves the development of group interaction skills. It takes at least two people to communicate—a *sender* and a *receiver.* If both people talk simultaneously, no one is listening, so children need to learn not to speak when someone else is speaking. This is something that the kindergarteners need to be constantly reminded of, in varying degrees, depending upon their level of social development.

Discuss the appropriateness of loud and soft voices—sometimes referred to as outdoor voices and indoor voices. When is it polite to speak? When is it polite to refrain from speaking? When is it polite to whisper, or not to whisper? Talk it out during Circle Time. In the social context of the classroom, keep working daily on interaction skills. Tell children what is expected of them so that they can learn this.

Tell Me with Your Voice, Not with Your Hands

During class discussions that help "set the tone" for the day, encourage children to work on this skill. Impress upon them that they need to use words to get their message across, and not their hands (pushing, shoving, hitting, and so on).

When two children have been in a physical altercation, the teacher needs to turn to one and say, "Tell me what happened from your point of view," and teacher and other child will listen. Then repeat the statement for the second child, and listen. Sometimes it is necessary, or even desirable, to ask a third-party witness to tell the story in the spirit of mediation-assistant. As prime mediator, the teacher must help resolve the issue, and remind the children to use their words, not their hands. At the end of the retelling, the teacher can say, "Instead of using your hands, what should you have used?" Teach children to answer with the phrase "my words," and soon the response will be automatic. An apology may be in order, and children should be asked to shake hands and be friends.

Classroom rules should be discussed at the beginning of the school year and whenever necessary, and posted. This helps to take care of many behavior issues. (See Classroom Rules under the Classroom Management section.)

How Did We Do Today? Let's Talk About It

At the end of your session for the day, sit down and have a talk about some of the things you have been working on. Ask, "How did we do when we were cleaning up?" "How did we do during free time?" "How did we do with listening today?" These can be changed depending upon what skills you are stressing. Have children give their input. Then make plans to improve if they feel the need to do so. Be reassuring and say something like, "Well, Dominic has a good point. We need to work on that." "Thanks, Novriyaldi, for your comment. Perhaps tomorrow we can all try to do better with our voices when the loudspeaker is on," and so on. For a child who has special needs, an individual daily evaluation may be necessary, so that the child can be praised for effort being put forth and reminded of areas that need work.

The Four Seasons

The changing seasons are important to children because changing seasons mean a change of activities; a change of scenery; a change of plant life, birds, and animals in their environment; a change of weather, clothing; and so on. All of these changes personally affect the child.

Help children to name the four seasons, and to recognize the vocabulary words *autumn, winter, spring, summer*. Make four charts and hang them in the classroom, one for each season. As each season is discussed, write or draw information about holidays, sports, and so on, on the chart.

The charts can be in different shapes, such as:

- **Autumn**—leaf, pumpkin, cornstalk
- **Winter**—snowman, snowflake, sled
- **Spring**—flower, bird's nest, egg
- **Summer**—kite, sun, ball and bat

Cut out colored pictures that can be stored in little envelopes and categorized by seasons.

Who's in Your Backyard?

Birds come and birds go; this is called "migration." During the autumn and spring, especially, there is bird activity with many birds leaving the colder climates (some staying) and many birds arriving in warmer climates. Set up a bird-watching station with an outdoor birdfeeder that has a suction cup so that it can be attached to the window. Introduce binoculars and the care and handling required for their use. Give children an opportunity to look through the binoculars. Go to the library for several colorful bird books. Have children be on the alert for the birds they see in their own backyard. It's a good time to paint birds at the easel.

Before birds migrate, they gather in flocks in trees. Create your own classroom tree on a bulletin board and have each child make a construction paper bird to perch on a branch, getting ready for the takeoff. Or, bring in a real tree branch you find on the ground in a wooded area. Attach it to a bulletin board and tie the birds to the branches with strings so that they wave in the breeze, ready for the takeoff.

Some students may be ready for "migration routes" on the globe.

Who's Going to Tough It Out for Winter?

"Not I," says the turtle. "I'm going under the mud."

"Not I," says the snake. "I'm going underground."

"Not I," says the bear. "I'm going into a cave to sleep."

"I'll stay," says the rabbit. "I can change my fur to white like the snow."

"I'll stay," says the cardinal. "I can crack seeds with my beak."

"I'll stay," says the fox. "My hair will grow longer."

Use multiple stick puppets of a variety of animals, and distribute them to students sitting on the circle. Go around the circle, asking who's going to hibernate and who's staying outdoors for the winter; who's going to migrate and who's staying right here. (Children need to look at their animal or bird, and then answer. Perhaps a Rebus clue can be given on the reverse side.) When animals do stay and take cover for the winter, it's called "HIBERNATION." (There's a new vocabulary word and a new concept for children to learn!) Use a variety of children's magazines for bright colorful pictures including *My Big Backyard, Ranger Rick,* and *US World.*

If children are hesitant to answer, don't insist on an answer. Perhaps the puppet isn't talking that day. Perhaps the puppet will say something if it is passed along the circle to someone who can respond.

A Mural of Birds in Winter

"Winter Is for the Birds" is a catchy title for a mural of birds that stay in your area during the winter. Children can work in groups to make a mural. Start with blue kraft paper as the background for the mural, and tear large sheets of brown to construct a tree or trees. Have some children tear brown branches (strips) to paste on the big tree. All children can make construction paper birds for the mural, or paint on their bird using tempera paint. Finally, add dabs of white paint, or use real cottonballs, for snowflakes.

Then, find bird poems to read aloud as the children sit in front of the mural and admire this work of art.

A Mural of Animals in Winter

This mural can be the joint effort of the kindergarteners and some student assistants from an upper grade. First, decide who is going to be represented on the mural—underground and above ground.

- **underground**—turtle, fish, bear in cave, etc.
- **on the ground**—fox, white rabbit, spotted deer, etc.
- **above ground**—bluejay, cardinal, etc.

Older children can begin the mural by dividing it in half: half for underground and half for above ground. The bottom half can be painted brown, or can be covered with brown construction paper to represent the earth. A blue pond can be painted so that we barely see it above ground, but see it below (with hibernating turtles, fish, snakes, and so on). A beaver dam adds a bit of interest underground and above ground as well.

Use chalk to have students draw in the animal and bird figures. Then use tempera paint to fill in the forms. Add snowflakes and have students print a title for their mural.

Fins, Hoofs, Beaks, Feathers and Such

Animals and birds have a variety of coverings, a fact children will learn over a period of time and through experience. They may be quite familiar with a dog or cat, or even a pet canary, because it has been in their immediate environment.

A good picture book to read aloud is *Fish Is Fish* by Leo Lionni. A frog sets out to see the world and comes back to tell a fish about the animals it sees with feathers, and a trunk, etc. But the fish to whom he is speaking can only visualize the shape of a fish with feathers, the shape of a fish with claws, and so on. Children enjoy this book and will look through it again and again. They are being introduced to the concept of *point-of-view.*

The Clock Man

Have a large clock hanging at eye-level. Make the face of the clock into the face of a person by attaching construction paper eyes, ears, nose, mouth, and a hat that is representative of the season or month.

When the calendar changes, so does "Clock Man." The changes can be representative of a special upcoming holiday for the month. This creates interest in the face of the clock itself, and the length of the hour and minute hands, and their location. See representative samples below:

Scarecrow . . . September

Snowman . . . January

Queen of Hearts . . . February

The Smells of the Seasons

Appeal to the child's sense of smell when referring to seasons and to special events or holidays during each season. Researchers have discovered that the sense of smell is powerful for evoking memories of events in the past. As children discuss their activities from summer and the cook-out they enjoyed, elicit sensory words that describe the experience. An experience at the seashore may bring back a host of smells. What does the seashore smell like?

"What does Summer smell like?" "What does Autumn smell like?" This is a good activity to do when the season is in the midst of change, and children can be on the alert for the smells (both indoor and outdoor) of their world.

An excellent poetry book that appeals to the senses is *Hailstones and Halibut Bones* by Mary O'Neill. In this book, the author describes colors in terms of their appeal to the five senses.

Provide a cooking experience in the classroom so that children can smell the cookies baking, or smell the popcorn popping, or smell the waffles warming in the toaster. Elicit descriptive words for these wonderful indoor smells.

Communication in Our World

The world in which kindergarteners live is one of almost instant communication. We have newscasters "breaking in" to the regular TV programming to give us news of what's going on right now somewhere in our city, state, country, or world! This can be overwhelming for the kindergartener, so let's go slowly with communication.

First, begin with language (words). You speak, I listen. Communication has taken place. Have a discussion of how children get their information. This list will help you get started:

direct conversation   computer
telephone   movies
television   videos
car phone   cassette tapes
radio

How Do We Communicate with Print?

Children need to be made aware that we gain information from the printed word. This calls for a discussion of the many ways print conveys information to us. List some:

writing a note/reading a note
writing a story/reading a story
newspaper
magazines
billboards
signs in store windows
signs on gas station pumps
advertising on buses
"junque mail"
commercials

This new awareness of print calls for a new supply of magazines and some fresh paper and pencils at the writing center.

Let's Write Rebus Stories

An excellent book that incorporates pictures and print is *Rebus Treasury,* compiled by the editors of *Highlights.* Supply children a variety of pictures (sun, clouds, tree, lion, cat, dog) and have them practice writing some sentences using words and the pictures.

Let's Communicate Without Words

Nonverbal communication is a way of communicating with "body language." Demonstrate a "look of surprise" and have students mimic this look. What other emotions can we communicate with our eyes, eyebrows, mouth, hands, arms, shoulders, feet, body stance, and so on? Here are some emotions to practice, but children can think of more:

anger	wonder	joy
impatience	sympathy	gratitude

Faces in Picture Books

Begin to look for a nonverbal display of emotions by characters in picture books. How do the animals' facial expressions change from page to page in *What's for Lunch?* by John Schindel and Kevin O'Malley, as each animal changes from one who is seeking lunch, to one who may *become* lunch? How does the African-American grandmother look and feel when she gets her Easter hat in *Chicken Sunday* by Patricia Polacco? And what emotions do the many animals communicate to us in the glorious picture book *My Very First Mother Goose,* edited by Iona Opie and illustrated by Rosemary Wells?

In *Grandpa's Face* written by Eloise Greenfield, with illustrations by Floyd Cooper, a little girl is very much affected by what she interprets her African-American grandfather's face to be communicating. In *The Chanukkah Guest* by Eric A. Kimmel, with illustrations by Giora Carmi, grandmother Bubba Brayna, who is ninety-seven, neither sees nor hears so well as she used to, and children will laugh right out loud when she mistakes a sleepy bear for the rabbi.

Once children begin to look for emotions on faces, they will get much more information and enjoyment from the illustrations in picture books.

It's Time for a Project

Social studies lends itself to hands-on projects throughout the year. No sooner are we finished with one, then we have an idea for another. This can stem from interest generated by the children, or can be initiated by the teacher in relation to the social studies curriculum.

Building a City Children like to build, and they can construct a city using a collection of cardboard boxes and containers, string, and anything else you can locate in the classroom. This big city can aid with your discussions of transportation (**outdoor:** car, bus, taxi, van, bicycle, motorcycle, truck, trolley, train, boat, subway; **indoor:** elevator, escalator, moving sidewalk), and communication within the city (telephone, mail, e-mail, fax).

This poses many questions for problem solving. Where do the stop signs, traffic lights, yield signs, and other signs go? Where do we place the telephone poles? What about the overhead wires? What safety factors do we need to keep in mind?

Building Inside a Shallow Box   We can use materials such as playdough, construction paper, and found objects to build an airport in a box, a subway in a box, a harbor in a box, a mall in a box, a grocery store in a box. This calls for planning, cooperation, and compromise.

When I Grow Up I'm Going to Be a Worker in the Community

Let's make a list of all the workers in our community, starting with the police officers, firefighters, mail carriers, truck delivery people, doctors, nurses, bus drivers, reporters, and so on.

Ask each student which role appeals to him or her and why. Write letters to community people, and invite them to come to your classroom to talk about what they do.

Secure books about careers, and set up a Learning Center. Include a variety of hats (nurse cap, chef hat, police cap, etc.) so that children can role-play. Have a variety of shoes in a box entitled "Whose Shoes Are These?" Children can use them during role-play. (Ask parents for a shoe loan.)

Get styrofoam bust mannekins, the type used to display wigs, and have students transform them into community workers. You will need yarn for hair and construction paper or felt for features. Students can make hats for them. These can be used during role play.

One book that both you and the children will enjoy reading aloud is the 1996 Caldecott Award-winning *Officer Buckle and Gloria* by Peggy Rathman. Police Officer Buckle gives safety talks and tips to school children, and Gloria steals the show. In addition to being a highly amusing story, children will learn many good safety tips.

For career investigation, two other helpful books are: *Whose Shoe?* by Margaret Miller and *Whose Hat Is That?* by Ron Roy, with photographs by Rosemarie Hausherr.

A Multicultural Focus on Holidays and Festivals

AUTUMN

Around the world, many cultures have harvest festivals in autumn, for that is the time the crops come in. It's also a time to celebrate with friends before people begin to retreat indoors for the winter months (northern areas).

USA Festivals

In the United States, there are Corn Festivals, Apple Butter Stirrin' Festivals, Pumpkin Festivals, and even Popcorn Festivals at this time of year. We have American Education Week, Children's Book Week, and United Nations Day to celebrate. In addition, there are traditional holidays in the United States, such as Columbus Day and Halloween in October, and Veterans Day and Thanksgiving in November.

A Salute to Autumn

Set up an autumn display in the classroom for a festive atmosphere. Use the following:

- Cornstalks, Indian corn, gourds, and squash of all colors.
- Encourage students to bring in weeds, and make a weed bouquet for the table.
- Make scarecrows by stuffing real blue jeans and a plaid shirt with paper. The head can be made from a pumpkin or a paper bag. You'll need a straw hat, gloves (or straw sticking out of the long sleeves). Prop up the scarecrow in a corner, or settle it down in the corner with a good book.
- Encourage children to bring in colorful leaves and then identify them.

Mask Making

If you plan to make masks for Halloween, it can be turned into a multicultural mask-making time of year.

- Native Americans (Iroquois) make false faces, which they believe prevent and cure illness. Other clans make masks to resemble animals, birds, mice, frogs, and so on. Feathers and beads are used.
- Curing masks of Sri Lanka are very important: light colors for wealth, and red and green for demons.
- The Mischievous Barong of Bali, Indonesia is a character masked as a cow, tiger, or dragon.
- The Gelede masks of Africa are made from wood. Africa has a wealth of mask-making tra-

dition. To simulate bark, use crinkled-up paper bags. Add bright paint, and shells, if possible.

An excellent resource book on masks is *Traditions Around the World: Masks* by Amanda Earl and Danielle Sensier. Also in this series is *Costumes*. Kindergarteners would be interested in the colorful pictures. (Text is for older readers.)

National Popcorn Week

Popcorn is a good snack because it is low in calories. Some dentists even say it helps to clean the teeth and massage the gums. Try this recipe for Popcorn Balls:

Materials Needed:

2 cups sugar   1 cup light corn syrup
1 cup water   3 tablespoons butter

Procedure:

Combine ingredients and bring to a boil. Mix with a wooden spoon. Pour the mixture over 2 quarts of salted popcorn. Mix thoroughly. Wait until mixture cools, then mold into balls. **Caution:** Only the teacher works with the hot syrup. *Tip for molding balls:* Use latex gloves.

It's Pumpkin Time

Pumpkin is rich in calcium, iron, phosphorus, and vitamins A and C. In Europe, little pumpkins (and gourds, too) were carved out and used at night as candleholders to light the way along a garden path. These are the forerunners of our jack-o'-lanterns that grin at us during this time of year.

Storytime Zest

To put some zip into storytime, carve out a pumpkin and light it from the inside with a flashlight. Then turn out the overhead lights, light up a large flashlight, gather around, and read a scary story by the light of the large flashlight.

Pumpkin Math Activities

Children can estimate the weight of real pumpkins (small, medium, large) and then check the actual weight on a scale.

Have children draw a face on the pumpkin. (Teacher carves it into a jack-o'-lantern, because only the teacher handles the sharp knife.) If the weather is mild, do this outdoors.

Children can scoop out the seeds. Let each child get a chance to do this. Then the seeds can be washed and dried.

Time for more estimation . . . How many seeds were in that pumpkin? Make a chart and have children record their estimate. Then count them by one's, two's, and also by five's. Here's a good pumpkin seed recipe that involves measurement and time:

Roasted Pumpkin Seeds

Preheat toaster oven to 250 degrees. Mix 2 cups of seeds (cleaned and dried) with 1 teaspoon salt, and 1-1/2 tablespoons of vegetable oil. Spread seeds on cookie sheet. Bake for approximately 30 minutes until they are crispy and golden.

Fire Prevention Week

October serves as a good reminder that we need to take precaution when it comes to fire. Conduct practice fire drills regularly during this week.

Also, review the *Stop, Drop, Roll* method of putting out a fire if your clothing should catch on fire. Running will only make the fire burn faster, whereas rolling is similar to trying to put the fire out with a wet blanket.

Ask Parents to Map a Fire Route at Home

In your letter to parents, remind them of Fire Prevention Week and ask them to practice a fire drill at home—to set up a procedure for getting out of the house and for meeting outside. Then, ask the children to discuss this in class.

Practice Reporting a Fire

Have students calmly practice dialing 911 on a toy telephone (stress that this is for emergency use only). Tell the operator you want to report a fire and where it is. Be prepared to answer questions. (This gives incentive to children to learn their full name, address, phone number, and the closest intersection by their home.) Some students even learn the full name of their grandmother and grandfather and their address (the Smythes at 4713 Hummelberger Road).

Smokey the Bear

Smokey has been a long-time symbol in the United States for helping to prevent forest fires. All of the teddy bears in the classroom can be renamed "Smokey" for this week. Children can tie a red ribbon around their Smokey's wrist as a reminder to prevent fires. Have children help each other tie a red ribbon around their upper arm to show they are Smokey's helpers. If someone asks why they are wearing a red ribbon, have them answer: "I'm Smokey the Bear's helper. Don't start a fire!"

Thanksgiving Day

In Canada, this is celebrated in October. In the United States, it is celebrated on the last Thursday in November. The first celebration was in Plymouth, Massachusetts, with the Pilgrim settlers from the Old World (Europe) and the Native Americans in the New World (United States). Turkeys were plentiful, and were first domesticated by the Native Americans in Mexico and called "uexolotl."

Tom Turkey on a Bun

turkey meat (small chunks or pieces)	carrot sticks (for tail)
chopped celery	celery stalk (for neck)
low-fat mayonnaise	ruffly potato chips
hamburger buns	green olive (eye)
	pimento from olive (wattle)

Mix together turkey, chopped celery, and mayo for a spread. Spread mix between hamburger buns. Place bun on a paper plate, and—to construct a turkey on the plate—have students use carrot sticks for tail feathers, a celery stalk for the neck, a ruffly potato chip for the head, an olive for the eye, and pimento from olive for wattle. Gobble, gobble!

Ren Bear's Apple 'Nana Treat

4 apples (diced)
4 bananas (sliced)
1 cup milk
1/2 tray crushed ice cubes

Blend all ingredients in a blender. Pour into paper cups. Serves 16.

There is a traditional Macy's Day Parade in New York City that is nationally televised so children all over can see many of their favorite giant balloon characters, along with floats, marching bands from high schools across the United States, singers, and dancers. The teacher can videotape this and use it in the classroom for a representative look at America across the land.

Read *Stone Soup* by Marcia Brown and reenact the story. Start with a large crock pot, chicken or beef stock, and have students bring in vegetables for the pot (have extras, too). Scrub, peel, and cut vegetables (teacher handles the knife). Cook on high and enjoy the aroma. Then ladle it into styrofoam cups, and serve it with cornbread. This is a good lesson in sharing.

Griddle Maize Cakes (Corncakes)

2 cups Indian meal (cornmeal)
1 tablespoon dark molasses
1 cup flour
1 teaspoon baking soda
enough sour milk to make a stiff batter
    (to make sour milk, add 1 teaspoon vinegar to 1 cup milk)
butter and maple syrup
shortening

Mix the dry ingredients, and add molasses. Add sour milk and mix until batter is stiff. Drop by spoonfuls into an electric frypan, greased with shortening. Serve with butter and maple syrup.

Giving Thanks

Native Americans have many corn ceremonies, as well as other types of ceremonies. The Salish Indians have a ceremony of giving thanks for the wild raspberries. The berries were cooked and passed around a circle in a newly carved bowl.

We can give thanks and have a bounty of fruit in a bowl to be passed around (e.g., grapes). Have each child say, "I am thankful for the grapes and for . . ." (Their thanks can be related to their family, school, friends, and so on.)

Storytelling Festival

A favorite activity for Native American, Asian, African, European, and Island cultures at festivals was "storytelling." Children were encouraged to tell stories and act them out, so that they, too, would become good storytellers when they grew up. This might be an excellent time to have a Storytelling Festival. (Children can retell a picture book story, or you can use a "show and tell" format so children can share something interesting or unusual.)

<u>WINTER</u>

There are many celebrations around the world during the winter months, especially in the Northern Hemisphere. It is an opportunity for snow sports and contests and for ice sculptures. Perhaps the most popular one around the world is Christmas.

Christmas Celebrations

There is no "right way" to celebrate Christmas, but there are many "different ways," and here is some information to enrich us all.

- **Germany.** Many of our traditional customs were brought to these shores by German settlers. The custom of trimming a Christmas tree began in Germany. Originally, trees were decorated with nuts, fruits, gingerbread, candy, and homemade ornaments. Students can fold a 12" x 18" sheet of green paper in half (the long way) to make a tree, cut out shapes from foil paper, and glue them to their tree.

- **The Netherlands.** St. Nicholas, or Sinter Klaas, drops little gifts into stockings hanging over the fireplace to dry. Family gifts are often "double wrapped." Each member carefully unwraps a gift, locates the name of the family member on it, and presents it to that person, who then unwraps the second layer.

- **Mexico.** We can thank Mexico for the beautiful red poinsettia that has come to be associated with Christmas. It is called Flower of the Holy Night, or Flor de la Noche Buena. Also, the custom of putting little candies and trinkets inside a piñata is from Mexico. Children are blindfolded, given a stick, and gently tap the piñata until it breaks—then they scramble for the goodies!

- **Poland, Czech Republic, and Slovakia.** Christmas Eve is when the feasting and exchange of presents begin. At what time? When the first star appears in the sky—so children can be seen with their noses pressed against the windows and, when they see it, dinner is served. The Polish Wigilia meal is a feast and guests are welcome. An old Polish proverb is, "A guest in the house is God in the house."

- **Finland—Share with the Animals and Birds.** On the day of Christmas Eve, children leave nuts, suet, and corn outdoors in the trees for the birds. Then they decorate their indoor Christmas tree with small, delicately carved wooden ornaments hung with red ribbons.

- **United States.** Do you plan a Christmas party? Get input from the room mother regarding the menu and keep it simple—such as cookies and a festive drink. Children are very excited during the time before Christmas, and could use some quiet activities, stories, and games. The kindergartener, who is at the center of his or her world, is by nature far more interested in what he or she will *get* rather than give for the holiday.

To present a classroom focus upon giving, write a letter home to parents asking them to donate a pair of new mittens for children who are less fortunate. Have students bring in a pair of mittens from home and decorate a classroom mitten tree. Then, these can be wrapped by children and donated to a local agency.

Children enjoy making a greeting card for the family. They can also make a red or green fingerpainting. Mount the painting and give as a Christmas gift or use as gift wrapping paper.

Make a cassette recording of students singing familiar Christmas carols. The recording can be donated to a nursing home or to a children's ward in a local hospital as a Christmas gift. (Keep a copy for the classroom, too.)

Santa's Ribbon Jello (red and green)

Make cherry jello and lime jello. Pour the jello into a 9" x 12" glass pan, one layer at a time. Start with cherry red and pour 1/4 inch of jello, then let that set. Next pour a layer of lime green and let that set. Repeat with alternate colors. Because there is not a great mass of jello, it sets up relatively quickly, but be prepared for a couple of hours to make this dessert. (It would be helpful to have a parent volunteer carry out this activity.) Children really enjoy watching the dessert build up from the bottom. Put dots of snow (whipped dessert mix or miniature marshmallows) on top.

Hanukkah Joy!

This Jewish holiday is referred to as the "Festival of Lights." Some of the customs associated with Hanukkah are the lighting of a candle in the menorah each of the eight nights of Hanukkah, playing the dreidel game, making potato latkes and serving them with applesauce or sour cream, and the giving of gifts.

Potato Latkes

4 potatoes, grated   melted margarine
1 small onion, grated   applesauce
1 egg   sour cream
1 tablespoon flour
a pinch of salt

Children can help mix all ingredients together. Then an adult can drop the mixture by large rounded spoonfuls into a hot electric frypan that has been coated with spray, and greased with melted margarine. Fry latkes on both sides until brown. Serve piping hot with applesauce or sour cream.

One Potato, Two Potato

One potato, two potato,   *(make fists, and*
three potato, four;   *alternate hands with*
Five potato, six potato,   *pounding motions)*
Seven potato, more;
Eight potato, nine potato,
Ten potato—STOP.
1-2-3-4-5-6-7-8-9-10   *(pound fists, count faster)*
10-9-8-7-6-5-4-3-2-1
Mashed Potatoes!   *(mixing motion)*

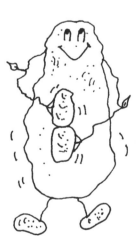

Class Menorah

Make a classroom menorah from tag board. Cut candles from construction paper, and have children put one candle on top for each day of the celebration.
A good resource book is *Jewish Holiday Fun* by Judith Hoffman Corwin.

It's Time for Kwanzaa!

This African-American holiday has steadily gained in popularity during the 1990s. It originated in California in the 1960s, and means "first fruits." On

December 26, the seven-day festival begins with the lighting of a candle. Each night a candle is lit at home and the family discusses one of the seven principles of African-American family life. These seven principles are: unity, self-determination, work and responsibility, cooperative economics, purpose, creativity, and faith.

A good read-aloud picture book for this holiday is *Seven Candles for Kwanzaa* by Andrea Davis Pinkney, illustrated by Brian Pinkney. A fine resource book is *Kwanzaa Karamu, Cooking and Crafts for a Kwanzaa Feast* by April A. Brady, with illustrations by Barbara Knutson and photographs by Robert L. and Diane Wolfe.

Kwanzaa Symbols

Introduce the following vocabulary words for those children who may not be familiar with them:

kinara (kee-NAR-ah)—candleholder for seven candles

mkeka (m-KAY-kah)—a straw mat to place under items

muhindi (muh-HIN-dee)—ears of corn to represent the children in the family

matunda (ma-TOON-dah)—fruit in a basket to represent harvest

kikombe cha umoja (KI-kohm-bay cha oo-MO-jah)—a cup from which to drink, representing unity

Happy New Year! Ring Out the Old, Ring in the New

It's a brand new year and people celebrate in many ways, with different customs. In many European countries, church bells are rung to scare away the old spirits of the past and to welcome the new year.

- **The Chinese New Year!** In many cultures (China, for example), everyone had a common birthday on New Year's Day. Everyone added another year to his or her age. The colorful Chinese New Year Dragon, held up by many people, is a common sight wending its way through the crowds on New Year's Eve in large cities that have a large Chinese population. Two good books about the beautiful Chinese dragon are *The Dragon's Robe* by Deborah Norse Lattimore and *The Last Dragon* by Susan Miho Nunes, with illustrations by Chris K. Soentpiet. Perhaps the story could be told by the teacher, while the pictures are enjoyed by the children. For a different eating experience, cut vegetables into tiny pieces and have students pick them up with chopsticks. Fortune cookies provide fun and laughter for your celebration.

- **The Peille Fete** (New Year in France). For the New Year, the children write letters and send them to their mother with good wishes and apologies for any wrongdoings during the past year. This may be a good January writing project in the classroom.

- **Open an Old Window, Open a New Door**. In Great Britain, at midnight, on the stroke of ONE the back door is opened to release the Old Year. Then the door is locked to keep in the luck and the front door is opened at the stroke of TWELVE to let in the New Year. In the classroom on the first day of the new year, open a window to let out the old year, lock it to keep in the luck, and open the door to let in the New Year!

Celebrate Winter—Build an Ice Castle

For building a castle, you will need a collection of molds (avoid glass) such as muffin tins, funnels, or yogurt containers. In cold areas, these may be filled with water and left outside overnight to freeze.

1. Fill molds and freeze.
2. Select a cool place to work indoors.
3. Put on warm, woolen gloves.
4. Unmold ice shapes by dipping containers into lukewarm water.
5. Make a solid foundation (use ice slush to help).
6. Build the castle. Put parts together with ice slush or a spray of lukewarm water.

This can be done outdoors in northern parts of the country as an outdoor play activity. In warmer climates, it can be done indoors, but don't expect it to last too long.

Ptarmigans vs. Ducks (Eskimo Tug of War)

The Eskimos use a seal rope, but any rope will be fine. The Ptarmigans represent those students who were born in winter and the Ducks represent those students born in the summer. So, line up the teams on either side of the rope accordingly (winter/fall vs. summer/spring) and *pull*. The contest is helpful in deciding how severe the winter will be—if the Ptarmigans win, we're in for some blustery, winter days!

Celebrate Winter Sports

How many winter sports can we name? Let's make a list. If it's a Winter Olympics year, we're in luck because the events are broadcast daily and in the evenings on television. As the teacher, you can make a videotape of some of the night-time events (while the kindergarteners are fast asleep) and show them the next day. The ice skating events are enjoyed by the kindergarteners, along with the downhill ski events.

Secure a copy of the newspaper *USA Today* for the Sports section. Also, note the weather map on the last page of Section One. It gives us a great deal of information about the weather in our country during this time of year.

Martin Luther King, Jr. Celebration in January

On January 15, we celebrate Dr. Martin Luther King, Jr. Day. He was a black minister and civil rights leader. He believed that people of all races and color should work and live together in harmony. It was his dream that one day this would come about.

Discuss issues of "peace in the world" and let children express their hopes and dreams.

February—Black History Month

We can celebrate this month in the United States at the kindergarten level by having a folktale and modern-day storybook festival. During the 1990s there was an *explosion* of African tales and African-American tales in children's picture books, so there are many old and new splendid picture books to read to children! Your local librarian will have a list of the Coretta Scott King Award-winning picture books that young children will enjoy.

In African tribes the storyteller is a very special person who paints beautiful pictures with words. Here are some recommended story books to read aloud:

Aardema, Verna. *Rabbit Makes a Monkey of Lion*. Pictures by Jerry Pinkney (NY: Dial Books, 1989). This author has many African tales to tell, so look for them at the library.

Crews, Donald. *Shortcut* (NY: Greenwillow, 1992). A modern-day story, from the author's experience. Also wrote *Big Mama*.

Gerson, Mary Joan. *Why the Sky Is Far Away: A Nigerian Folktale*. Illustrated by Carla Golembe (Boston: Little, Brown, 1992). Told in the true folktale tradition.

Gray, Nigel. *A Country Far Away*. Pictures by Philippe Dupasquier (NY: Orchard Books, 1988). A look at Africa.

Harris, Joel Chandler. *The Classic Tales of Brer Rabbit*. Retold by David Borgenicht, from stories collected by J. C. Harris. Illustrated by Don Daily (Philadelphia: Courage Books, 1995). The interplay of text and illustrations in this collection is stunningly beautiful.

Howard, Elizabeth Fitzgerald. *Papa Tells Chita a Story* (NY: Simon & Schuster, 1995). There are several in this series of Papa and Chita, which take place in Baltimore, MD.

Lester, Julius. *Last Tales of Uncle Remus*. Illustrated by Jerry Pinkney (NY: Dial, 1994). An excellent collection with lovely illustrations.

McDermott, Gerald. *Zomo the Rabbit: A Trickster Tale from West Africa* (NY: Harcourt, Brace, 1992). Bright and bold. Also look for *Anansi the Spider* by this author.

McKissock, Patricia. *Flossie & The Fox*. Illustrated by Rachel Isadora (NY: Dial, 1986). A Red-Riding Hood variant tale.

Thomas, Joyce Carol. *Brown Honey in Broomwheat Tea*. Illustrated by Floyd Cooper (NY: HarperCollins, 1993). A book of poetry with soft, warm illustrations.

"Koni-Koni Says"

Koni Koni is a Caribbean rabbit-like animal, similar to Cunnie-Rabbit of Sierra Leone. Koni-Koni is associated with many proverbs, and his name is used as a preface. For example "Koni-Koni says . . ." or "Koni-Koni says that one must not . . ." When playing the popular *Simon Says* game this month, substitute the name Koni-Koni.

St. Valentine's Day!

St. Valentine of Italy in the 1200s was the patron saint of lovers. This is celebrated in February, where it is

the custom to give valentine cards, candies, and tiny gifts as a gesture of love and friendship. Have everyone wear something red on February 14 to celebrate the day! Exchange valentines. Make valentines for the school personnel (principal, secretary, nurse, crossing guard, bus driver, and so on).

You can learn to say and write love messages in several languages. Here are some:

Navaho—Ayor anosh ni

French—Je t'aime

Chinese—Wo ai ni

Spanish—Te a mo

Have students write their name on a heart-shaped piece of paper and put it in a bag. Each student can reach in and draw out a name (privately) and then do something nice for that person today.

February—Month of Presidents

In the United States, we celebrate the birthdays of George Washington, our first president, and Abraham Lincoln, both of whom were born in February. We also celebrate all of our presidents during this patriotic month. Declare a red/white/blue day, and ask children to remember to wear something that contains any or all of those colors. Tie a little red or blue piece of yarn to their hand the day before as a reminder when they go home.

SPRING

There are Spring Festivals the world over, as the Earth renews itself for a new season. People who have spent many winter months indoors are joyous to be outdoors once again. Spring flowers are blooming, the trees are budding, and everything looks "alive" after a gray, dormant winter.

Tulips and Daffodils

From construction paper and tissue paper, make giant red tulips and giant yellow daffodils. Tape them to the classroom door, both inside and out. Spray some cologne onto the display for the "smell of spring flowers."

It's a Day for the Wearin' o' the Green

St. Patrick's Day is an Irish celebration on March 17. Have students wear something green on that day. Put fresh light green, dark green, and yellow paint at the easel, and invite students to paint a fancy leprechaun. We think they wear pointed hats and shoes with pointed toes, but nobody knows what a real leprechaun looks like, so there are no right or wrong paintings!

Happy Easter!

This well-known Christian holiday is celebrated in many lands. Easter may fall in March or April, depending upon the time of the full moon in March. It is a time for shedding the old and putting on the new, so many people traditionally have received new clothes for Easter. We can make a bulletin board Easter Bunny with a large Easter Bonnet (hat) shape. Children can decorate the hat with red, orange, and yellow tissue paper flowers so that it is a glorious, colorful Easter bonnet!

My, These Eggs Are Heavy!

Collect a variety of oval-shaped pebbles and small rocks, wash and dry them, and place them in a colorful basket. Have children look them over, and help come to the conclusion that they would look "just like Easter eggs" if they were painted with flowers, dots, filled-in shapes, and line designs. Use pink, purple, yellow, and white tempera paint and let the children become Easter bunny helpers. (These eggs become colorful paperweights that children can take home and give as a gift.)

Twig Decoration

In Sweden and Germany, it is the custom to decorate small branches or twigs at Easter. Twigs can be gathered from the playground, or along the walk, and brought into school. Cut designs from metallic paper and use fringe to hang from the twig. Place the twig in a plasticine ball as an anchor.

Celebrate Earth Day

Seek permission to "adopt" a section of the ground in your schoolyard. Ask for parent help so that the soil can be turned over and flower seeds or a small bush can be planted and tended by the students. Also, go on a "weed pulling spree" in the area in front of the school.

April Fool's Day!

It's fun to wear something that doesn't match and see if people can guess what it is (e.g., unmatched socks, a Christmas sweater, a Halloween costume, and so on). Why do we have such a foolish day, where we try to trick people?

It has been said that in France, many years ago, the new year began on April 1 but was changed to January 1. Because news traveled so slowly in those bygone days, some people did not "catch up with the news" for many months and were teased for being "fools" or "fish." In France, it was the custom for many years to try to pin a paper fish on someone's back on April 1, so they would become an "April Fish." This was done in the spirit of good fun.

Today we can play an April Fool's variation of "Duck, Duck, Goose" and call it "Duck, Duck, Fish."

A Day for Poetry

Set aside a day in Spring for poetry, just as they do in some European countries. Have children enjoy the rhythm and the rhyme of poems, and make up some of their own. Some good books to help with your poetry celebration include the following: *July Is a Mad Mosquito* by J. Patrick Lewis, illustrated by Melanie W. Hall; *A House Is a House for Me* by Mary Ann Hoberman, illustrated by Betty Fraser; *Bird Poems* by Arnold Adoff, illustrated by Troy Howell; *When It Comes to Bugs* by Aileen Fisher, illustrated by Chris and Bruce Degen; *The Singing Green: New and Selected Poems for All Seasons* by Eve Merriam, illustrated by Kathleen Collins Howell; and *Poems of A. Nonny Mouse* by Jack Prelutsky.

Other Special Days

There are many holidays awaiting our attention during the early and late Spring months, such as Passover, May Day, Mother's Day, Father's Day, the patriotic Memorial Day with parades and picnics, Flag Day, and the beginning of baseball season . . . it leaves us breathless. Check your calendar for local, state, and national holidays.

Remember Your Patriotic Manners for Celebrations

At many sporting events and parades, the flag of the United States of America is prominent. Let children know that even the flag has *nicknames* like

"Old Glory" and "The Stars and Stripes." Use the flag for the following instruction:

- the 50 stars on the blue field represent the 50 states (Count them.)
- the 13 stripes represent the original colonies (How many red? How many blue? Count them.)
- stand up and take off your hat when the flag is passing by
- learn the Pledge of Allegiance; stand tall, place your right hand over your heart, and say:

> I pledge allegiance to the flag
> of the United States of America
> and to the Republic for which it stands,
> one nation under God, indivisible, with
> liberty and justice for all.

(See reproducible activity pages for the Pledge of Allegiance.)

Explain the vocabulary words such as *pledge* (promise), *allegiance* (loyalty), *flag* (symbol), *United States of America* (the name of our country), *Republic* (our form of government), *for which it stands* (that which it represents), *one nation under God* (we are a religious people with values), *indivisible* (cannot be broken apart), *liberty* (freedom with the accompanying responsibility), *justice* (fairness), *for all* (everyone regardless of race, color, creed, gender, rich and poor, and those with handicaps).

Resources for the teacher: *I Pledge Allegiance* by June Swanson, pictures by Rick Hanson; *The American Flag* by Ann Armburster; for more information about the flag, write to the U.S. Capitol Historical Society, 200 Maryland Avenue, N.E., Washington, D.C. 20002.

E Pluribus Unum

This is a Latin phrase that means "one nation, made up of many." Look for this on coins and paper money. We have a right to be here, and with that right comes responsibility. We all have to obey the laws of our country so all people can live in peace. Kindergarteners are receptive to this idea, and want everyone to "play fair."

Social Studies Survival Tips

Some New, Some Review

1. Keep a bulletin board of newspaper clippings and current events so that your classroom reflects what's going on in the world. Invite children to contribute to this—bring in an article and tell something about the information that's in it.

2. Keep newspapers in the classroom for reading purposes (browsing, location of weather maps, and photographs related to areas of the world).

3. Check with the librarian for computer programs and media resources to accompany and enrich your units.

4. The local library or your school library should have beautiful picture information books on every subject you are introducing. Be sure to have a collection for your study.

5. Bring in "realia" whenever possible. That is, bring in real items for children to examine, such as postage stamps, articles of clothing, quilts, timepieces, shoes, clocks, books, etc.

6. Bring in, and encourage parents to loan, items from their trips to distant cities or distant lands that are pertinent to your study.

7. Set up a birdfeeder on the windowpane and fill it with wild bird seed that attracts a particular type of bird in the area. Shh! Quiet Zone—Birds in Your Backyard! Have many picture books of birds here, and a chart and pencil to record the birds that are spotted. Also, bring in binoculars for students to observe birds up close.

8. This area of the curriculum is rich with opportunities for field trips—zoo, firehouse, bakery, grocery store, and so on. The field trips become a common experience, and new learning can be built upon that.

9. Invite guest speakers into the classroom from the community to tell about their work—carpenter, dentist, nurse, physician, and so on.

10. Go on a "Clean-Up-the-Schoolyard Walk" with a big bag and garden gloves. Take along kitchen prongs, as well, for picking up items and for good hygiene.

11. Plant bulbs outdoors in the autumn and watch them come up in the spring. "Leave the environment just a bit better than you found it" is a key phrase.

12. Write letters to community workers seeking answers to specific questions.

13. Write thank-you notes to community workers at holiday time—Thanksgiving, Christmas, Kwanzaa, and so on—for keeping your community humming.

14. Have a phone book available and teach children how to "read" the Yellow Pages. There are many Rebus symbols to help find information about cars, shoes, pets, etc., and it's good practice for working with the alphabet.

15. Have a map and globe in the classroom for easy location of areas that are referred to on TV and in the newspaper.

16. Encourage parents to send in outdated copies of news magazines. Children can "read" them for photographs of people in the world.

17. Foster respect for "Planet Earth." Engage children in a discussion of how they, in particular, can help. (Don't throw paper out of the window of a moving car; throw all waste in containers; recycle paper and cans; turn off the tap water while brushing your teeth and then turn it back on again to rinse in an effort to conserve water.)

18. Read children's books on topics that deal with friendship, getting along, the playground bully, interaction with siblings, etc., so that children are receiving positive socialization messages.

19. Paste maps and photographs onto heavy posterboard. Cover with laminated paper. Cut into puzzle pieces. Place in an envelope for free-choice time.

20. Find out what computer programs are available at the library for areas that you will be studying and order them well in advance.

21. Order films and videotapes from the media center or the public library well in advance for your units of study.

22. By using a doll or stuffed toy, model for the children how to hold and talk to a baby.

23. Model for the children how to hold and take care of a pet in the same manner—with your class pet or with a stuffed animal.

24. Invite a parent to bring in a young baby, so that the mother can talk about its care. The necessity of nurturing an infant can be reinforced.

25. Children need to survive and thrive with some "Social Skills Sense" discussions that involve not going along with something that they know or sense is wrong; not trying food/drink/drugs "just for the fun of it"; practicing safety when a stranger approaches them with gifts, and so on.

26. Discuss with children the procedure to follow when they are *home alone* and the phone rings and someone asks for a parent. (If they say, "My mom can't come to the phone right now," they are not telling a fib or a lie because the parent *can't* come to the phone right now.) Get off the phone as soon as possible and do not give out any information.

27. Discuss with children the desired procedure to follow when they are home with a parent who cannot come to the telephone upon request. ("My daddy is busy. Please call back.") This can be used when a parent is in the bathroom; the child does not need to be explicit.

28. Many neighborhoods have a specific sticker or relatively large sign in the front window that serves as a signal to children that this is a "safe home" to go to if they are in trouble (need to use the bathroom, fear that someone is following them, and so on). Find out if this is a practice in your community.

29. "I don't do dares" can be one response when a child dares another to do something—"I dare you to cross the street before the light turns green," etc. Impress upon children that *dares* are usually something unsafe.

30. If a child continually harrasses another (on the schoolbus, on the playground, in line), the child should report the situation to her or his teacher. Children need to learn the difference between "tattling" and "telling an important fact that is bothersome or hurtful or unsafe."

31. Have extra articles of clothing and socks for rainy days. In fact the nurse could have a little supply of dry underpants, too.

32. If a child has a bathroom accident, this is a case for the school nurse who is trained in such matters. (Use kitty litter and call for the custodian.)

33. Discuss the telephone purpose of "911" in an emergency—and encourage children to tell what they have heard about it (usually from TV). Leave the children knowing what constitutes an emergency, and feeling positive and empowered. Don't frighten them unnecessarily.

34. Have children learn that a police officer is someone to turn to in case of trouble. Learn the local police number—have children practice dialing it. Discuss when you would use this number rather than calling 911. Leave children feeling positive and empowered.

35. Many kindergarteners learn their own phone number. Next, have them learn the phone number of their nearest relative. Work on it. Memorize it.

36. Use puppets to help get your message across. Sing it.

37. Arrange to have "study buddies" or a "big sister/big brother program" with upper-grade students who can come to the kindergarten class to read stories to the students and to help them with small tasks.

SOCIAL STUDIES ACTIVITY PAGES

Learn the Pledge of Allegiance (*practice*)
My Country 'Tis of Thee (*song practice*)
Meet the Family—Caribbean Style (*family*)
Folktales from Various Cultures Series:
    Native American Storyteller
    Asian Storyteller
    African Storyteller
    Latin American Storyteller
    East Europe Storyteller (A)
    East Europe Storyteller (B)
Multicultural Holidays:
    Tom Turkey on a Bun (*recipe*)
    United States Holiday Concentration (*game*)
    Time for Christmas (*Santa Claus*)
    Hanukkah Holiday (*meaning*)
    Kwanzaa Craft (*holiday banner*)
    Santa Learns About Kwanzaa (*meaning*)
    Gung Hay Fat Choy (*Chinese New Year*)
    Martin Luther King, Jr. (*dreams*)
    Celebrate Black History Month (*folktales*)
    Abraham Lincoln and George Washington (*bookmarks*)
    Leprechaun Good-Listener Award
    The Giant Easter Egg (*design*)
Community Worker Hats
    Police Officer
    Firefighter
    Health Technician
Snow Sports (*winter fun*)
Warm-Weather Sports

Learn the Pledge of Allegiance

I PLEDGE ALLEGIANCE

TO THE FLAG

OF THE UNITED STATES
OF AMERICA

AND TO THE REPUBLIC

FOR WHICH IT STANDS

ONE NATION UNDER
GOD,

INDIVISIBLE,

WITH LIBERTY

AND JUSTICE

FOR ALL

My Country 'Tis of Thee

MY COUNTRY 'TIS OF THEE

SWEET LAND OF LIBERTY

OF THEE I SING.

LAND WHERE MY FATHERS DIED

LAND OF THE PILGRIMS PRIDE

FROM EVERY MOUNTAIN SIDE

LET FREEDOM RING!

Meet the Family—Caribbean Style

On some Caribbean Islands, children call their mother "Mooma," and their aunt is "Tanty."

This is Mooma.
She wants to meet your family.
Draw your family in this space.
Tell us about them.

Native American Storyteller

This is Frank's doll and they tell each other Native American tales. Do you know one? Please find a Native American folktale book in the library. Who will read it to you? Who will you tell it to?

Asian Storyteller

This is Budi's doll. The doll likes to tell folktales from Japan, China, Indonesia, and other areas in Asia. Find an Asian tale at the library. Have someone read it to you. Memorize it. Retell it.

African Storyteller

This is Agoi's doll. It can tell African tales AND African-American tales. The doll wants to hear an African tale from Agoi. Can you help? Find one at the library. Who will you tell it to?

Latin American Storyteller

This is Maria Christina and her doll who likes to tell many stories, and sing too. Find a Spanish or Mexican tale at the library for Maria Christina and her doll.

Listen to it.

Memorize it.

Retell it.

East Europe Storyteller (A)

Color and cut out this Matroyshka Doll from Russia. Use it as a big stick puppet OR as a cover for a Big Book of tales from Europe.

My Big
Book of
Folktales

Tom Turkey on a Bun

To make this yummy turkey treat, you will need:

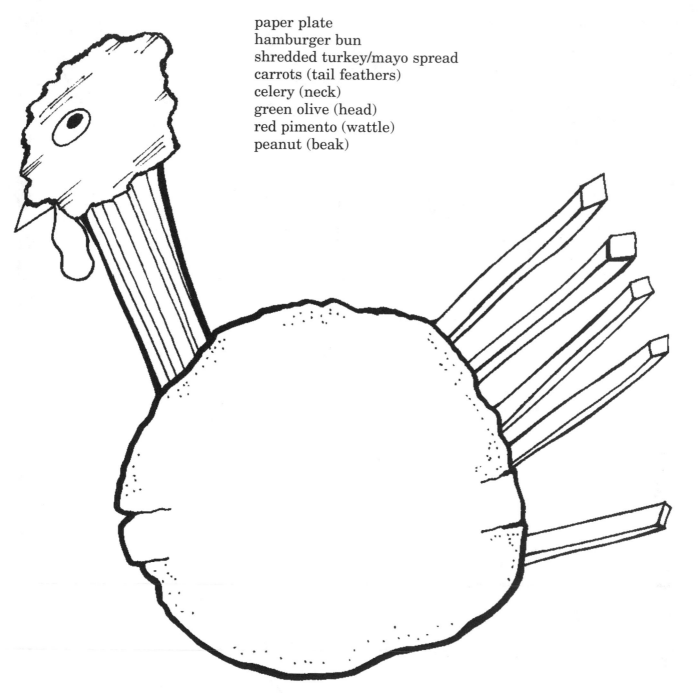

paper plate
hamburger bun
shredded turkey/mayo spread
carrots (tail feathers)
celery (neck)
green olive (head)
red pimento (wattle)
peanut (beak)

Use your crayons to show what Tom Turkey will look like.

United States Holiday Concentration

Look carefully at the holidays here. Learn what goes together as you color them. Then cut the squares on the lines. Place them on a grid. Turn two over to see if they match. If they do, keep them. If not, put them back, AND remember where. This can be played with one or two players. The winner: The one with more matching cards.

Time for Christmas

Christmas is celebrated in December. The holiday was brought to the United States from Europe and is celebrated around the world.

Show what's in Santa's pack.

Color me red and merry!

_____

Hanukkah Holiday

Hanukkah means "Festival of Lights." It's celebrated for seven days in December. This holiday means different things to different people. Use your crayons to SHOW what it means to you.

Kwanzaa Craft

HOW TO MAKE A KWANZAA BANNER
1. Cut a 2-foot long strip of blue paper or cloth. (Blue like the indigo plant dye.)
2. Paint the word "Kwanzaa" on it with black felt pen or fabric crayon.
3. Make designs on it. (In Ghana, the comb design is very popular.)
4. Wear this for your festival.

Santa Learns About Kwanzaa

Find out more about Kwanzaa and what these symbols mean. Also, learn about Hanukkah and Christmas and other December celebrations in the United States.

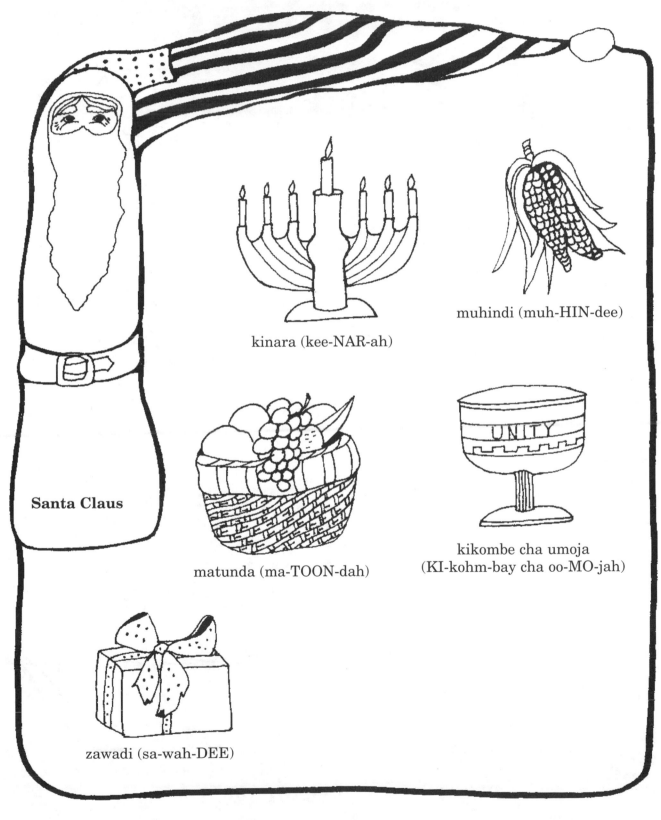

Santa Claus

kinara (kee-NAR-ah)

muhindi (muh-HIN-dee)

matunda (ma-TOON-dah)

kikombe cha umoja
(KI-kohm-bay cha oo-MO-jah)

zawadi (sa-wah-DEE)

Gung Hay Fat Choy

It's the Chinese New Year. This dragon wants you to celebrate by naming what you will work on in school for improvement.

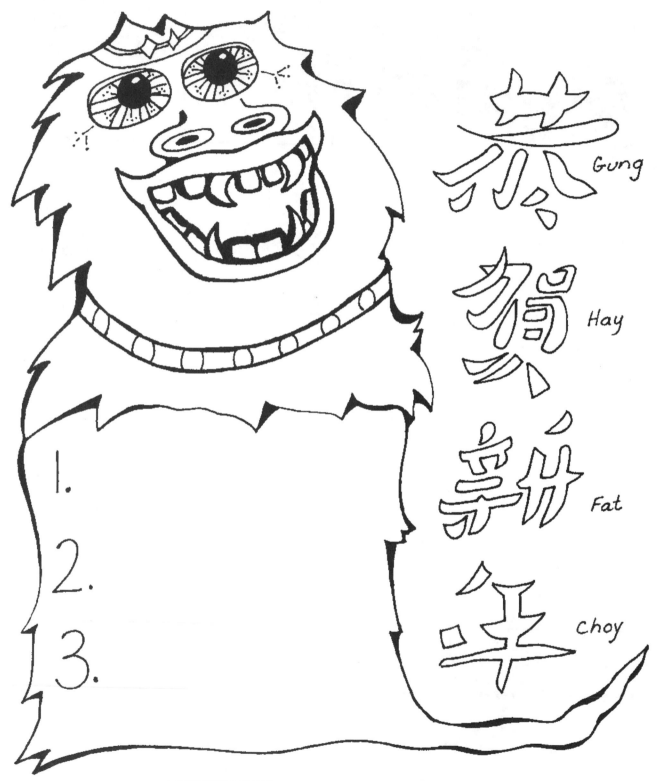

Gung

Hay

Fat

Choy

OUT WITH THE OLD. IN WITH THE NEW.

Name _____

Martin Luther King, Jr.

As we celebrate this day in January, show us what YOU look like. Write down YOUR dream.

Celebrate Black History Month

Listen to some African folktales. Then draw your favorite character in the middle of this space. Can you tell the story?

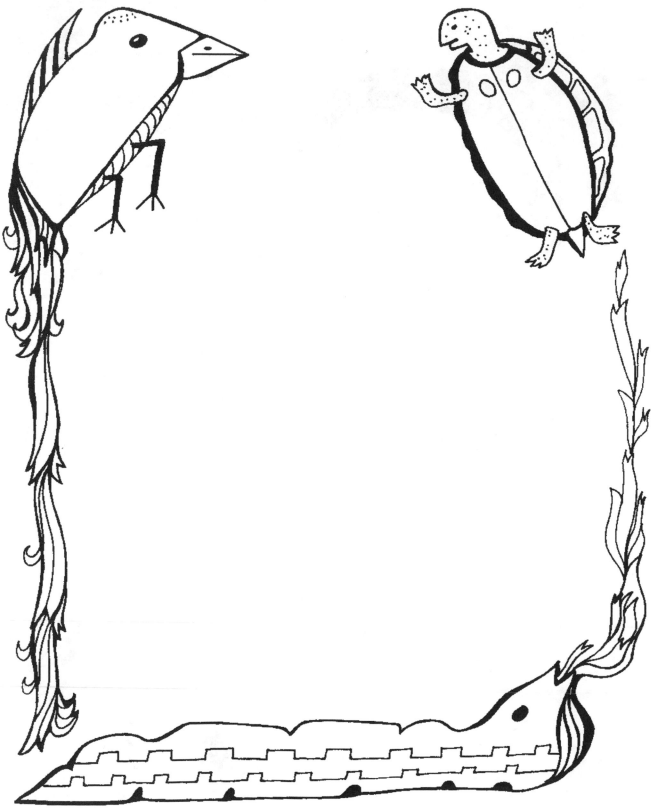

Name _____

HONEST ABE LIKES GOOD BOOKS.

Name _____

"I CANNOT TELL A LIE. I LOVE TO READ."

Leprechaun Good-Listener Award

SHH! Leprechauns are on the look-out for good listeners.

you are a good listener

Name _____

Date _____

The Giant Easter Egg

In Spring we think of the Easter holiday and colorful eggs. R-R-R-RING! Mr. E. Bunny got another phone order and wants YOU to finish decorating this egg. He likes bright colors. Thank you!

Community Worker Hat—Police Officer

Color me. Cut me out. Use blue yarn to tie me around your head. Fold the brim forward.

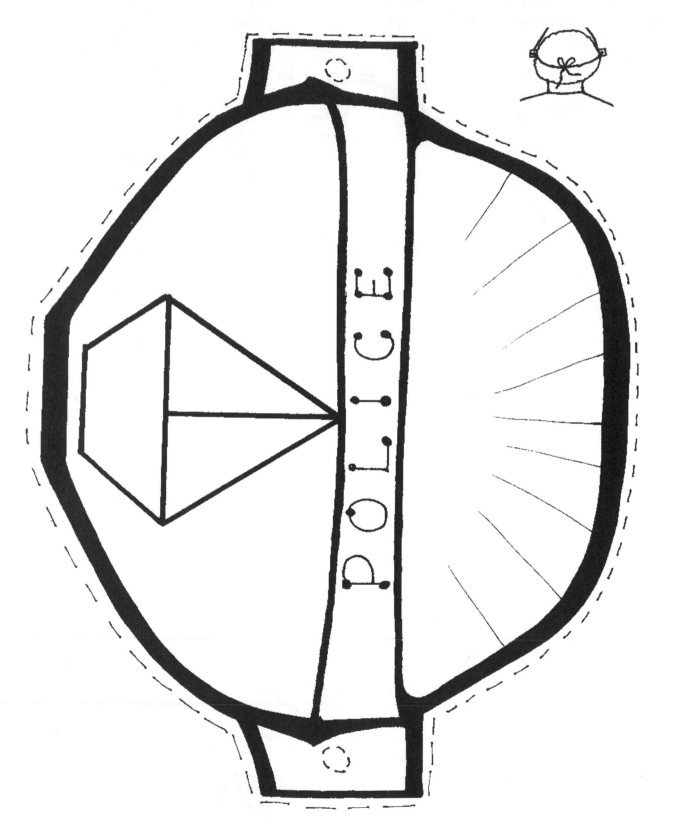

Community Worker Hat—Firefighter

Use your bright red crayon to color Winfield Bear's fire hat. Cut it out. Use red yarn to tie it on.

Wear the hat after a fire drill.

Stop Drop Roll

Winfield

W.F.F.

Fire Fighter

Plan A Fire Drill At Home

Community Worker Hat
—Health Technician

Color the hat red and blue. Cut it out. Use yarn to tie it on. Learn the local police number and write it on your hat.

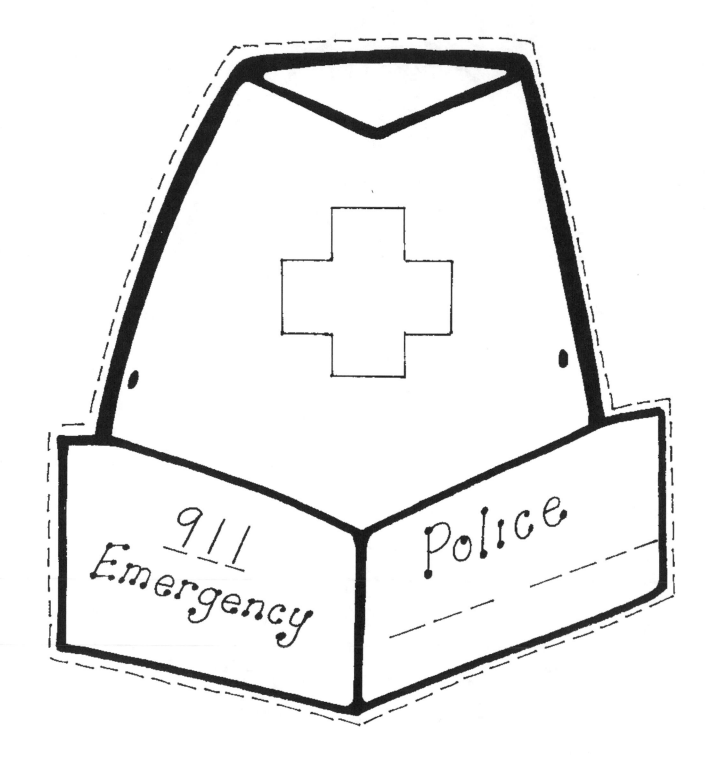

Name _____

SNOW SPORTS

This snowman wants you to use your crayons to show two winter outdoor snowy-day sports.

Warm-Weather Sports

Frankie Frog needs to know two warm-weather outdoor sports. Draw them in the spaces below.

Color Frankie in her new outfit.

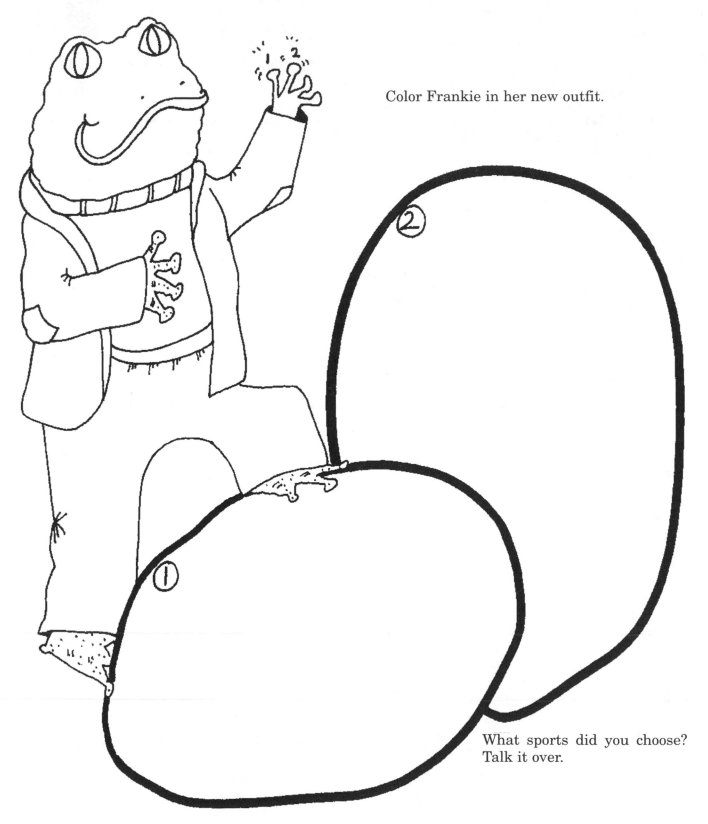

What sports did you choose? Talk it over.

HEALTH and SCIENCE

Mrs. Zifchock

Health and Science

Introduction

In addition to factual knowledge, kindergarteners need to develop inquiry skills and become problem solvers in our rapidly changing world. At this level they can *obtain data* by observing and manipulating items in their environment (rocks, shells, seeds, plants, weeds) in a hands-on approach. They can *organize data* by classifying materials that they manipulate, and then *analyze* and *record data.* Kindergarteners like to *question* and this should be encouraged along with the *communication* of their ideas. They can be encouraged to make *predictions*, to *estimate,* and to draw conclusions with assistance from you when necessary. These skills enable budding young scientists to engage in the *decision-making* and *problem-solving process* which is necessary for building a foundation for success.

The Curious Kindergarteners

In this stage of development, young children are interested in the world around them. They learn from first-hand experiences. For example, it is better for them to hold a real magnet in hand and to work with it (concrete) than it is for them to see a picture of a magnet (semi-concrete) and to listen to the teacher tell them what it can do (abstract). Science has to be something that children observe, experience, and reflect upon. They need positive experiences and reinforcement in the classroom setting.

To feel the grass beneath your feet, you need to take off your shoes and walk in it. This is a concrete example of direct contact. The science program needs to be concrete, rich, and varied, so that children can observe, explore, experience, make inquiries, and begin to develop concepts.

The Five Senses

The kindergartener is egocentric, and so an investigation of the senses is a natural study for children of this age because they carry their own laboratory around with them.

Smell

Smell and Tell

Set up a center for investigation of different odors. Collect small frozen juice cans, preferably cardboard, and put prepasted paper around the cylinder portion.

Put different herbs and spices or other odorous ingredients in each can. Over the top, place aluminum foil and secure it with a rubber band. Poke tiny holes in the top so children can smell what is inside. They may not be able to tell the exact item, but they can describe their reaction to the odor—is it a strong smell, a weak smell, a sweet smell, a pleasant smell, an offensive smell? Do they agree in their observations? Can they classify their observations on a chart? New vocabulary words can be introduced, such as a *pungent* odor.

Some items to put inside the "smell and tell" cans include:

- whole cloves
- parsley
- pumpkin pie spice
- onion flakes or real onion slices
- garlic
- orange peels
- cotton ball soaked with perfume
- other

The Nose Knows What Your Tongue Likes

Encourage students to talk about their favorite smells when they walk into a restaurant, the mall, the cafeteria, their kitchen, or a movie theatre. Take a survey to find out how many like the smell of pizza, popcorn, hamburgers, roast beef, spaghetti sauce, and so on. Make a large graph of "Our Favorite Smells in Room _____."

If appropriate, work on the concept of the relationship between smelling and tasting. For example, if something smells peculiar we are not interested in eating it. Some people like the smell of something while others do not. Encourage children to give examples of their experiences with smell. Since most children like oranges, have several oranges available to peel, to smell, and enjoy the aroma and taste.

Other food activities that give off good smells include: popping popcorn (see below), making toast, and baking brownies or cookies in a small portable toaster-oven.

Measure How Far a Smell Can Travel

If you have a microwave oven available in the classroom, this is a good time to pop popcorn, and have the children just sit quietly and s-m-e-l-l the experience. Or, you can use an electric popper and observe and smell at the same time. Does it smell in the whole room? Does it smell out in the hallway? Have students use the trundle wheel or a yardstick and *measure how far a smell can reach.*

Touch

It Feels Pinchy!

Get a sturdy cardboard box and cover it with attractive paper. Make four partitions, or sections, inside the box. Next, cut out four circular holes on the outside of the box so that children can reach through and touch the items that you have placed inside, one at a time. (To ensure that students cannot peek inside, get four socks and cut the feet off. Glue them to the inside of the hole. This way, students have to reach through a sock top to touch and investigate the items within.)

Next, ask them to *describe the feel* of the item inside. Make a chart—before long there will be plenty of descriptive words (adjectives) such as fluffy, pinchy, wet, soggy, crisp, hard, soft, and so on.

A Tubfull of Touching Going On!

Bring in a plastic tub and start filling it with objects that are soft and cuddly (teddy bears and other stuffed animals), objects that are hard and smooth (plastic), objects that are rough (twigs), and so on. Have students classify the items by touch.

Work with a partner. First person places hands behind their back, and the second person gently puts something in their hands from the tub. The person has to give two descriptive words, and then try to guess exactly what the item is.

Satin, Denim, and Lace—The Swatch Touch

Start a box of material swatches, perhaps 4" x 4" in size. Encourage parents to send in materials for the swatch touch experience, such as corduroy, satin, denim, flannel, wood, angora, lace, mohair, and so on. (Parents could send in the actual clothing items, and you can cut off a swatch and then use the item of clothing in the dress-up area.)

If you have enough material, make two sample swatches of the same material. Put them in two piles, and bind each one together, so that they make sample books just like those used in a department store for fabric selection. Now that you have two books, have students match the identical fabrics in book one and book two. Then, challenge them to do this while wearing a blindfold.

What Happens If?

Use an eyedropper and water to discover which fabrics absorb water and which ones repel water. Wash the fabrics. Which ones shrink? Which ones are not color-fast? What generalizations can we make from this information to the care of clothing?

Fingertip News

To help convince students of the importance of fingertips for receiving sensory information, have them put on a rubber glove, a garden glove, or a plastic glove to pick up items. First, it's awkward, and second, they don't get the same information (rough, smooth, silky) that the fingertips give. An excellent and sensitive poetry book to read aloud is *Fingers Are Always Bringing Me News* by Mary O'Neill. Other good books include *The Wonder of Hands* by Edith Baer, with photographs by Tana Hoban, and *My Hands Can* by Jean Holzenthaler, with pictures by Nancy Tafuri.

Hearing

Sound Off!

If you have a piano in the classroom, you are fortunate because you can demonstrate high and low sounds (pitch) by striking the keyboard. High-pitched notes come from things that vibrate rapidly. Have a variety of simple musical instruments available, such as a drum, rhythm sticks, finger cymbals, and rattle. Encourage children to listen for high sounds, low sounds, short sounds, sustained sounds, and loud and soft sounds. There are about 400,000 sounds in the environment for us to hear. What are the most common sounds? Make a list.

Make a Thumb Piano (Kenya, Africa)

You will need a block of wood and popsicle sticks. Nail the sticks into the wood, so that they extend over the edge of the wood at varying lengths. Gently flick the edge of each stick with the thumbnail to make the sounds.

Story String Sounds

Have a variety of stringed instruments available and introduce them one at a time. (Perhaps this is a good time to invite a member of a community orchestra for about a half-hour visit to demonstrate several instruments.) Play music for students that includes a banjo, violin, guitar, dulcimer, and so on. Audiocassettes or videocassetes that feature particular instruments can be secured for this purpose from your local library. One good introductory record for music, story, and sound is *Peter and the Wolf* by Prokofiev.

If you do not have access to stringed instruments, you can make one from a shoe box. Stretch the rubber bands of varying widths over the box, and strum the bands. Note that the bands move (vibrate) to make the sounds. A sound is made by something moving (solid, liquid, air). Children can use this information to create background sounds for a story.

Story Sounds

Make a cassette recording of environmental sounds (horn tooting, doorbell buzzing, microwave timer signal, telephone ringing, door closing, dog barking, laughter, and so on). Work these sounds into a background for a story being read or a song that is being learned. Or, create an original story using the story sounds as a starting point for the plot. Attention to the sounds will automatically lead the children to engage in listening.

Play Classical Music

Recent studies show that classical music makes different pathways (circuits) in the brain, and that it is helpful for students to listen to this music for there is a correlation between the music and the development of a greater capacity for learning spatial relationships. So, during rest time introduce music by Mozart, lullabies by Chopin, and concertos by Tchaikovsky. For the child with an attention deficit disorder, as well as for all children, background music for listening is a soothing experience.

Taste

Mr. Tongue—The Taste Taster

There are four tastes that can be distinguished, and they are: salty, bitter, sweet, and sour. For a taste-testing experience, try a food from each of the four groups on four different days. The following suggestions may be helpful:

A salty day—pretzels
A bitter day—cranberry juice

A sweet day—raisins

A sour day—pickles

Make a little page-a-day book to accompany the Mr. Tongue tasting experience. Print the name of the item at the bottom of the page, and students can draw and color the illustration using crayons or felt pens.

Smells Good! How Does It Taste?

Cooking with children is one way to get them interested in tasting the items that are being measured, mixed, and cooked or baked in the classroom. The smell of toast appeals to most children, so bring in a toaster, a loaf of bread, jams and jellies, and a plastic knife. Cut the toast into quarters, and the children can decide if they would like to taste it with, for example, strawberry or raspberry preserves (sweet) or orange marmalade or quince jelly (tart, or bitter to some taste testers).

Sight

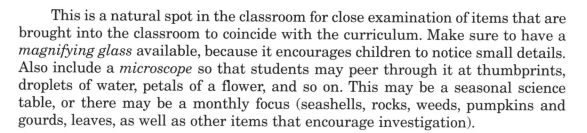

Science Table

This is a natural spot in the classroom for close examination of items that are brought into the classroom to coincide with the curriculum. Make sure to have a *magnifying glass* available, because it encourages children to notice small details. Also include a *microscope* so that students may peer through it at thumbprints, droplets of water, petals of a flower, and so on. This may be a seasonal science table, or there may be a monthly focus (seashells, rocks, weeds, pumpkins and gourds, leaves, as well as other items that encourage investigation).

The Great Cover Up

Cut out a collection of large pictures from magazines, such as the giant head of a dog, a large turtle, a cat, a house, an automobile. Then make a peek-through sheet that has a circular hole in the middle. Place the peek sheet on top of the pictures, and have students try to guess what the object is. An excellent picture book to encourage close looking is *Look Again* by Tana Hoban.

The Seeing Eye Dog

Some people have no vision, or partial vision or blurred vision, and need assistance with sight. Discuss the role of the seeing eye dog in the lives of people who are visually impaired. During playtime, have a simulation whereby one student wears a blindfold and another student leads him or her around, giving verbal directions so that the simulation takes into account the safety factor for the students.

Who's Wearing Glasses?

This is a good opportunity to talk about vision. The book *Arthur's Glasses* by Marc Brown addresses the topic of Arthur's need for glasses and the resistance that he feels about wearing them, which would be helpful for the kindergartener to know. Another good one is *Baby Duck and the Bad Eyeglasses* by Amy Hest, with illustrations by Jill Barton. They would be good read-aloud books for storytime.

It Makes Sense to Take Care of Your Senses

Discuss daily health care of the body with children. Give some do's and don'ts about eye care (regular examinations, don't look directly at the sun, don't rub your eyes); ear care (wash gently with a soft cloth both inside and out, don't poke anything into the ear); mouth care (brush teeth twice per day and floss once per day, don't put foreign objects into your mouth); hand care (wash before meals, wash after using the bathroom, protect them in cold weather by wearing gloves); nose care (blow your nose gently, cover it up with a tissue when you sneeze). Have children contribute information from their own experiences that help to enrich the pool of information.

A good picture book entitled *Livingstone Mouse* by Pamela Duncan Edwards and Henry Cole, about a mouse who searches for a home that satisfies his senses of touch, taste, sight, and sound, would add a dimension of adventure to this unit.

Additional Health and Science Activities

Growing Things

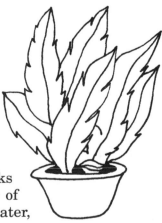

Make your kindergarten a magical place for growing plants. Have a wide variety of hardy potted plants (cactus, ivy, philodendron) in the classroom that children are responsible for watering and fertilizing. Write a note home to parents offering to take in their plants over the winter, or during a dry or rainy spell.

A sweet potato makes a plentiful vine. Insert toothpicks into three sides of the potato, and set it onto a container of water. The bottom of the potato should be submerged in water, but not touching the bottom of the container. Do the same for an avocado seed and for carrot tops.

Set aside a countertop space or a table by the window to ensure plenty of sunshine for your classroom garden. Have a watering can with a long thin spout available, and a tiny garden fork for aerating the soil occasionally. You may be able to have a real tree growing in a keg of dirt on the floor. Children can sit under it and read or do their paper work in this area. Two good picture books for growing things are *Growing Vegetable* Soup and *Planting a Rainbow,* both by Lois Ehlert.

This Seed Is for the Birds

Sprinkle mixed bird seed on a wet sponge and watch it sprout in just a few days. This is sure to attract attention. Then, get a number of sponges and wet them. Next, sprinkle a variety of bird seed on the sponges and encourage students to observe the growth. Invite them to note differences, to make comparisons, to ask questions, and to do their own experiments with seeds. A good read-aloud book for storytime is *The Tiny Seed* by Eric Carle.

Collecting Seeds in Autumn

Take several bags, garden gloves, and large snippers with safety lock (carried by the teacher) and go on an Autumn Seed Walk. Collect seeds, seed pods, dried flowers, etc. Bring them back to the classroom in the bag. Shake the bag so that loose seeds fall to the bottom. Plant the seeds.

Ways to Germinate Seeds

To observe the growth of seeds you can do the following:

- Sprinkle seeds on a wet sponge.
- Sprinkle seeds on a wet paper toweling.
- Wet a rectangular piece of blotter and place the blotter around inside a plastic see-through cup with 1 inch of water in the bottom. Tuck seeds around the glass and observe the growth.

Mr. MacGregor's Gift to Peter Rabbit

Here's a good recipe to go with your plant study in which you will need:

- crumbled chocolate cookies (dirt)

- nuts (pebbles, stones)
- butterscotch or chocolate pudding
  (Mr. MacGregor's garden)
- carrot sticks
- tiny pieces of lettuce leaf

Prepare pudding according to directions. Mix the nuts and three-fourths of crumbled cookies into pudding mix. Pour into plastic see-through glasses (enough so that each child gets one). Sprinkle the rest of the cookie mixture on top (dirt). Poke two or three carrot sticks into the pudding mix (or have students do it). Poke lettuce piece so that it rests on top of carrot stick. Read *The Adventure of Peter Rabbit* by Beatrix Potter and then enjoy this garden delight, compliments of Mr. MacGregor.

Milk Carton Garden

Place a milk carton (quart or half-gallon size) on its side. Cut out one lengthwise section. Then fill three-fourths full with potting soil. Children can plant their seeds in rows in this large garden.

Busy Bodies—You and Me!

Explain to the students that our body is very busy at work, and is *very, very quiet* for all of the work that it is doing. Children enjoy helping to make a list of some of the work that our busy body is doing, and then they like to make up motions to accompany the list. Here are some ideas to get you started:

- Brain is thinking and making connections
- Eyes are looking and blinking
- Nose is smelling and taking in air
- Lungs are expanding and contracting (breathing)
- Food is digesting
- Heart is beating (can hear with stethoscope, can feel with hand)
- Ears are hearing
- Fingers are feeling
- Knees are bending
- Ankles are rolling

Busy Body Diagram

Have two students, one boy and one girl, lie down on a long piece of butcher paper, and trace around their body. Label each one "MY BUSY BODY." Have students make face, hair (yarn), and clothing with crayons, felt pen, construction paper, or real clothing. Captions can be printed alongside the body at appropriate places indicating that the body is at work (for example, my ears are listening, my brain is thinking, and so on). Use the motions from the previous activity to help get the points across. The kinesthetic learner especially enjoys this activity, and the busy body diagram is helpful, too.

Seeds, Roots, Stems, Leaves—Let's Eat!

What parts of plants do we eat? Point out the roots, stems, and leaves of vegetables (carrots, celery, turnip, sweet potato, etc.). What's good to eat? Have a vegetable party, and eat a sample of each (**seeds:** crackers with a variety of seeds on top; **root:** radish, turnip, carrots; **stem:** celery stalk, rhubarb; **leaves:** lettuce). An amusing picture book to read is *Tops and Bottoms* by Janet Stevens.

Nutritious Snacks

Have a "Healthy Snack Week" and encourage parents to send a healthy snack to school with their youngsters. Give suggestions such as: grapes, apples, plum, pear, peach, orange, carrot sticks, celery sticks, raisins, banana. Make a graph of these healthy foods that we can eat "in between" meals, rather than a candy bar or a drink of soda.

Hot, Humid, and Thirsty?

One way to avoid a steady run to the drinking fountain on extremely hot and humid days (if there is no air conditioning in the building) is to allow children to bring in small plastic water containers that are approved by the school, or by you. Students will need their name on the little bottle. This encourages children to drink water, which is healthy for them especially during a heat wave. At other times, use your discretion. (Perhaps the water only comes out during snack time, for example.)

It's a Balancing Act

Children playing with blocks are in the process of learning to balance when they build bridges and skyscrapers. Provide other opportunities for students to balance using their body as well as objects. Encourage children to practice and strengthen their ability to balance in the following ways:

- on tiptoes
- while standing on one leg
- stand up from a sitting position (folded arms)
- walk along a balance beam, or a piece of tape attached to the floor or rug
- walk along a low wall of blocks
- USING ONE FINGER, balance a ruler or pencil
- a lunch tray with play items on either end

An excellent book is *Make It Balance* by David Evans and Claudette Williams in the *Let's Explore Science* series.

Making Mobiles

Use bold, colorful plastic hangers and have students work with a partner to make a mobile. You will need construction paper, scissors, and string or yarn. Challenge students to hang three items from their mobile for a start; later, some may want to add two more.

Students will discover with the aid of the teacher that to create a balance they will have to move certain items to the left or right in an effort to even the weight. (**Note:** If students are having trouble after having tried, use a tiny bit of plasticene on one of the objects to make it heavier, and then the balancing may be easier.)

Making a Simple Pulley Clothesline

A pulley is the concept behind the ski lift, and curtains that open and close with the pull of a dangling string. For this experiment, you will need two squares of wood, two wooden spools to affix to the center of the wood, and a string. Make a loop of the string and place it over both spools. Pull the string and it will move. The students have made a movable clothesline.

To make a longer clothesline, just lengthen the string. Have students use clothespins to clip items to the middle of the line and then pull them to one side or the other for removal. Students can use this line imaginatively during play-time.

Simple Machines

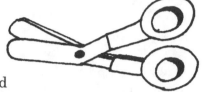

We use simple machines every day and don't even think about it. For example, a pair of scissors is a simple machine. We provide the power to make them cut when we move our fingers back and forth. Have students practice cutting with their simple machines. (Many students need practice with this skill.) For the children who are developmentally challenged, paint a wide stripe along a large piece of kraft paper and have the students cut it with the scissors. It's easier to stay within a broad line, and the child will feel successful.

For more practice with cutting, secure an outdated wallpaper sample book from a paint store. Have students find the paper with vertical lines and remove the page. Then they can practice cutting the straight lines. Later, they can move to rounded edges, but initially, focus upon managing the scissors.

Collect a variety of simple machines, and let children discover how they work. Use an old-fashioned egg beater, doorknob, padlock, and so on. A good resource book is *Simple Machines* by Anne Horvatic, with photographs by Stephen Bruner.

Wheels Help Us Move

People who are physically challenged are able to get around by using a wheelchair, or a chair that has large wheels on it. This would not be possible in a chair *without* wheels. It wouldn't move smoothly. (Students can try this.)

Wheels also help us to move things—the wheels on a cart, the wheel on a wheelbarrow, and the wheels on our wagon.

People use wheels for recreation, too. Think of the wheels on roller skates, bikes, and the giant ferris wheel at the carnival.

Have students try to push a box of items. Then place that same box on a wagon with wheels and see if the pushing gets easier!

Set Up an Aquarium

You will need a fish tank, water, some gravel and rocks at the bottom, and fish (especially guppies and goldfish)—that's the simple aquarium. If you want to get more complex, you might want to add snails because they help keep the water clean. Then, you might want a filtering system, a lighting system, and more exotic fish and water plants.

BUT, initially, you can begin with a fishbowl, stones, water, two goldfish, and a supply of commercially prepared fish food flakes to sprinkle on top for the fish. One visit to a local pet shop, and you can get helpful information about fish tanks, water temperature guides, a filtering system, and so on. Perhaps parents might be interested in helping with this project.

Arrange to visit an aquarium, if you are fortunate enough to live near one. If not, you can introduce students to the colorful and informative book *My Visit to the Aquarium* by Aliki. Have it available in your reading area so that students can examine the colorful fish and other interesting sea creatures.

What Sinks, What Floats?

You will need an aquarium or a plastic see-through bowl that is half filled with water. Have a collection of items on a tray, and place them one by one, gently, into the container. (Teacher needs to model this.) See if the items sink or float. Children can be asked to place items into the water to determine if they sink or float.

Variation: Have students predict whether the item will sink or float. Then verify the prediction.

Who Needs a Bath? Who Needs to Clean the Room?

We all need to bathe daily to maintain a healthy body, especially if students roll and play in the dirt on the playground during and after school. Sometimes children's books can help to get the message across. A good read aloud book is *Harry the Dirty Dog* by Gene Zion. Harry, a white dog with black spots who dislikes bathing, wants to become a black dog with white spots.

Another thing kindergarteners need to learn is responsibility for taking care of their things, and for helping to clean up after themselves. A fanciful picture book of poems that may help to get the message across in an amusing way is *Animals That Ought to Be: Poems About Imaginary Pets* by Richard Michelson, illustrated by Leonard Baskin. In this book there is, for example, an imaginary pet named "Roombroom" who does the cleaning up, and "Buscatcher" who chases the bus and catches it for you.

Teeth—You Get Two Sets

Kindergarteners are at various stages when it comes to losing their teeth. Some important information to convey to the students include:

- Primary teeth save a space for permanent teeth.
- Teeth need to be brushed daily to keep cavities from forming.
- Become accustomed to brushing, flossing, and rinsing.
- Good gums are pink and firm, not red.
- Too much sugar candy (lollipops, caramel) is not good for our teeth.
- Some foods help us to keep teeth clean (carrots, apples, celery).
- Teeth do different work—some cut, some break, and some grind food.

Children can make a Tooth Fairy Puppet or a puppet of a talking tooth or of their dentist, so that they can repeat information about good health care for their teeth.

February—Dental Health Month

During this month make a special effort to focus upon good dental hygiene. Send a letter home to parents and encourage them to give their children a toothbrush as a Valentine's present from the Tooth Fairy, because the Tooth Fairy likes to collect nice white teeth—first set only.

Make a tooth-shaped name tag to wear this month. Have students print the number of primary teeth they have lost. Are any teeth loose? Print that numeral and draw a circle around it.

A Discovery of Magnets

Have a new focus to your Science Area by introducing magnets and their care. Place different types of magnets (bar, horseshoe) on the table and let children explore with them. Children find magnets fascinating.

Locate a box of metal and non-metal objects and two trays. If the object is attracted by the magnet, place it on the designated tray. If an object is not attracted, place it on the other tray. This is a beginning classification exercise.

Encourage children to make a string of paper clips, with a magnet attached to the first clip. They learn that the magnetic force can travel *through* some objects, and not others.

Let's go fishing by attaching a magnet to the end of a string and then fastening it to a ruler or stick. In a large plastic tub, have a variety of cut-outs of items from magazines with a paper clip on each one. Children can "go fishing" and name the items they catch. Can they name the beginning sound? Are there words in there, also, that can be matched to a picture?

What's It Made From?

Have a sample of each of these four materials: (a) wood, (b) plastic, (c) chrome, (d) tile. Let children feel them, hold them, and make observations about them. Then look around the room and find all of the items made from wood and list them. Do this for each of the other three materials, too.

As a homework assignment, have children look for these items in their own home. Make a list of these items, too, and let children illustrate the items and learn how they are used in their environment (home surroundings).

A Live Classroom Pet

Children learn a great deal from first-hand observation of a classroom pet such as a rabbit, gerbils, fish, turtle, guinea pig, or even a parrot in a cage. They watch the pet in action and at rest, they observe the pet as it eats and breathes, and how it moves, and how it reacts, etc. In addition, they learn how to take care of a pet—fresh food, the type of food, fresh water daily, fresh paper at bottom of cage, and so on. (Check with parents regarding allergies.) A pet is dependent upon humans for its well-being, and this is a good lesson for children to learn: How to care and nurture a living thing.

The library has an abundance of picture books and information books about animals. What will the children name the pet? How old is it? Does it make sounds? Children can make puppets of their classroom pet, and communicate information or make-believe stories involving the pet.

A Trip to the Zoo

This is an excellent kindergarten field trip. Make sure you have a date set and everything in order *before* you tell the children. They can help plan from there. Some teachers like to go in advance and then tell the children what they can expect. Some teachers prefer to ask children what they can expect. Some teachers prefer to ask children what they think they will see on a zoo visit. (Make a list, and later see if their predictions were on target.) Some students have been to the zoo many times, and some may never have been to the zoo. Some zoo territory is roped off for a "petting zoo" and many children enjoy this experience while others prefer to watch from afar. (Be sure to get permission from parents for this aspect of the zoo experience.)

Upon return to the classroom, children will be filled with excitement about their zoo trip. This is a wonderful opportunity for reading about the animals, painting pictures, making puppets, painting a mural, and writing stories about their trip. An experience chart is a good culminating activity that same day. And don't forget the thank-you notes to the zookeeper. Children's magazines such as *Ranger Rick, Your Big Backyard, National Wildlife* as well as *National Geographic World* will provide many splendid opportunities for viewing close-up photographs of animals and birds.

What's Hot? What's Cold?

Have two or three thermometers in the classroom so that students can measure the temperature of a variety of items and record these numerals. For example, what is the temperature of:

- a glass of ice water
- the countertop in the glaring sun
- a thermos of soup

Children will soon come to realize that the higher the number, the warmer the item. Or, the higher up the mercury climbs, the hotter the temperature. High means hot, low means cold.

Rhyming with Tom Thumb Thermometer

Here's a rhyme that can help children to catch the rhythm of what's hot and what's cold. See reproducible activity pages for Tom Thumb puppets, or you can use teddy bears to help.

Tom Thumb Thermometer
Tell me please
How do you feel
At 33 degrees?   (*Shiver and shake body. Use a white teddy bear.*)

Tom Thumb Thermometer
Tell me please

How do you feel
At 90 degrees?   *(Wipe brow and make sound of WHEW! Use a tan teddy bear.)*

Keep repeating numbers over 90 degrees and under 33 degrees. Then work on numbers in between and have children determine what motions they will use for words such as "cool," "warm," "mild," and so on. Make a *Cold and Hot Teddy Bear Book.* (See reproducible activity pages.)

The Language of High and Low

When working with the thermometer and temperature, make associations that are *opposites* and meaningful to children. For example:

High means sunshine.   High means swimming.
High means bathing suit.   High means _____.

Low means snow.   Low means ice skates.
Low means snowsuit.   Low means _____.

Let's Balance Rocks

Encourage students to bring in a variety of rocks for the science table. Place in a large container on the floor. Use a balance scale to determine how many little rocks it takes to equal the largest one.

We Can Categorize Rocks

A practical and easy container that will help students begin to categorize small rocks is an empty egg container. There are twelve sockets readily available, although all twelve may not be needed.

When a group of students has categorized the rocks (color, size, shape), let them explain their rationale for their categories. Then, have another group see if they can categorize them in a different way.

Categorizing Items

The teacher can demonstrate the process of categorizing by having about five items at hand, and discussing how the items are alike and different, and which ones would "go together."

Have students work in small groups. In advance, make up envelopes that contain a variety of items and let each group categorize the items on a tray. Then, have each group tell how it categorized the items, and why it arranged them in that way, while the others carefully listen. Children can learn different techniques of categorizing through this process. (For example: Some children may put a red paper clip, a red button, and a red piece of paper together because of the color, so they create a *color category*. Whereas, another group may put the red paper clip with a brown pencil and an envelope, thus creating a *writing category*.) It is important for the teacher to *accept all ideas that can be explained*.

Some envelope items to get you started include:

- button (any color or size)
- penny
- pencil
- paper clip
- envelope
- plastic cup
- plastic fork
- seashell

Venn Diagrams: Making Sets

Use colorful, loopy yarn to make two large circles that intersect, or use two plastic hula hoops on the floor. Have a set of animal pictures and a set of flower pictures on 3" x 5" cards, that you cut from magazines and laminated. Have children classify them into two sets.

Next, sort 3" x 5" picture cards that you have made of living/non-living items. How can some be placed in the middle of the Venn Diagram, so that they include *both* living and non-living items? For your pictures, these ideas can help to get you started:

- picture of a child (living or L)
- picture of a birthday cake with candles (non-living or NL)
- picture of a child blowing out candles on a birthday cake (L, NL)
- a picture of a boy (L)
- a picture of a football (NL)
- a picture of a boy kicking a football (L, NL)

Are You Interested in the Terrible Lizard?

Tyrannosaurus Rex was so tall that he could have peeked into your upstairs window on the second floor! A study of dinosaurs is usually fascinating to kindergarteners. It offers an opportunity for many new vocabulary words such as the names of dinosaurs, as well as *paleontologist* (a scientist who studies fossil remains of life) and *monstrous* (huge like a monster). Here is an opportunity to categorize the dinosaurs as meat eaters and plant eaters:

PLANT EATERS	MEAT EATERS
Brontosaurus	Ceratosaurus
Anklylosaurus	Tyrannosaurus Rex
Stegosaurus	Velociraptor
Triceratops	Allosaurus
Protoceratops	Megalosaurus
Iguanodon	Stenonychosaurus
Pteranodon	

See if children can add to the list of plant and meat eaters. Have them consider those that live in the sea and in the air.

We Can Make Fossils

Fossils are remains of bones or animals, plants, or marks in mud that have hardened. A fossil is a record of the past. Scientists have learned many things about dinosaurs because of their fossil remains.

To make fossils, press a figure into clay (this becomes the mold). Then, pour plaster of Paris into the mold. Allow to thoroughly dry. Remove when the mold has set. This is a "fake" fossil.

Let's Make Dinosaurs from Clay

Give children ample opportunity to study photographs and drawings of dinosaurs before they create their clay model. Are they going to have two legs or four? Will their teeth show? Are they upright or crawling on the ground? Will they have wings, a suit of armor, or rough-looking skin?

Display the clay dinosaurs on colored paper plates so that the colors match (red dough/red plate, green dough/green plate, blue dough/blue plate). This way, the dinosaur blends in with its surroundings. Have the artists name their dinosaur and tell something about it. (Write the information on a 3 x 5 display card.)

Some good picture books include *Bones, Bones, Dinosaur Bones* by Byron Barton and *Tyrannosaurus Rex, A New True Book* by David Petersen.

Getting Help from Dinosaurs

Dinosaurs Divorce and *Dinosaurs, BEWARE! A Safety Guide* by Marc Brown and Stephen Krensky are two picture books that teachers will find helpful. Many kindergarten teachers have found the first book to be helpful for the child whose parents are divorcing or who are divorced. If a child learns that dinosaurs divorce, well, then, perhaps they can find it not so dreadful in their own family situation. There are reassuring tips here for the child. The latter can be included in your talks on safety during meals, on the playground, at home, on wheels, while camping, and so on.

Tools Help Us to Do Work

Children can be exposed to a variety of tools that help people do work. At the center include a hammer with wood and nails, a stapler and colored paper squares, a variety of padlocks with keys, and also include a wrench, pliers, screwdriver, and measuring rule. Allow students to take apart an appliance that has been donated for the purpose of exploring the insides. (**Caution:** Alert children that they are not to do this at home on their own. They don't play with appliances that are plugged into the wall, and they are never to use tools without adult supervision.)

The Tools of the Trade

Talk about the tools that help us do our school work, and make a list. Here are some to get you started:

chalk	pencils
crayons	scissors
glue	stapler

Then talk about the tools that people use in their careers. Discuss and list with the children the tools of:

firefighter	doctor	police officer
mail carrier	carpenter	dentist
TV repairman	custodian	principal
artist	chef	secretary
teacher	waitress/waiter	TV reporter

We All Need Water!

In just one day, we use water in a variety of ways—some for health, some for work, some for play. How many ways do we use water? Discuss and list with the children:

drinking	bathing
watering plants	brushing teeth
watering the lawn	filling a pet's dish
washing our hands	cleaning up a spill

There are many other ways that water is used. Most cities are built along waterways (rivers, lakes). Some cities are built near shores of the ocean and become important for their imports/exports. There are many animals that live in the water. We use the waterways for a variety of our recreation, especially in warm weather. Water is critical to our well being—so enjoy a glass right now!

Two good resource books are *Wonderful Water* by Bobbie Kalman and Janine Schaub and *Rivers and Oceans, a Young Discoverer's Book* by Barbara Taylor.

When Garbage Gets Rotten, Where Does It Go?

Some students may be familiar with the term *landfill,* whereas others may not. But our trash and garbage is buried underneath the ground. Some of it breaks down, and some of it does not.

Here is a simple experiment. You will need food scraps, a plastic wrapper, a paper wrapper, and an aluminum foil wrapper. Place food scraps in all three wrappers and seal them. Then, dig a spot far out on the playground along the fence and bury them. About a month later, dig this area up to see which items are in the process of becoming biodegradable (breaking down) and which are still intact. What does this tell us about the importance of recycling? Also what does it tell us when we learn that our landfills are becoming full? What does it mean to live in a "throw-away world"? An excellent resource book to help with this topic is *Garbage! Where It Comes From, Where It Goes* by Evan and Janet Hadingham. This is one in a series of NOVABOOKS.

Other Topics for Children to Explore with the Aid of Picture Books

Some good resource books are available for your use in the NOVABOOK series, published by Simon & Schuster Books for Young Readers. While the text in this series is too complicated for kindergarteners, the information is helpful for the teacher, and the pictures, photographs and diagrams are meaningful to young children. Some topics include: *Radical Robots, Can You Be Replaced?* by George Harrar, *Junk in Space* by Richard Maurer, *Dmitri, The Astronaut* by Jon Agee, *The City Kid's Field Guide* by Ethan Herberman, and *The Great Butterfly Hunt: The Mystery of the Migrating Monarchs* by Ethan Herberman.

You Have a Problem-Solving Attitude

That's a compliment! Remember, these are the key steps we are working with in Science. Post them in the classroom. Talk about them.

- What is the problem?
- What do we already know?
- What do we need to know?
- What do we need to do? (How can we find this out?)
- Can we do it? (Do we need help, or permission?)
- How will we determine when/if the problem is solved?
- If we can't solve it, what steps do we take to at least try?
- If we can't solve it, what steps do we take to live with it?

If the problem is not solved, do we give up? No, we can start again or we can learn ways to manage the problem. Children need to learn this "science attitude."

Some problems cannot be solved so that everyone is joyous. For example, an outdoor field trip may be canceled at the last minute because of rain. But, is it the end of the world? No. We can go again another day when the weather is just right. Meanwhile, take advantage of the "gift of time" you were just given because of the weather—explain to the children that it is a disappointment, but that it would be a waste of time and energy to pout about it. Get out some rainy-day activities and enjoy this time. Children will "pick up" the attitude and mood of the teacher—be a positive role model.

A picture book that deals with a trickster troublemaker is *Aunt Nancy and Old Man Trouble* by Phyllis Root, with illustrations by David Parsons.

Memorize and Use the Unicorn Chant

Introduce children to unicorns, the make-believe animal with the body of a horse and a long horn attached to the top of its head that has magic powers. For example, it can touch a polluted pond with its horn and turn it into fresh water; it can touch a scratched knee and make it better; and so on. Children can use their imaginations to tell what else the unicorn might be able to mend and fix. Have them memorize the Unicorn Problem-Solving Chant. This is an especially helpful, handy reminder for the child with special needs:

Think with your head,
Feel with your heart,
Don't scream and shout,
Let's work it out!

How to Get Better!

In kindergarten, children are exposed to a variety of strains of germs as they progress through the year. One book that can be helpful for the teacher is *Buz* by Richard Egielski. In this book a child "catches a bug" and has to go to the doctor. The giant, colorful illustrations help to tell the story of pills as germ fighters. The book may help allay fears about going to a friendly doctor and since there is relatively little text, it can generate much conversation about the topic of germs.

Students can make an "I'm a Germ Fighter" Badge (see reproducible activity pages) and tell how they can help fight germs. Make a large Germ Fighter Bug Chart. Some tips to get you started are:

- Wash hands before eating.
- Don't put your mouth directly on the drinking fountain nozzle.
- Cover up your mouth when you cough.
- Cover up your nose when you sneeze.

(*Note to teacher:* If you have not already done so in your weekly note to parents, this is a good time to include a request for a large box of tissues from each household.)

What Makes Us Feel Good?

We need a caring family, friends, and familiar surroundings in order to "thrive." As you gather together for storytime, some fine picture books for young children that may help them have good feelings about themselves are:

- *What You Know First* by Patricia MacLachlan, drawings by Barry Moser (family and a sense of self)
- *The Rooster's Gift* by Pam Conrad, pictures by Eric Beddows (self-affirmation)
- *Grandmother Bryant's Pocket* by Jacqueline Briggs Martin, pictures by Petra Mathers (dealing with fears of fire)
- *Happy Adoption Day!* lyrics by John McCutcheon, illustrations by Julie Paschkis (an original song, multi-ethnic family and friends)
- *White Wave* by Diane Wolkstein, illustrations by Ed Young (Chinese tale, good read-aloud to soothe the child who has just broken something, or done something wrong)
- *Old Home Days* by Donald Hall, illustrations by Emily Arnold McCully (roots, family)

Healthy Snacks and Recipes

Some healthy snacks for children to bring to school include:

oranges	plums	cheese and crackers
apples	apricots	peanut butter crackers
bananas	raisins	cheese chunks
tangerines	dried fruit	cauliflower pieces
pears	pretzels	carrot sticks
peaches	crackers	celery sticks

Apple Peanut Butter Snack Man

You will need: apple
                     peanut butter
                     raisins
                     (knife)
Procedure: 1. Cut an apple in half.
                    2. Spread peanut butter on the sliced part.
                    3. Then use raisins for eyes, nose, and mouth.

Peanut Butter Balls

You will need: 1 cup honey
                    1 cup peanut butter
                    1-1/2 cups powdered milk
                    graham cracker crumbs
Procedure: 1. Combine all ingredients until well mixed.
                    2. Shape into little balls.
                    3. Roll in cracker crumbs.

Snack Chow

You will need: a variety of dried fruit (apples, apricots, raisins,
                        pineapple)
                    a variety of nuts
                    a variety of seeds (sunflower, pumpkin)
                    small paper cups
Procedure: 1. Combine in a heavy-duty bag and let children help
                        shake the mixture.
                    2. Scoop mixture into small paper cups.

Banana Apple Frosty

You will need: 4 apples (diced)
                    4 sliced bananas
                    1 cup milk
                    6 to 8 ice cubes
                    blender
                    cups
Procedure: 1. Blend ingredients in a blender.
                    2. Pour into serving cups.

Individual Vegetable Pizzas

You will need: English muffins (cut in half)
pizza sauce
grated mozzarella cheese
chopped carrots, cauliflower,
zucchini

Procedure: 1. Children are each given half a muffin and they can help spread the sauce, sprinkle the cheese, and put vegetables of their choice on top.
2. Toast in toaster oven at 375 degrees until cheese melts.

Stuffed Peanut Butter Dates

You will need: dates
peanut butter
granulated sugar

Procedure: 1. Slit dates and remove pits.
2. Insert peanut butter into the center.
3. Close date around filling and roll in granulated sugar.

Individual Banana Lunch Salad

You will need: lettuce leaf
1/2 banana slice (from top to bottom)
1 tsp. peanut butter and 1 tsp. vanilla yogurt (mixed together)
crushed peanuts
maraschino cherry
sturdy paper plate

Procedure (Children can construct their own salad):
1. Place banana slice on lettuce leaf.
2. Put dollop of peanut butter/yogurt mixture on top of banana.
3. Sprinkle with crushed nuts.
4. Place maraschino cherry on top.

Health and Science Survival Tips

Some New, Some Review

1. Have a Science Table in the classroom, and keep changing the theme: rocks; seashells; insects; birds; magnets; inventions; etc.

2. Have a magnifying glass available. Teach children the proper way to use this equipment.

3. Have a microscope available, if possible, and teach children the proper way to use this equipment.

4. Use a multi-media approach with your Science Table. Have books on the subject, models, pictures or photographs, actual items or objects, a videocassette, or a computer program (CD-ROM) that deals with the particular topic.

5. Decide how many people can be at this area at one time (2 or 3) and stick with it.

6. Encourage children to discuss what they are investigating and discovering.

7. Have writing paper and pencils at this area for diagrams, notes, etc.

8. Science provides many opportunities to reinforce sorting and categorizing items from nature.

9. Be sure to use plastic containers rather than glass.

10. Keep the area cleaned up. Keep adding items, subtracting items.

11. Change the theme of the Science Table when interest begins to wane.

12. Buy old tools at garage sales (free from rust), or ask for donations of hammer, screwdriver, nails, screws, wrench, and so on.

13. Make a habit of picking up old items at garage sales that children can take apart. Kitchen items are especially good for your study of levers, pulleys, and other simple machines.

14. Put a prism on a countertop on a sunny day to catch the children's attention and to launch a unit on color, sunlight, refraction.

15. Keep a weather chart to track the weather daily—record temperature, and use a symbol for rain, snow, sun, wind, clouds. At the end of the month, graph the information. (Good math/science correlation)

16. Have "Closed" and "Open" signs available to use at the Science Table. Let the signs "do the telling."

17. Memorization is not the key at this level. Exploration and discovery are important. Explain that real scientists work in this way, too.

18. Encourage questions. Don't always think that as the teacher you have to know the exact answer for everything. Guide students to be resourceful in terms of where they can search for information and how they can become problem-solvers.

HEALTH and SCIENCE
ACTIVITY PAGES

Planet Earth Needs Your Magic Touch (*awareness*)

The Rebus Butterfly Story (A) (*color; cut*)

The Rebus Butterfly Story (B)

Six Legs, Three Body Parts (*insects*)

Make a Sound Box (*high sounds; low sounds*)

Make a Pickosaurus (*dinosaurs from clay*)

Science in a Bag (*an outdoor hunt; classification*)

What Belongs in the Ocean? (*pollution*)

Use Your Good "Horse Sense" About Germs (*discussion*)

Tooth Fairy Time (*dental health month*)

Hot Chocolate Fit for a Moose (*a br-r-r day drink*)

Popcorn Ball Recipe (*cooking; measuring; timing*)

Cold and Hot Teddy Bear Book (A) (*temperature*)

Cold and Hot Teddy Bear Book (B)

Tom Thumb Puppets (*for rhyming with Tom Thumb Thermometer*)

"I'm a Germ Fighter" Badge

Name _____

Planet Earth Needs Your Magic Touch

You don't need to do magic tricks to help clean up Planet Earth. Show two things YOU can do to help.

The Rebus Butterfly Story (A)

This is the story of my life. Color me. Cut out my circles. Paste me on my butterfly shape.

The Rebus Butterfly Story (B)

Paste on my story. Color me beautiful!

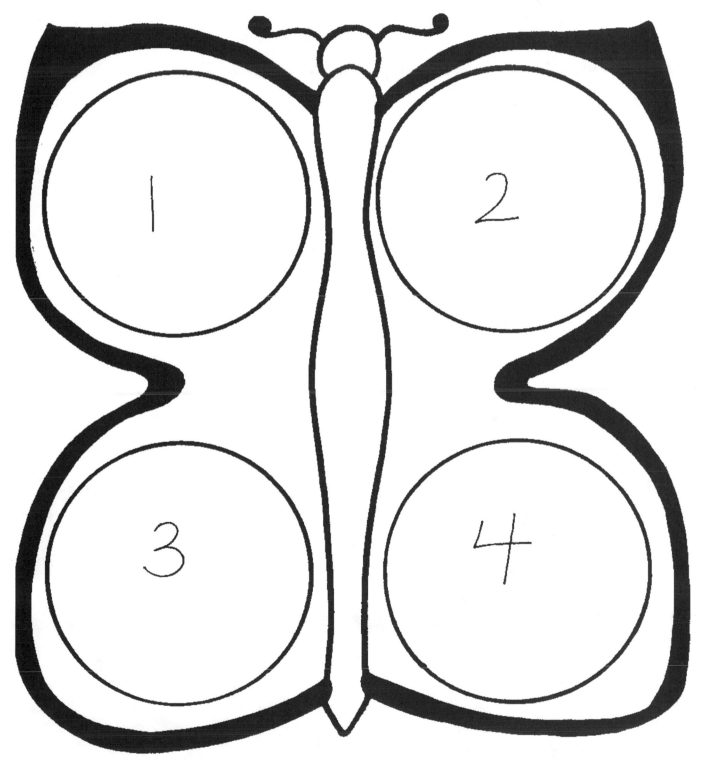

Name ______________________________

Six Legs, Three Body Parts

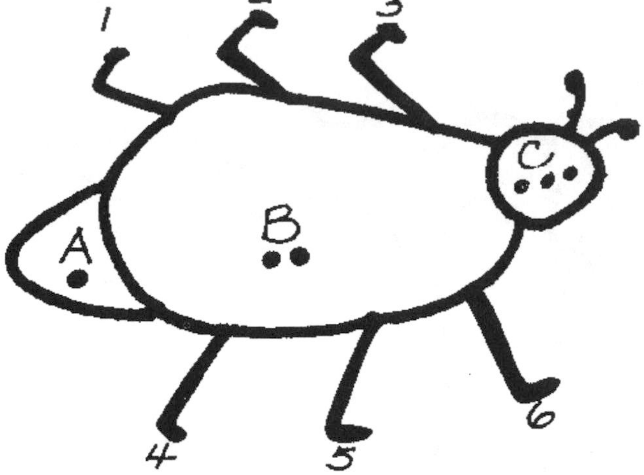

It's a secret
I'll share with thee
Remember 6
Remember 3.
WHO AM I?

Make the shapes below into insects.
How?
6—legs
3—body parts

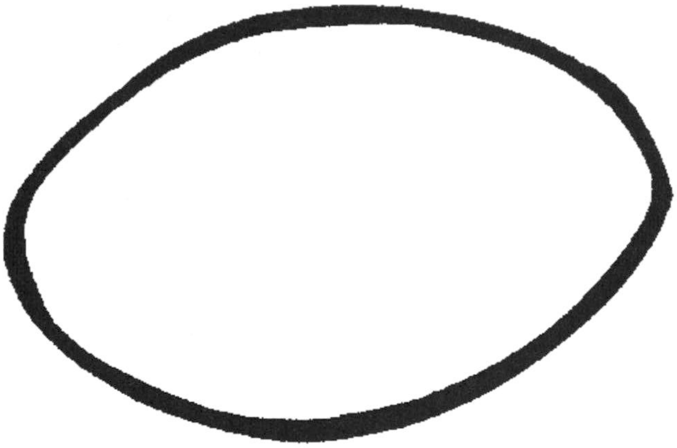

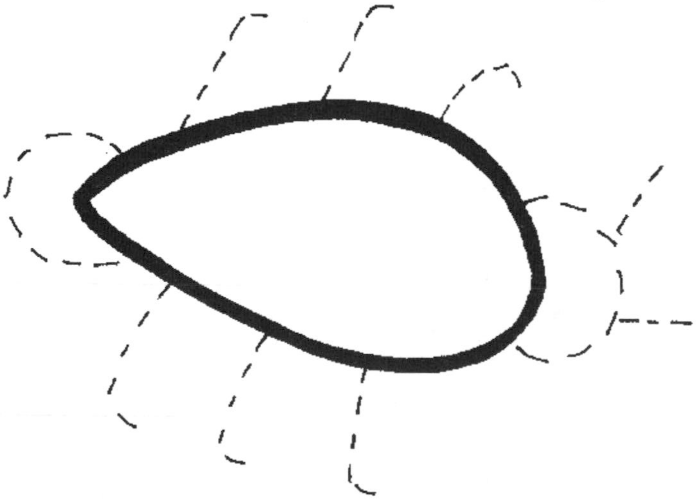

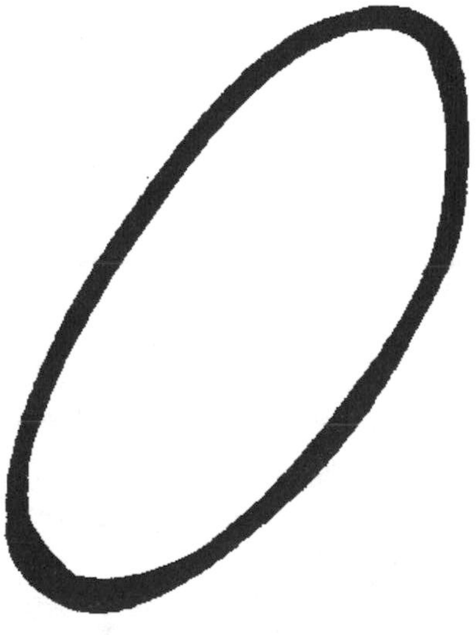

Use your crayons to make beautiful insects.

Name _____

Make a Sound Box

You will need:

1. box
2. rubber bands (thick and thin)

Place the around .

Pluck each .

Let's find out:

1. Pluck the bands.
2. Is the sound high or low when the bands move fast? when the bands move slow?

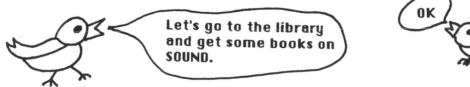

Let's go to the library and get some books on SOUND.

OK

Make a Pickosaurus

You will need:
clay
toothpicks

Display your animal on this spot.

This is my Pickosaurus.

My name is_____

I eat _____

I'm as big as a _____

Name _____

Science in a Bag

Collect 10 different things from the ground. Empty the bag indoors. How can you classify the items?

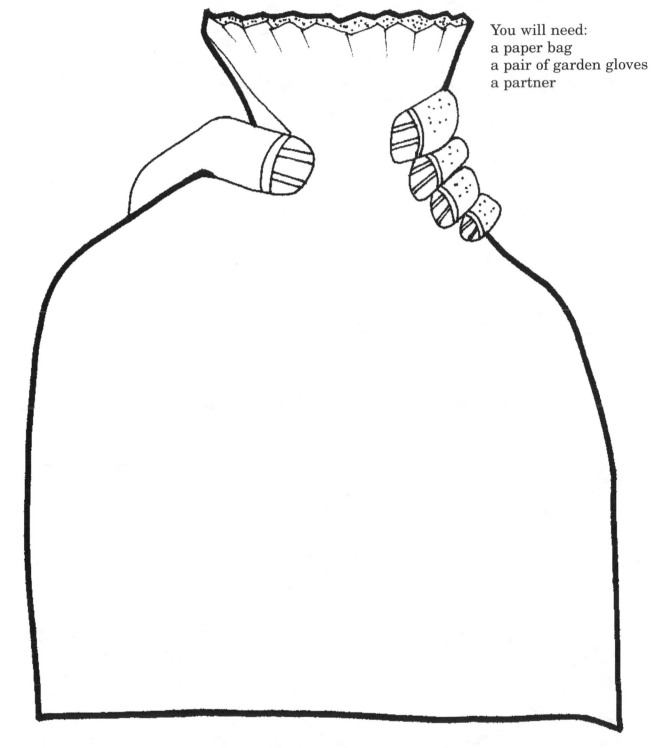

You will need:
a paper bag
a pair of garden gloves
a partner

Use your crayons to show WHAT'S IN THE BAG?

Name _____

What Belongs in the Ocean?

Color only those things that belong in the ocean. Put an X on those that do not belong. Talk about it.

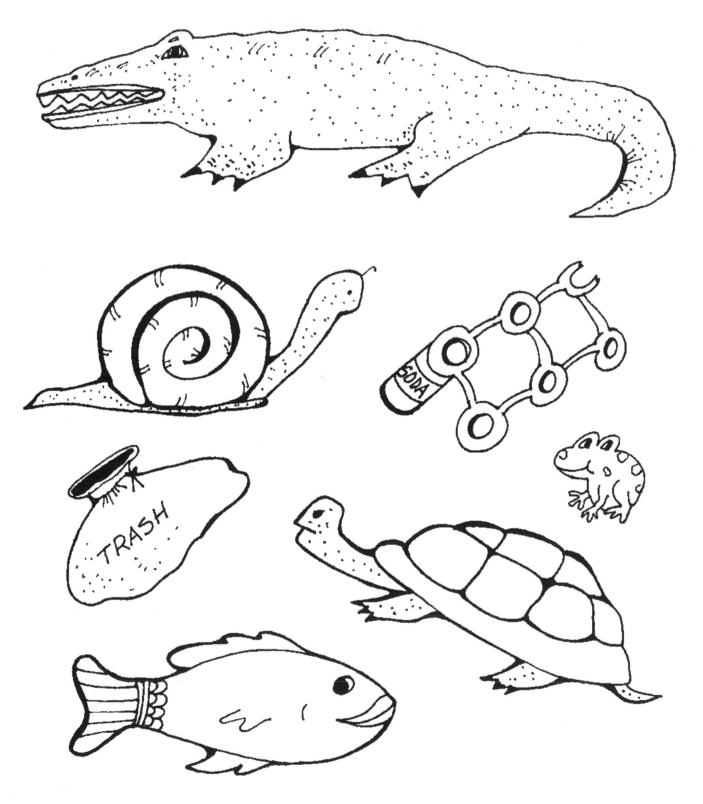

Use Your Good "Horse Sense" About Germs

Cover your nose when you feel a sneeze coming on. Wash your hands before eating. How many other "Good Horse Sense" rules can you think of?

Tooth Fairy Time

February is Dental Health Month and the Tooth Fairy is in charge of baby teeth. Use your crayons to show us what the Tooth Fairy looks like.

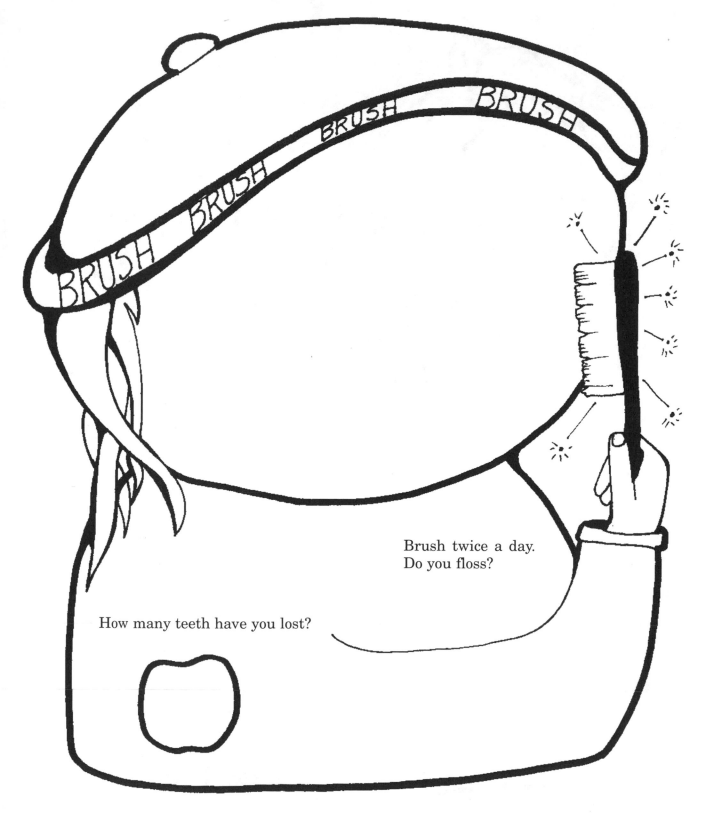

BRUSH BRUSH BRUSH BRUSH BRUSH

Brush twice a day.
Do you floss?

How many teeth have you lost?

Hot Chocolate Fit for a Moose

IT'S A GOOD BR-R-R DAY DRINK

YOU WILL NEED:

1 tsp. dry chocolate mix
1 cup warm milk or warm water

WHAT TO DO:
Stir.
Add tiny marshmallows.

Popcorn Ball Recipe

What do scarecrows do with all that corn? They make popcorn balls. You can, too. Here's the recipe.

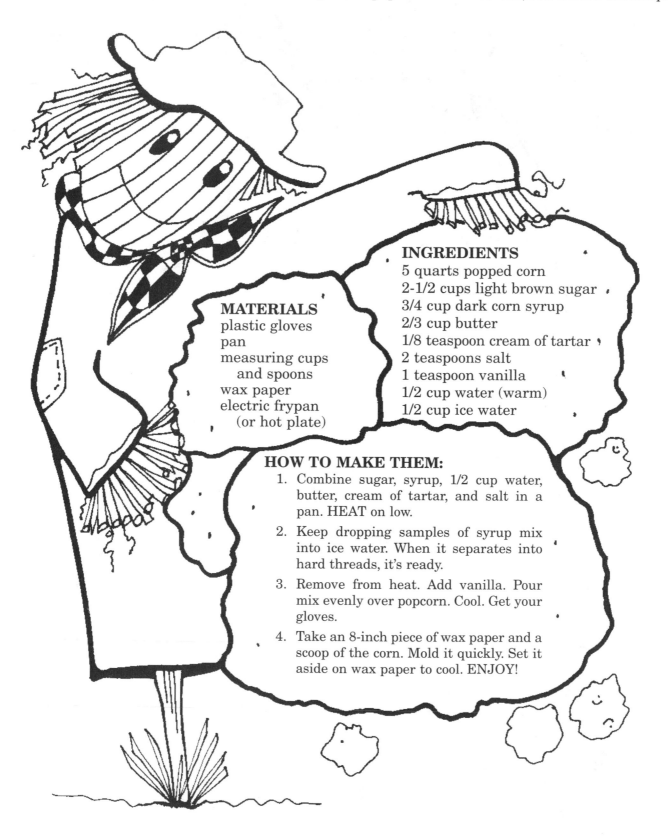

MATERIALS
plastic gloves
pan
measuring cups
  and spoons
wax paper
electric frypan
  (or hot plate)

INGREDIENTS
5 quarts popped corn
2-1/2 cups light brown sugar
3/4 cup dark corn syrup
2/3 cup butter
1/8 teaspoon cream of tartar
2 teaspoons salt
1 teaspoon vanilla
1/2 cup water (warm)
1/2 cup ice water

HOW TO MAKE THEM:

1. Combine sugar, syrup, 1/2 cup water, butter, cream of tartar, and salt in a pan. HEAT on low.

2. Keep dropping samples of syrup mix into ice water. When it separates into hard threads, it's ready.

3. Remove from heat. Add vanilla. Pour mix evenly over popcorn. Cool. Get your gloves.

4. Take an 8-inch piece of wax paper and a scoop of the corn. Mold it quickly. Set it aside on wax paper to cool. ENJOY!

Cold and Hot Teddy Bear Book (A)

Make a book along with your study of temperature. If you agree that it's a hot day activity, color Teddy *red*. If it's a cold day activity, color Teddy *blue*.

snowy day

cut the grass

go iceskating

play football

Cold and Hot Teddy Bear Book (B)

Cut the pages apart on the lines. Make a cover. Then staple the book together and read it.
RED = hot or warm
BLUE = cold or cool

go sledding

plant flowers

go swimming

play in the sand

Tom Thumb Puppets

Color the puppet thermometers. Trace around the edge onto red (hot) and blue (cold) paper. Cut and staple them to make hand mitts. Hold up the appropriate hand for the rhymes.

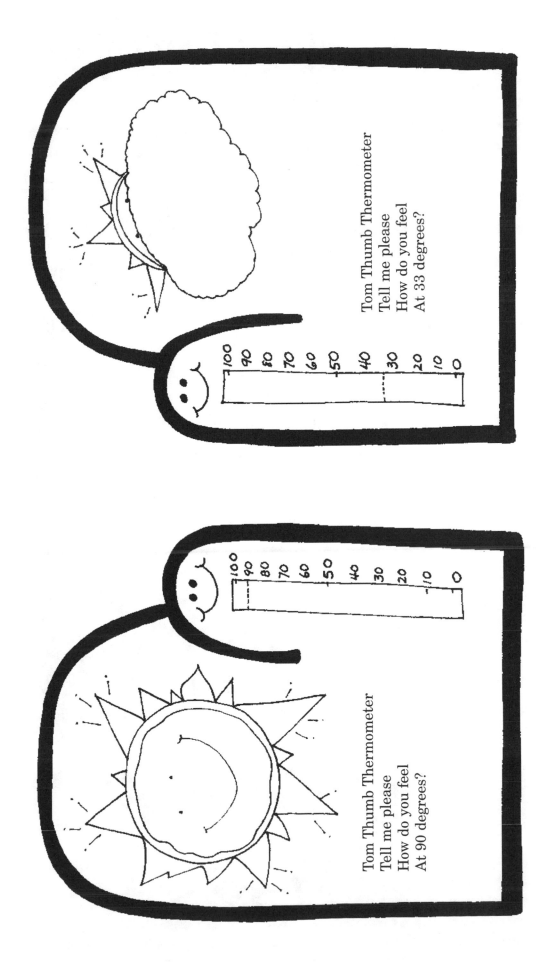

Tom Thumb Thermometer
Tell me please
How do you feel
At 90 degrees?

Tom Thumb Thermometer
Tell me please
How do you feel
At 33 degrees?

"I'm a Germ Fighter" Badge

Color me. Cut me out. Wear me with pride.

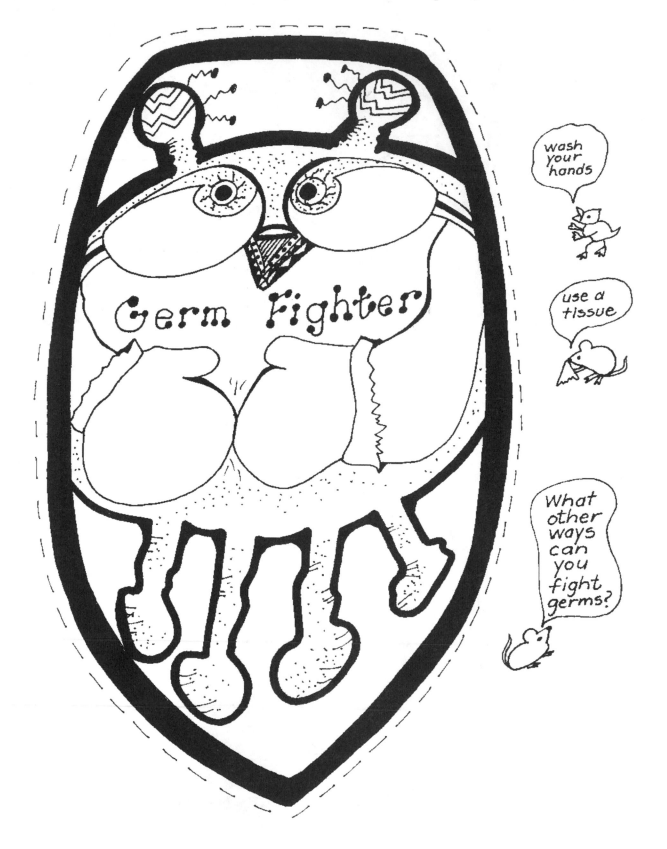

ART

Mrs. Boyd-Brooks

Art

Introduction

The kindergartener is primarily in the "Preschematic Stage, Four to Seven Years" in terms of art development according to Lowenfeld and Brittain, *Creative and Mental Growth, 6th edition* (NY: Macmillan Co., 1975). Children's art experiences vary widely prior to the kindergarten experience. Children the world over begin their art work by scribbling, and some kindergarteners may still be in this stage. The more a child employs his or her senses into the art experience, the happier the child will be.

Keep in mind that most kindergarten children are interested in the *process* rather than the *product*. For this reason, grading of art is to be avoided. You can explain a procedure, and the child takes it from there. Take fingerpainting, for example. Children need to be able to fingerpaint freely, enjoying the experience itself, rather than having to "make something" during this time. The sheer joy of getting involved with the gushy, runny paint is a pleasurable art experience. Some children will get involved with two hands, some get involved with fingertips on one hand only, and some are almost too shy to try. They will say, "My mother doesn't want me to get my hands dirty." These children need reassurance that their hands can be washed clean after the experience; but it's best not to force the issue.

At this stage, allow the child to explore with a variety of media (for example, chalk, painting with sponges, easel painting, gadget painting, modeling clay).

Above all, the child's drawing stems from his or her *experience*. You cannot just tell a child to "draw a flower" or "make a flower." First, a child must examine flowers, smell flowers, run a fingertip along the petals of a flower, learn the shape of a flower leaf by touching the leaf. After repetitions of this experience, a child may begin to "draw a flower."

Tracing large patterns and cutting with scissors has yet to be mastered by many children of this age. Rather than calling such an experience "art," it is more a form of visual and eye-hand coordination training

For many, coloring within designated lines is still a challenge. Some children like coloring books while others do not. The very process of moving a crayon repeatedly back and forth across a shape is a good exercise for strengthening small motor coordination.

Setting Up an Art Center

An Art Center can be stationary, or activities can be moved away from this area from time to time. Some things to remember about setting up the art center:

1. Have plenty of newspapers to spread on table and floor.
2. You may want to cover the floor surface with oil-cloth, or a plastic cover that can be easily washed.
3. You will need to be close to the sink, or a water supply.
4. Be away from the classroom's regular traffic flow.
5. Have a designated area to place finished work.
6. Keep it clean, uncluttered, and attractive.
7. Display children's art on the door, on the walls inside and outside the classroom, on countertops, in display cases in the hall.
8. Put lids on tempera paint overnight (easel) and clean brushes regularly.

Do You Plan to Set Up a Woodworking Center?

A Woodworking Center may be set up once the classroom is humming along. This area needs to be carefully selected *and* carefully supervised. Definite rules need to be established. Get an adult volunteer to help with this area, if at all possible; perhaps a retired woodworker if you're lucky. Some helpful tips are:

1. Select an area that is spacious and well lit.
2. The area needs to be out of the pattern of traffic.
3. Only _____ students at a time can be working here.
4. Equipment should be durable.

5. Equipment does not leave the workplace (trace around it with a felt pen, and return equipment to the proper place—the shape will help).
6. Stress that this is a work area, and the tools are not toys.
7. Safety is a prime factor.
8. Guidance is an important factor.

Some "starter equipment" would be: heavy-duty surface, nails, wood, sandpaper, hammer. Initially, it is the *experience* that the child needs, so the "product" is unplanned. For example, pounding nails into soft pine wood scraps helps to develop eye-hand coordination and large muscle control.

If you do not have the space to set up a permanent woodworking center, you might want to consider this. At various times, bring in a fireplace log, two hammers, a container of nails, and allow children to pound the nails into the wood. Again, safety needs to be stressed and the area needs to be in an out-of-the-flow-of-traffic setting.

Time to Set Up the Easels!

Try to secure a triangular back-to-back easel for your classroom so that two students may paint at one time. This can be set up after the first two weeks, or later, depending upon the group. Have smocks available at this area, so that students may put one on (an adult's shirt worn backwards) to protect their clothing. Also, have fresh newspaper under the easel each day.

Initially, introduce students to the easel and its purpose, which is for their painting pleasure. *Demonstrate* for them how to slowly remove the brush from the paint container and wipe off the edges on the rim of the container before they lift the brush up to the easel. Otherwise, they will have many drips and runs. *Demonstrate* how to use the brush (back and forth movements rather than scrubbing). *Demonstrate* for them the practice of returning the brush to the same container from which it was taken. For example, return the yellow to the yellow container, return the red to the red container. Otherwise, the paint will all get a "muddy" look to it. (Be prepared for brushes to get into the wrong containers and for colors to get mixed; it's all a part of maintaining an easel. Try to wash the brushes daily, and lay them out to dry on a paper toweling.)

Initially, limit the colors to three (red, yellow, blue) and add more as children gain experience with the medium.

Do not be concerned that a child may paint a person with green paint and raindrops with red paint. Many children do not make a color connection until later.

Variety with Brushes

When children have had quite a bit of experience at the easel, change the brush sizes. Secure inexpensive throw-away brushes at a paint company, and get wide ones, thick ones, and very narrow ones so that students can experiment with the medium. This will add zest to your easel painting experiences.

Art Activities

Holiday Colors at the Easel

Give students an opportunity to paint with orange, black, and white during late October; and red, green, and yellow during the holiday seasons in December. Pastels for spring (pink, violet, light blue) will create renewed interest in the easel in spring and will brighten up your classroom with these works of art!

Oops! Dip a Fingertip, Don't Squeeze

Save the screw caps from soft drink bottles, juice bottles, and soap containers. Ask parents to save them and send them in so that you have a large bag of screw-top caps. Then, when needed, the teacher can squeeze small amounts of glue into the caps, and place one at each work station. Children will have more control over the amount of glue they use, and won't end up with a heap of glue or runny paste on a sopping wet project.

 Children can dip a fingertip into the glue and won't have to squeeze the glue bottle. (The bottle of glue seems to have a mind of its own for some children who cannot yet gauge the strength needed for just the right amount of glue for their paper.)

Pound, Roll, Bend, Twist

Use plasticene and playdough so that students can explore with this medium. Have them roll out coils, make round balls, and roll the clay flat and use cookie cutters to make shapes. Separate the clay by colors, and store it in different containers. Use coffee cans, and put bright red, yellow, blue, and green construction paper or prepasted paper around the cans to help students color-code the clay storage. Some clay will become blended, so eventually you can have a container for the blended colors.

After children become familiar with the medium, they can create items that come naturally from their own experiences—perhaps they saw a bird, so they will create a clay bird. Encourage them to tell you something about their bird or experience and write it down on a sheet of paper labeled: "What the Artist Says." Then display the clay item and the notation on different bright colored plastic-coated paper plates for all to admire and enjoy.

Sometimes the clay table can provide a common experience for all students. For example, after reading *The Very Grouchy Ladybug* by Eric Carle, all children can be encouraged to make their version of a ladybug in clay. After a reading of *Where the Wild Things Are* by Maurice Sendak, the clay area may call out for a wild thing creation. (This is a busy time at the easel, too, as scary monsters become a theme.) When children create scary things, *they* are in control of the experience and can work through some of their own fears in this manner.

The Magic Porridge Pot

Being able to cut paper with scissors is a skill to be mastered. Some need more experience. Put Strega Nona's Magic Pot in the center of the table, and have children cut spaghetti from newsprint to put into the pot. This is a good accompaniment to the book *Strega Nona* by Tomi dePaola. Children who need practice can keep that pot overflowing!

Springtime with Sponges

Cut up old sponges in a variety of shapes (not all square). Put out some inviting lilac-colored paint in foil pie tins. *Demonstrate* how to paint with sponges—show them how to take the sponge and "hop like a bunny" (rather than dragging the sponge over the paper "like an elephant"—a brush can do the elephant work).

If you can have a bouquet of real lilacs in the classroom, it will enhance the experience. Work at a table or on the floor with groups of two or three children at a time. They can select a background color (dark purple, white, violet, maroon) from 12" x 18" construction paper. Have them cut out a vase shape from a different complimentary color. Then, have students use crayon or felt pen to draw brown stems above the vase. Now for the masterpiece! Using the sponges and varieties of purple paint housed in aluminum pie plates, create the splashy, filmy bouquet of lilacs, using dabbing motions. Children enjoy the process, and end up with a product as well for this particular art activity.

You can also make a dazzling mural of purples and pinks for spring.

Mask Making

Students enjoy making masks from paper plates. Have bright colored paints available, and a variety of items to glue onto the mask such as buttons, feathers, and beads. Students may be inspired to make a variety of masks after hearing stories about masks and their use at festival time in a variety of cultures. If an exploration of real masks is not possible, picture books would be excellent for helping with this project.

Later, students can wear their masks for a storytelling festival, or for acting out a particular story.

Art Talk

For this age, the child should be praised for the way he or she is working, rather than for the product itself. If the product is praised, many children will want to do the same thing and become frustrated when they cannot.

Also, since the child's representation is personal, do not ask, "What is it?" Rather, comment about an interesting shape or color, and then through your conversation you will discover more about what the child is trying to portray.

If a child finishes very early with a painting of a dog, for example, encourage the child to *add information* to the painting by showing the viewer where the dog lives, or where the dog has ventured (into the busy street, into the forest, and so on), or invite the child to depict the dog's collar, or his dish. Suggest only one, and let the child take it from there.

Torn Paper Collage

Tearing paper with small motions (rather than ripping it with large motions) is a skill that children can learn to master. Tearing the paper into tiny bits and pasting it onto paper is a skill that many children need time to develop. Working with bright colors that a child can personally select will help sustain interest in this activity. For example, in your art corner, save paper scraps so that bits and pieces can be torn from a variety of colors and textures and placed on larger sheets of paper with no thought to a specific "picture" but for creating an abstract collage.

Scissor Rules

For many, scissors have been "off limits" until now, so rules about scissors need to be established. These include: "Scissors Are for Cutting Paper," "Scissors Do Not Move With You, They Stay on the Table." When someone says, "Please Pass the Scissors," you pass them by holding the straight edge (closed) so that the finger holes are pointed toward the receiver. Keep the thumb on the top. Have a plastic berry container with holes, turned upside down, for storage of scissors on each worktable so that students do not have to get up to get them and return them. Both right- and left-handed scissors with blunt safety edges should be made available.

Media in a Tub

If students are working at tables in small groups on art projects, it is helpful to have small plastic tubs at each table that contain the following: felt pens, crayons in a container, scissors in a container, glue and screw-top caps, sponges, paint (on some days), paper towels, and so on. This helps to minimize trips and spills.

Cutting Fringes

Give students long strips of paper and have them make repeated cuts for a fringe, from one end to the other. This is good practice for the kindergartener who is still working on the control of small hand muscles. Allow extra time for the child with special needs to develop muscle control to a greater degree.

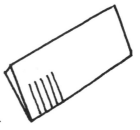

Art Appreciation

Line, color, form, and texture are all elements of art to enjoy and share. Introduce these concepts to kindergarteners by having lovely items available to share that have been created for everyone to enjoy. Take time to show and share art objects with children. Bring in an unusual basket and encourage comments about its shape, line, texture. From time to time, or on a more regular basis, share sculptures (wire, metal, stone) that have been created for pleasure. Bring in art prints and introduce children to the works of famous artists. Many of these items are available from your local public library.

Some schools have an "Artist in the School Program" and invite an artist for the day. The artist usually sets up in the main hall or in a designated room, and students rotate through that room during the day to watch the artist at work, and to note how a sculpture or painting has changed since they last walked through the area. The finished work may be displayed in the school for a week following this event. (Some schools arrange to buy one of the pieces so that they can hang it in their main hall area.)

A Multicultural Display and Some Art Experiences

Encourage parents to share items from their culture by making them available, or by sharing them in person with a fifteen-minute talk. Some parents will send in items such as festive clothing, colorful tablecloths, brightly woven rugs, masks, jewelry, and artifacts for children to admire. Perhaps a "just for looking" area can be established for these special items.

An examination of dolls, puppets, and marionettes from other cultures enables students to see variations in skin color, dress design, patterns, and textures of materials.

Along with a display from a foreign country, be sure to have folktales or fairy tales and information books about that country or region of the world on display.

Mosaics

Mosaics have been used since ancient times to cover walls, ceilings, and floors of palaces in Europe and East Europe, and temples in Asia. Some city walls in Indonesia are covered with these tile designs. Mosaic designs are common in Mexico, Costa Rica, Guatemala, and other areas of Central America and in South America as well. Children can create with *paper mosaic* by cutting pieces of construction paper or bright glossy paper from magazines. Then, have the children tear them into small pieces that are no larger than their thumbnail. They can outline the shape of a bird, animal, or tree on an 8-1/2" x 11" sheet of colorful construction paper, and then fill in the space using a repeat pattern.

Blue Indigo Cloth

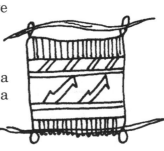

Did you know that there is an indigo plant? The dye from the leaves is a deep blue. Knowledge of the plant and the process of making dye was brought to Africa from India. Students can dye a white square of cotton with a cold-water dye of blue. Allow it to dry. Make a "combed pattern," which is popular in Ghana, by taking a comb with large teeth, dipping it into black tempera paint, and making a swirling pattern on the blue cloth. An excellent resource book is *The Art of Africa* by Shirley Glubok, designed by Gerard Nook, with special photography by Alfred H. Tamarin.

A Maori "Heitike"

A heitike is a Maori (mow' ree) ornament that is carved from pounamu (greenstone) and worn around the neck in New Zealand. Greenstone is a form of jade. Students can use modeling clay to create a small heitike (an animal, face, or design) that they can glaze and also wear around their necks.

Bright Birds of the Caribbean Isles

Birds in this area of the world have dazzling, colorful feathers. The parrot, especially, is a flying color machine. Students can create large-sized parrots from glossy construction paper. Refer to *basic shapes* for this lesson—an oval shape for the body, a round head, then a circle and dot for the eye, a triangle shaped beak, straight-line legs, and curved-line claws. Use curved lines for the wings. Then, use a wide range of colors for those beautiful feathers. If possible, use phosphorescent and gold and silver felt-tipped markers for these beautiful birds. Locate *The Calypso Alphabet* by John Agard, with illustrations by Jennifer Brent, for a colorful scratchboard (art technique) journey to the Caribbean.

Just Like Picasso

Pablo Picasso, a Latin American artist, was an explorer, not of the land or sea, but of ideas for creating works of art. What did he do? Well, for one thing he created sculpture from old, discarded items. This is called "found art." He once assembled a sculpture from the seat and handlebars of an old bicycle and called it "Bull's Head" (1942). Set up a table of old, discarded items. Ask parents to contribute. Have students take the items apart and reassemble them in new ways, just like Picasso. Ask, "What do you see in this shape?" Make a display of the new works of art. On a small card, print the title and the name of the artist.

The Art of Papermaking

During the Han Dynasty (202 B.C.–A.D. 220), the Chinese invented the art of making paper. For a student activity, paper can be made in the classroom. Then, students can draw or paint on the paper, or use it as a background for a work of art that they make from cut paper. (See "Recipe for Paper Making" in reproducible activity pages.) One American picture book award-winning artist *makes* the paper for her colorful book pages and illustrations. (Get a copy of the lush book *In the Tall, Tall Grass* by Denise Flemming, examine the pictures, and enjoy the story. This artist has a paper-making kit available at local bookstores that have a children's section.)

Making Masks

In many cultures, masks play a powerful role in the lives of the people, the theatre, and the arts. In the Native American culture, the mask is used in cere-monies to cover the face or to be worn on the top of the head.

Full-face or partial masks are used in Asia, Africa, Europe, East Europe, and in the Americas. We can begin to cre-ate simple masks by using a paper plate (or a paper bag) and adding designs with paint or felt-tipped pen. For a more elaborate mask, glue on feathers, sequins, seeds, or felt shapes.

Masks can be used to enrich language development and storytelling in your own classroom.

Be on the Lookout for Shapes

Once students have the concept of a circle and a square, look for them in a big book of quilts and quilt designs. Have a variety of sizes and col-ors of shapes made from felt available so that stu-dents can create shape designs and pictures on a large flannel board or felt board. Attractive and helpful quilt books to use include *My Grandmother's Patchwork Quilt* and *Mrs. Noah's Patchwork Quilt,* both by Janet Bolton.

Another good book to use is *Shapes and Things* by Tana Hoban. After exploring the book, try some sun-printing on a shelf by a sunny window. Use 8-1/2" x 11" dark blue construction paper for back-ground, and set several items on top of the paper. The sun rays will fade the paper within a week, and the shape of the objects will remain in darker color to create a shape print. For more of a contrast, leave the items on longer. Encourage students to keep trying a variety of shape prints.

Make Beanbag Shapes

Use heavy felt, and cut out circles, squares and triangles. Perhaps a parent or an aide can sew the edges together on a sewing machine, leaving enough room to fill the pocket with lentils or white beans. A funnel can be used by the children for the filling process. Then the aide can sew up the remainder of the material around the edge. Students can decorate the beanbags with pieces of cut-out felt that is glued onto the bag.

For a matching experience, students can toss the round, red beanbags, for example, into a round, red container. Toss the green, square ones into a green, square container, and so on. In addition to helping with visual acuity—and the force needed to throw the beanbag accurately—it will reinforce the concepts of shape and color.

Dots, Circles, and Lines

Have children look for dots (circular shapes filled in with color), circles (rounded shapes, not colored in), and lines (straight, curved, angular). They can look for these in their clothing, around the classroom, outdoors, and so on. For example, examine a flower. Does it have dots? circle shapes? straight or curved or angular lines? Have students use a felt pen to draw this flower, thinking of it in terms of dots, circles, and lines.

Have students practice making dots. They can make small and large ones all over their paper. This is familiarizing them with the concept of a dot.

Make circles on a paper. Do you want them to *overlap*? (This is a new term.)

Make lines on a paper from one end to the other. Make a straight line, a curvy line, and a straight line that suddenly decides to go in a different direction (an angular line).

Soon children will begin to "see" in terms of dots, circles, and lines. Keep pointing this out to them. (See "Zuni Zebra's Art Studio" in reproducible activity pages.)

Creating with Dots, Circles, and Lines

Use construction paper, in a variety of colors, and have students create a bird, using only straight lines or using only curved lines. There are no "right and wrong" birds—just fancy birds. (Demonstrate a straight-lined bird for the students. Cut out a variety of squares or rectangles of different sizes and colors. Select a large rectangle for the body, a smaller square for the head, stick-like rectangles for the legs and claws, a small square eye, a smaller square pupil, a rectangular-shaped beak. Everything on this bird is in straight lines—even the feathers.) Next, create one with circles and ovals. Children will enjoy watching. *Then take your samples away*, and let them create their own. These can be hung with yarn or string from the ceiling or on a tree branch.

SAMPLE:  straight-line bird    curved-line bird

Weaving In and Out

Create a large loom from a giant-size piece of cardboard (the side of a large appliance box) so that children can stand up and weave. Cut slots (2 inches in depth) along the top and bottom, and then use string to dress the loom. It can be labeled with signs such as "top," "bottom," "left," and "right."

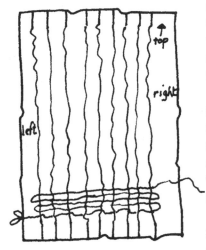

Start out with one yarn color and gradually add choices. Demonstrate for students how to go over and under and over and under the string; then let them try it. Remember, it is the experience of the weaving that we are after in the beginning.

Later, when a variety of color is available and children have learned the right amount of tension on the yarn so that the edges remain reasonably straight, more thought can be given to changing colors. Multicolored yarn makes for a different visual effect, and eventually students may want to add beads.

The works of art produced here can be removed from the loom (knot the edges), hung from a tree branch, and displayed in a section of the room called "The Art Gallery."

Paper Weaving

Cut paper strips on the paper cutter. The base for the weaving may need to be cut for some children, or if working in groups of two or three, the adult can supervise the folding and cutting *on the fold*. The over/under, over/under pattern is a new experience for some, a challenge for others, and something others have mastered. For those who have mastered this, provide more of a variety of items with which to weave, either color or texture.

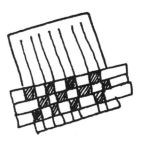

Bark Rubbings

Talk about smooth and rough textures, and have representative items for each. What about tree trunks? Are they smooth or rough? Armed with flat crayons and enough sheets of paper so that each child has two or three available, go out on the playground or on the school grounds to do bark rubbings. If this is not possible, secure fireplace logs and have children do the rubbings indoors. (This first-hand experience will have an effect on the way they create paintings of tree trunks at the easel and with felt pen or crayon.) A book entitled *Squirrels* by Brian Wildsmith is a good book to use along with this activity. The tree trunks in this book are not straight, dark brown representations. Rather, they are swirling designs of a variety of colors including pinks and blues. After this, tree trunks will definitely take on a different character.

Making Crayon Muffins

When crayons become broken and stepped on, gather them up and save them. They can be melted in individual small Pyrex® cups in an electric frypan half-filled with water (**teacher only is allowed to handle this**) OR they can be melted in a microwave oven. Then, wait until the Pyrex® cools and—using a mitt for handling the hot glass—pour the hot wax into small muffin tins that have been coated with cooking spray. They eventually form a large solid crayon of varigated colors and are fun for the children to use, and *promote the concept of recycling*. Again, caution is necessary when doing this as a *demonstration only* for children. They need to sit back and observe this activity and then enjoy the crayons.

Pictures from a Squiggly Line

On large paper, use a thick felt pen to draw a line (different on each paper). Then, after you have been examining lines and edges, distribute these to the students and have them complete the drawing. For some it is easy and for others it may be difficult, but once they gain practice with this activity, they will begin to have more ideas for completion of a picture.

What Do You Get If You Mix Red and Blue?

Children are curious about primary colors and secondary colors. Cut pieces of red, blue, and yellow cellophane squares so that each student can have one of each color. First, distribute just one color and have them put it up to their eyes and examine the world through that color. Encourage conversation. Then, add the other colors one by one.

Encourage students to overlap the colors. What happens when red and yellow are overlapped? (*orange*) What happens when red and blue are overlapped? (*purple*) What happens when blue and yellow are overlapped? (*green*)

The next step is to have children mix the actual paint at a painting station that has been set up for this purpose. Use muffin tins or styrofoam trays (from packaged fruits and vegetables) for this activity. Two or three children can work together at a time with adult supervision.

Another way to demonstrate color mixing is with the overhead projector. Use colored plastic see-through shapes or colored cellophane squares that project the actual colors on the screen. Then overlap the colors.

Another idea is to place two different colors of tempera paint inside a zip-lock baggie. Then double-bag it. Have children gently squish the colors together in a smooth motion. What's the result?

The Grass Is Pink, The Sky Is Green

Cover up the bottom part of a classroom window with large cellophane shapes of different colors and encourage the children to peer through them. How does it change the color of things in the environment? Perhaps they can experiment with different colors at the easel, making their tree trunk red and the grass pink. Be on the lookout for colorful illustrations in picture books or art books that depict items in colors other than those we are accustomed to seeing every day. Children will be delightfully surprised!

Secondary Color Days

During the following week, make a large color graph in the shape of an artist's pallet, in order to show at a glance the "secondary" colors such as orange, purple, green, etc., that are being worn by the students. Keep a daily tally of these colors for one week. A note home to parents will be helpful for this ongoing activity.

A storybook accompaniment for color mixing is the picture book *Little Blue and Little Yellow* by Leo Lionni, and the strikingly beautiful *Colors* by Ruth Heller. Also, *Mouse Paint* by Ellen Stoll Walsh is most enjoyable. (See more complete information on COLOR at the end of this section.)

More of the Beauty of Quilts

Treat the children to more picture books that explore quilts such as *My Grandmother's Patchwork Quilt* by Janet Bolton and *The Patchwork Quilt* by Valerie Flournoy, with illustrations by Jerry Pinkney. Another ABC book about quilts is *Eight Hands Round* by Ann Whitford Paul, with illustrations by Jeanette Winter, which shows various designs with fancy names. Children can work with geometric (paper or wooden) shapes to create their own quilt designs.

Give each child a square of white cotton cloth and have them draw a design or picture with fabric crayons. Put their initials in the lower right-hand corner. These can be stitched together with a paisley print border and backing, and hung in the classroom for all to enjoy.

Paper quilts can also be made by giving each student a square of paper and having them create a design using felt-tip pens. The quilt can have a theme (spring, winter) or it can be a general picture or design quilt. These squares can be pasted onto a large sheet of posterboard. Have students make yarn bows and place them on the corners where the squares meet.

Paper quilts can have a color theme, as well as a subject theme. A quilt done in varieties of orchids, purples, and pinks is effective, for example, as is a patriotic red, white, and blue quilt with symbols of our country (liberty bell, stars, stripes, Uncle Sam, Statue of Liberty, famous Americans, the shape of your state, and so on).

Fostering the Work of Artists

The book by Tomi dePaola entitled *The Art Lesson* is a helpful reminder for teachers and parents when working with children in the field of visual arts. They need freedom to paint and to produce works of art that do not follow a formula prescribed by the teacher. Put the materials out for them to use, be sure they know how to use them, and then stand back and just enjoy the results. If a child asks for a fresh piece of paper to start over, make sure it is available.

Those Paintings Just Sparkle!

And they do if you use the following Salt Paint recipe. Mix together:

2 cups salt
1/2 cup liquid starch
1 cup water
tempera powder paint OR food coloring

Mix the first three ingredients, then very slowly add the coloring. Use this as "salt paint." The pictures will sparkle when the salt paint dries.

Pardon Me, Are You Washing Dishes or Painting?

For a different type of painting experience, secure a number of detergent dispensers with the sponge tips. Instead of filling them with detergent, fill them with liquid tempera paint. This may be especially helpful for students who are disabled or delayed in their hand-coordination movements. Plan ahead. Have more than one of each color available so that when they are empty, children can get a full one, rather than having to go through the refilling process in the middle of an art experience.

Supplies, Supplies, Supplies

Here are some ideas for setting up an Art Center that ensures plenty of variety through the year.

brushes (variety)	scissors
sponges	glue or paste
easel	tape
felt-tip pens	screw-top caps
crayons	foil trays
styrofoam trays	berry containers
tempera paints	colored pencils
cans (for containers)	cloth scraps
newspapers	variety of construction paper
yarn	string
felt	wallpaper sample books
water containers	paint smocks (old shirts)
stamp pads	gadgets (for printing)
clay	plasticene
soap	toweling
zip-lock bags	straws
collage "stuff"	clothes hangers and clips
stapler	string
paper bags, cups, plates	cloth (variety)

Autumn Harvest for Winter Supplies

Start collecting dried plant stalks, pine cones, and dried flowers. During the winter these can be put out on a table with a pie plate container of relatively thick tempera paint for a different painting experience.

Buttermilk Chalk Paintings

Dip chalk into a container of buttermilk, or brush the buttermilk on a piece of manila paper. Have children create their art work on the damp surface.

Mixing Up Some Good Art Recipes

1. Uncooked Dough for Modeling

2 cups all-purpose flour
1/2 cup salt
food coloring

1/4 cup oil
1/2 cup water

Mix dry ingredients. Add oil. Add water until you get a consistency for molding (this may vary). Store in air-tight container.

2. Soap "Clay"

2 cups dry soap powder or detergent
1/2 cup water

Whip with beater. Keep adding soap until mixture is like dough. Dip hands into water before using. This can be molded and dried.

3. Sawdust "Clay"

3 cups sawdust
1 cup wallpaper paste

water

Mix together. Gradually add water until it is the consistency of biscuit dough. Mold, and allow to dry.

4. Papier-Mâché

1 cup flour
2 teaspoons liquid glue
cold water

2 cups boiling water
few drops oil of cloves

Make a creamy paste with flour and cold water. Then, add boiling water and other ingredients.

Tear newspaper into small bits and pieces. Soak overnight in a pail of warm water. Stir. Squeeze out excess water, and mash the paper. Add the paste to this mashed paper and shape as desired. Allow 1 to 2 days for drying.

5. Peanut Butter Dough (edible)

peanut butter
honey
powdered milk

Start by mixing dollops of peanut butter with powdered milk. A few table-spoons of honey can be added to hold it all together.

6. Plaster of Paris

Add dry plaster to a bucket of water until consistency is creamy but not runny. Stir well. Pour into mold (pie tins, small milk containers). This can be used for hand prints. Or items can be pressed into the mixture as it is "setting up."

All About Colors

Kindergarteners are very much in tune with the world of color. They like to be able to identify colors they are wearing, and colors in their classroom, colors at the easel, crayons and felt marking pens, colors in magazine pictures, and colors of birds and animals in the environment.

Some children have had more experience with colors than others. Ask one child to name his or her eye color and you may not get an answer. Ask another child, and the answer could be as sophisticated as "blue and white with a black dot in the middle."

At this age, keep calling attention to colors all around, and the child will respond.

Changing Colors (A Color Poem)

Here is a poem to learn.

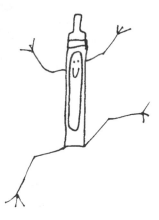

Changing Colors

Colors are sassy
Colors are bold
Colors are bright
Then some grow old.

But faded colors
are pretty too.
They just don't "gr-r-r,"
They pur-r-r "me-w."

Activities to Go with *Changing Colors* Poem

Language Development.   Talk about the meaning of the words "sassy" and "bold." Have concrete examples of glaring, shiny colors (for example, a glossy notebook cover, a plastic cup, or plastic dishes), and faded colors, too. The children's ABC book by Tana Hoban, *26 Letters and 99 Cents*, has excellent **bold** color examples to examine, whereas, the ABC book by Anita Lobel, *Allison's Zinnia*, has many fine examples of softer *faded* colors.

Color Experiment.   Put a 9" x 12" sheet of dark blue construction paper on the window ledge and place an object on part of it. Within the week the blue that has not been covered will fade. Note the difference in color tones. Try arranging different objects on the dark blue to make shapes and designs.

Fading   In autumn, colors of the trees are bright and then fade. Some "faded" clothing is popular, such as faded blue jeans. How many students are wearing blue jeans today? Compare the intensity of the blue colors from dark to light.

G-r-r-r and Pur-r-r.   The "gr-r-r" implies a loud sound way down in the back of the throat (like the roar of a lion in a bold, gold fur coat), whereas the "pur-r-r" and "me-w" are softer sounds (like a cat in a faded plaid hat). They are contrasting words to help get the message across of contrasting colors.

Colors I Know (A Color Poem)

Colors I Know

Colors are pretty,
Colors are gay,
Colors can help us
Brighten our day!
How many colors can you say?

Activities to Go with *Colors I Know* Poem

Do the "Color Cheer" to Accompany Colors I Know   Teacher serves as model. Get the rhythm and the movements going. Do this slowly at first. Practice daily. Say: "Stand at attention, feet together, arms at sides. Ready?"

RED	(*use both hands, touch your head*)
ORANGE	(*reach overhead*)
YELLOW	(*touch your shoulders*)
GREEN	(*arms outstretched at sides*)
BLUE	(*touch your knees*)
PURPLE	(*touch your toes*)
YEAH!	(*stand, stretch both arms high overhead, then down at sides*)

Color Identification   Here are some simple exercises to do daily during Circle Time:

1. **Color Plates**. Have a variety of colored plates and hold up one plate at a time. Call upon students who have raised their hand to identify the color. At other times, have the students say them together (choral speaking).
2. **Get the Yellow One.** Have a variety of crayons or material swatches on a table, and ask students to go and get a specific color, or point to the object that is the color that has been named.

Let's Move to the Colors

This is a good activity for movement and color identification at the same time. Teacher calls out all of the information *and* directions, and children respond by acting out the directions (in parentheses). Try to get a rhythm going:

If you're wearing any color at all	*(stand up tall)*
If you're wearing red	*(point to the wall)*
If you're wearing green	*(wiggle your nose)*
If you're wearing blue	*(wiggle your toes)*
If you're wearing yellow	*(reach up high)*
If you're wearing purple	*(wink one eye)*
If you're wearing orange	*(run in place)*
If you're wearing brown	*(wrinkle your face)*
If you're wearing white	*(turn out the light, snap fingers)*
If you're wearing black	*(sit down, good night)*
If you're wearing pink	*(reach up high)*
If you're wearing violet	*(wave good-bye)*
If you're wearing any color at all	*(sit down, cross your legs, fold your arms, close your eyes, take three deep breaths, AND REST)*

Purple Is the Color of My Brand New Shoes
(Poetry for listening)

Red is an apple.
Red is a rose.
And when I say, "A choo!"
Red is my nose.

***

Orange is a ribbon.
Tied in my hair.
Orange is the fur
Of my teddy bear.

***

Yellow is a school bus.
Yellow is a kitty.
Yellow is the sunshine
That makes the sky pretty!

***

Green is the grass
That's chewed by the cow.
Green is the traffic light
That says, "GO. NOW!"

***

Blue is the bluejay
Who squawks in its nest.
Blue is the color
Of my brand new vest.

***

Black is a choo choo train
Chugging on a track.
Black is the handle
Of my new backpack.

***

White is a feather
On a downy duck.
White is a chicken
That says, "cluck, cluck."

Purple is grape juice.
Purple prints the news.
And purple is the color
Of my brand new shoes.

***

Brown is a puppy.
Brown is a car.
Brown is the chocolate
On a candy bar.

***

Put colors together
What do they do?
They make plaids, stripes, and checks.
You can do that, too!

**Activities for *Purple Is the Color
of My Brand New Shoes* Poem**

1. **Make a Class Big Book.** Print the verse, and have students make the illustrations, using sponge paint or torn paper collage.

2. **Plaid Repeat Design.** Cut strips of various colored construction paper. Have students select three colors and create a plaid, repeat design.

3. **Plaids, Stripes, and Checks.** "Who is wearing plaid?" "Stand up." "Let's name the colors." Repeat for stripes and checks. Students can make plaid, striped, and/or checkered paper. Trim the edges to give the paper a rounded, oval look. Then have students make a person from this. Add a circular head, and rectangular arms and legs. Paper that has been cut off from the edges can be used to help decorate the figure (hat, eyes, gloves, shoes, and so on).

4. **Working with "Pl," "St," and "Ch"** (*Pl*aid, *St*ripes, *Ch*ecks). Look for examples of plaids, stripes, and checks in children's picture books. Many fanciful animals, clothing, and borders will have a variety. Use the people figures (#3 above) and make three colorful charts. Label the charts, place the figures around the edges, and go on a hunt for words that begin with these sounds. Students can print them on the chart and learn them.

Dress Up at "The Color Company"

Make several large color charts for a variety of colors, with a color-coded animal shape on each (for example, green crocodile, red cardinal, etc.). Do a *color check* each day to see who is wearing that color, and begin to graph it on the color company animal charts that you create. Note the synonyms for the word "company," such as corporation, shop, and factory. Point these out to the students. What are some store names in your area? Does the store have a logo and, if so, what color is it? Have students take notice and report their findings the next day. This information can be put along the bottom of the sheets. (See "Becca Bunny's Color Graph" activity pages for individual favorite color and graphing.) Following are suggestions for the clothing color charts.

The Green Crocodile Company Who is wearing green today? The Green Crocodile Company is in charge of green and wants to know the number, so take a count, and record it on the animal figure.

The Red Bird Factory Who is wearing red today? The Red Bird Company wants to know how many girls and how many boys are wearing red. Also, the Red Bird Company is interested in knowing how many are wearing red plaid (if time).

The Orange Pumpkin Company Who is wearing orange today? The Orange Pumpkin Company wants you to check your outer clothing (sweaters and jackets), too.

The Yellow Daffodil Shop   Who is wearing yellow today? The Yellow Daffodil Shop also wants to know how many lunchpails have yellow on them.

Ben Bear's Blue Shop   Ben Bear loves blue, and is eager to know if you do, too. If you aren't wearing something blue today, can you try to wear something blue this week? Or, can you hold up your blue crayon and say, "Let's Go, Blue"? (That's a sports cheer for the University of Michigan, a Big Ten University in the U.S.A.)

The Purple Mooooooo Cow Corporation   If you're wearing purple, record your mark on the purple cow, followed by a great big "Moo!" cheer.

Matching Colored Yarn

Cut two sets of various yarn colors, about three inches in length. Place each matching set in a zip-lock plastic bag and clip together. Students may take these from the "Color Shelf" and match the colors during free-choice time.

Colored Sock Match

Ask each parent to donate a set of socks. Place them in a little basket with a clothesline and clothespins. Students can match the socks and clip them together on the line.

What Color Are You Today?

Give each student a piece of colored yarn, and have them help each other gently tie the yarn around their wrist. Then, call students "by color" to line up, to play with various items (blocks, housekeeping corner, art center, writing center, and so on). These can be changed daily.

The Colorful Circus Clown

Make a clown on a large piece of posterboard with various colored pockets. Make a direction envelope for each pocket (Rebus style and color-coded). Example: "Put three crayons in the black pocket."

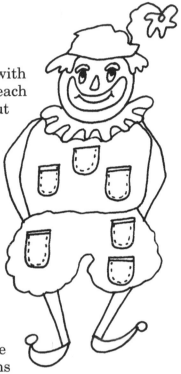

Have students follow the directions on the envelopes so they can place items in the clown pockets. They are reading, counting, following directions. Some suggestions for cards and pocket items:

- put 5 rubber bands in green pocket
- put 7 paper clips in red pocket
- put 3 pencils in yellow pocket
- put 1 eraser in blue pocket

When pockets are all full, children can use the envelopes as a directional guide and transfer the items from the pockets back to the proper envelopes.

White Cotton Gloves

Secure five sets of white cotton garden gloves at a variety store, along with some packets of dye. Dye the gloves in the classroom so that students can observe the process. When the desired color is reached, remove the set of gloves and hang to dry. You can get into the concept of secondary colors with this project (for example, red + yellow = orange; red + blue = purple). Once the gloves are dyed and dried, they can be mixed together and classified by color. Also, "tasks" can be assigned to certain gloves with labels, as follows:

YELLOW GLOVES—use when sweeping floor
BLUE GLOVES—use when emptying wastebasket
GREEN GLOVES—use when watering plants

RED GLOVES—use when helping with snacktime
ORANGE GLOVES—use when . . .

"What Is a Yellow?" (food)

In our vocabulary, one fruit is named for its color—the orange. If you say, "I'd like an orange, please," everyone would understand. But would people know what it meant if you said, "I'd like a yellow, please?" Chances are they would not! Let's have some fun with color words and fruits, and see if we can agree on fruits that the colors *could* represent. If we say, "I'd like a tan, please," what food might we be asking for? Solicit answers from students and then continue with more color words and associations.

"I'd like a red, please."	*(cherry, apple, and so on)*
"I'd like a yellow, please."	*(banana, and so on)*
"I'd like a green, please."	*(grapes, pear, kiwi, and so on)*
"I'd like a blue, please."	*(blueberry, grape, and so on)*
"I'd like a purple, please."	*(grape, plum, and so on)*

Look for colorful pictures of fruits in magazines. While we're at it, we can hunt for colorful vegetables also. Read Lois Ehlert's colorful picture books, *Planting a Rainbow* and *Growing Vegetable Soup*.

Yoo-Hoo! Do You Know Us? We're Colors, Too!

Can you find us? We're colors, too. And chances are, we belong to you. BUT, you may not know us by name. Write down our names on a big chart, and keep looking for us in picture books, colorful magazines, and pamphlets. Don't stop until you check off each one of us!

chartreuse (greenish yellow, or yellowish green)
puce (dark grayish purple, the color of a flea)
peach
fuschia
aqua
beige
teal
olive brown

You may get some help from a store that sells paint by gathering a variety of sample cards.

maroon

coral

charcoal

Use a wide assortment of colorful picture books and search for the different colors. Children can make a list of the book titles in which their favorite color appears.

Art Survival Tips

Some New, Some Review

1. Put newspapers under easels to catch paint drips. Then, bundle up paper with paint drips and throw it away at the end of each session. Replace paper immediately, so it's there when you need it.

2. Always cover tables with newspaper before doing art work.

3. Wash easel brushes every other day. Then thoroughly wash brushes on Friday, and line them up on the counter to dry over the weekend.

4. Cover paint containers at the easel at day's end to keep paint from getting too thick. (Some paint comes in plastic containers with covers.)

5. Use men's old, cotton, long-sleeve shirts for smocks—roll up or cut off sleeves so children's arms are covered. Have children put them on backwards so their entire front is also covered. A friend can button the top two buttons for them. (Teach children to help each other with the buttoning.)

6. Have left-handed scissors for those with left-hand preference.

7. Keep a Scrap Box. It can be covered with construction paper scraps and labeled "Art Scrap Box." Rather than throwing paper away, use it for projects (for details when making construction paper puppets, for projects, etc.).

8. When the Scrap Box gets filled to overflowing, have each student take a handful and use it to make a three-dimensional scrap design on a 9" x 12" piece of construction paper.

    Another idea for an overflowing Scrap Box is to have students do paper mosaic art. They can tear pieces of paper no larger than their thumbnail and outline an object (dog, TV set, flower). Some children may have time to fill this in. Remind them to keep gluing as they go along, and not wait until the end.

9. When plastic glue tops won't budge, soak them overnight in warm water.

10. *Teacher only* handles the paper cutter.

11. When demonstrating how to draw something, take your model and put it out of sight—otherwise, children will try to make theirs look just like it.

12. When making colored chalk drawings, use a sponge to wet the paper first. This eliminates a lot of chalk dust and mess. The teacher can keep circulating around the room to keep wetting the paper (and the results resemble a painted look).

13. Decide ahead of time where you want children to store their art work (countertop, on floor along edge of all). Some will be wet.

14. Keep looking for new ideas monthly in teacher magazines, such as *School Arts* or *Instructor*.

15. Don't ever try anything for the first time with the students without having tried it yourself; otherwise, you can't help them.

16. Backgrounds can be a problem for the new painter. Try having students paint the background first, then let it dry. Next day, paint objects over the background.

17. *Murals:* Have students draw their object on with chalk (not pencil) *before* they paint it. Chalk allows them more freedom.

18. *Kindergarteners draw what they know.* For example, if a car has four wheels, they will put four wheels on their drawing even though it may look like two of them are sticking out of the roof. This is a normal stage of art development and it's charming, so enjoy it while it lasts.

19. If a child seems to be "stuck" drawing the same thing over and over and over again, try a different media—such as clay—so the child can model it and rethink the shape.

20. NEVER ask, "What is it?" *Instead* say, "Tell me something about your painting," or "Hmmm, that's an interesting shape," or "That's a pretty shade of purple, isn't it?"

21. Foster the exuberance of art expression from the children, nurture their attempts, and display their art.

ART ACTIVITY PAGES

Recipe for Paper Making (*recycling*)

TEDDY BEAR VESTS, My Book of Colors: English and Spanish

- Title Page
- Red/Rojo
- Orange/Naranja
- Yellow/Amarillo
- Green/Verde
- Blue/Azul
- Purple/Morado

How to Make a Teddy Bear Color Vest (*directions*)

Zuni Zebra's Art Studio (*dots; circles; lines*)

Another Visit with Zuni (*vase design*)

A Bright Orange Pumpkin (*sponge painting opportunity*)

Turkey Feathers (*cutting fringes*)

A Winter Tree (*decorate a holiday tree or bird treat*)

Valentine Greetings (*gadget-printing opportunity*)

A Spring Basket (*construction paper opportunity*)

Becca Bunny's Color Graph (*colors; graphing*)

Recipe for Paper Making

MATERIALS: Old newspapers, egg beater or blender, dishpan, water, one-half teaspoon liquid detergent, 3" x 3" piece of window screen, wooden spoon, sponge, paper towels, iron.

PROCEDURE:

1. Tear newspaper into small pieces and drop into dishpan.

2. Half-fill dishpan with water and add detergent.

3. Beat mixture with egg beater (or blender) until it becomes mushy.

4. Scoop a spoonful of the mush (slurry) onto paper toweling.

5. Place window screen on top and gently rub with a moist sponge to spread slurry out. Press   down on screen, then remove it.

6. REPEAT STEPS 1,2,3,4,5 until layers are built up as thick as desired.

7. Place paper toweling over slurry.

8. Iron on low to medium heat.

9. Gently peel off paper toweling. Place newly made paper on slick countertop and allow two to three days for drying.

10. Print or draw on your recycled paper.

I can do this at home!

Make invitations, and note paper.

Teddy Bear Vests

MY BOOK OF COLORS
(English/Spanish)

red
rojo

(roh' hoh)

1

orange
naranja

(nah rahn' hah)

**yellow
amarillo**

(ah mah ree' lyoh)

green
verde

(vehr' deh)

**blue
azul**

(ah sool')

**purple
morado**

(moh rah' doh)

How to Make a Teddy Bear Color Vest

1. large paper bag

2. scissors

3. cut the neck
   cut the armholes
   cut the front

4. paint a design

5. Have a color vest party!

Zuni Zebra's Art Studio

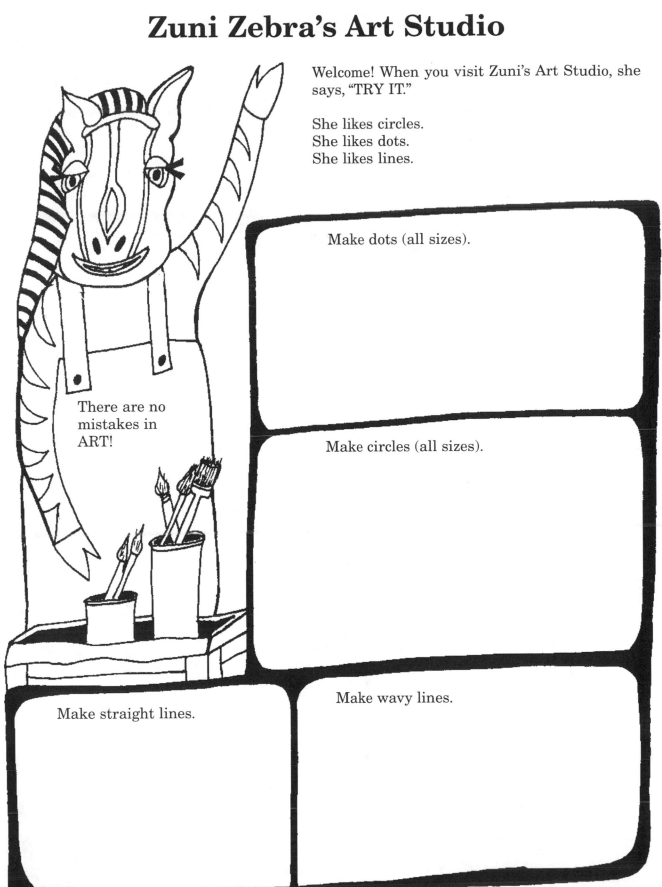

Welcome! When you visit Zuni's Art Studio, she says, "TRY IT."

She likes circles.
She likes dots.
She likes lines.

There are no mistakes in ART!

Make dots (all sizes).

Make circles (all sizes).

Make straight lines.

Make wavy lines.

Another Visit with Zuni

Since you visited Zuni, she made this giant vase and she chose YOU to put the designs on it with her favorite shapes—circles, dots, and lines. Good luck! Color Zuni, too.

Zuni
Loves Art

A Bright Orange Pumpkin

Make this into a bright orange pumpkin (or jack-o'-lantern) using small sponges and orange paint.

Turkey Feathers

Cut bright colored paper strips. Use your scissors to make feather fringes. Paste the feathers on the turkey to make it beautiful. Make the turkey a deep tan with your crayons. Put legs on your turkey.

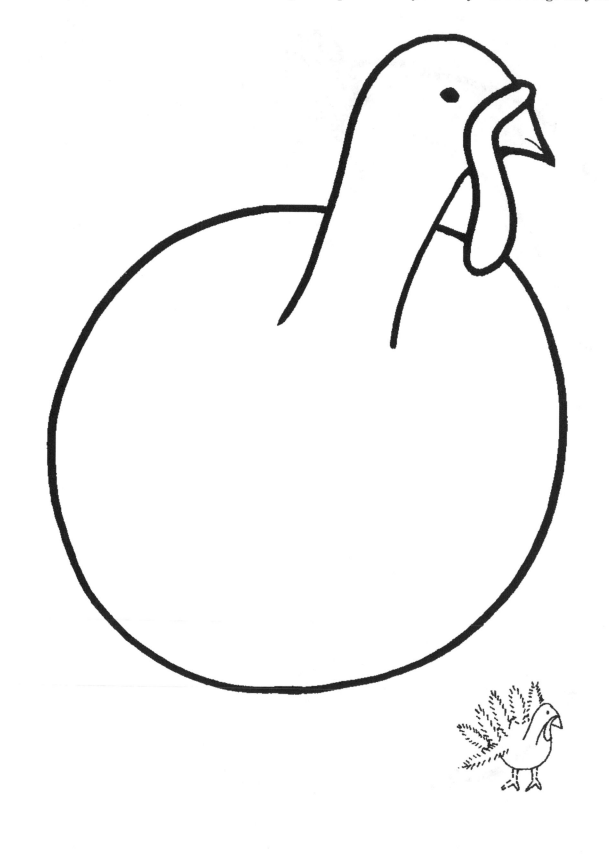

A Winter Tree

Make this tree a deep green. Then use construction paper to decorate it as an indoor tree for the holiday season OR as an outdoor tree for the birds.

Valentine Greetings

Use gadgets—along with red and pink paint—to decorate this pretty valentine heart.

Name _____

A Spring Basket

Use your construction paper and scissors to fill this space with colored eggs or flowers. OR, maybe a bird could build a nest in your spring basket.

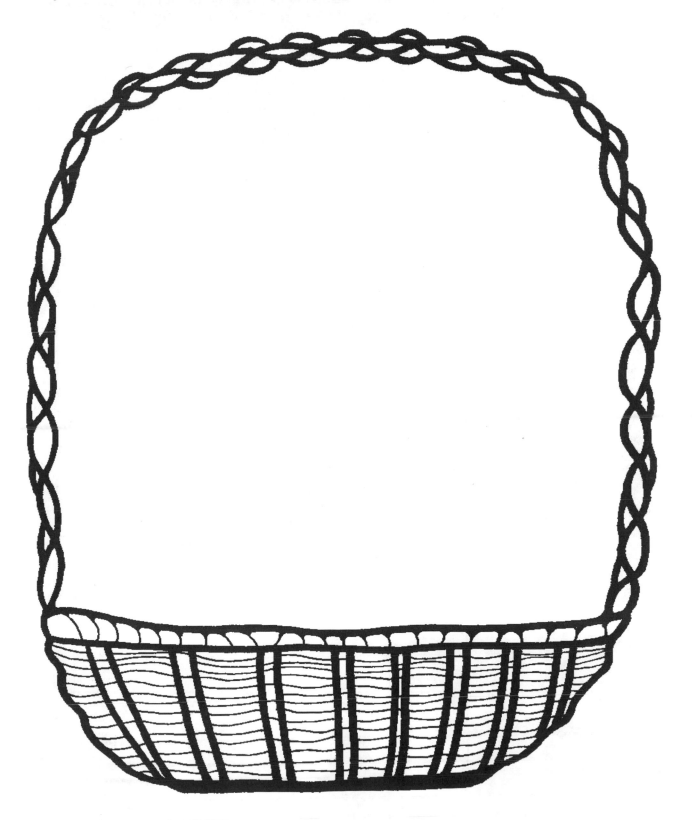

Becca Bunny's Color Graph

Becca Bunny wants a class graph of favorite colors. How many like red? How many like orange? Color in the squares with the appropriate color.

You can make a big class graph, too.

MUSIC and MOVEMENT

Mr. LaMar

Music and Movement

Introduction

Children enjoy rhythm and movement. They can remember jingles and simple songs, and enjoy moving to music, listening to music, painting to music, and learning fingerplays to accompany music. Most of all, they like to create their own music.

For quiet times, play soothing background music. It has been suggested by researchers that by playing the music of classical composers, such as Mozart, new pathways and connections are formed in the brain. These connections will help with learning, spatial awareness, and mathematical connections since areas for music and math are closely aligned in the brain.

An excellent resource book is *Go In and Out the Window, An Illustrated Songbook for Children* by The Metropolitan Museum of Art.

Musical Variety

Have a variety of music available for students. Audio cassettes may be secured from the local library for listening, and videotapes may be secured for listening as well as observing singing and dancing in different cultures.

In your music listening corner, have a cassette recorder with headphones. Be sure to include a variety of regional music here such as jazz, bluegrass, gospel and blues, polka, classical, opera, instrumental, choral groups, marching band music, and patriotic music. This cultural mix can be discussed, and the locations around the world of these music centers can be found on a map or globe. Cassettes and videotapes can be secured from the children's section of your public library.

Sing a Patriotic Song Daily

Children need to sing songs on a daily basis, and a good one to begin with each day is "My Country 'Tis of Thee." They begin to pick up the tune, the rhythm, and the words through repetition. Some countries have a custom of greeting visitors with a patriotic song or with a national song. Have children stand up tall, arms at sides, as they sing this one. Sing as a greeting when visitors come to the classroom:

"My Country 'Tis of Thee"

My country 'tis of thee
Sweet land of liberty
Of thee I sing.
Land where my father's died
Land of the Pilgrim's pride
From ev'ry mountain side
Let freedom ring.

"God Bless America"

God bless America
    Land that I love,
Stand beside her,
    And guide her,
Through the night
    With a light from above.
From the mountains
    To the prairies
To the oceans
    White with foam.
God bless America
    My home, sweet home.
God bless America
    My home, sweet home.

Music and Movement Activities

The Rhythm and Rhyme of Storytelling

Many stories, when read aloud or told by the teacher, invite children to join in by the very nature of the rhythm of the words. If the teacher catches and maintains the beat, this will be transmitted to the students. Make sure children are seated comfortably and they can hear. It is good to be able to maintain eye contact with the group when you tell or read a story. Some books to consider are *Tikki Tikki Tembo* by Arlene Mosel, *Millions of Cats* by Wanda Gag, *Ask Mr. Bear* by Marjorie Flack, *Old MacDonald Had a Farm* by Robert Quackenbush, and the tried-and-true series of "noisy" books that include *The City Noisy Book, The Quiet Noisy Book, The Seashore Noisy Book*, and *The Winter Noisy Book* by Margaret Wise Brown.

Jungle Make Believe

Get in large circle formation. Decide, with the children, which way they shall move (clockwise or counter clockwise). Children can do the accompanying movements to this rhyme. (Sing it to the tune of "The Wheels on the Bus.") *Variation:* Half of the children can sing, and half can do the movements; then change positions.

The trees grow tall in the hot, hot, jungle
Hot, hot, jungle
Hot, hot, jungle
The trees grow tall in the hot, hot jungle
Come take a trip with me.

   (*Stand on tip toes, reach arms up high, stretch and sway.*)
The leopard crawls through the tall, tall, grass
Tall, tall, grass
Tall, tall, grass
The leopard crawls through the tall, tall grass
In the jungle far away.

   (*Crawl on hands and feet, knees stiff.*)
The pretty bird flits in and out
In and out
In and out
The pretty bird flits in and out
In the jungle far away.

   (*Standing position: raise and lower arms, take small steps.*)
The crocodile jaw goes snap, snap, snap
Snap, snap, snap
Snap, snap, snap
The crocodile jaw goes snap, snap, snap
In a jungle far away.

   (*Stand in position, put both hands up to cheeks with fingers pointing out, and open and close fingers in time to music.*)
The big green snake goes hiss, hiss, hiss
Hiss, hiss, hiss
Hiss, hiss, hiss
The big green snake goes hiss, hiss, hiss
In a jungle far away.

   (*Slither on stomach and hiss in time to music.*)

The monkeys swing from branch to branch
Swing, swing, swing
Swing, swing, swing
The monkeys swing from branch to branch
In a jungle far away.

    (*Large arm movements, first left then right, while moving around circle.*)

The lion's prowling for a treat
Ha! Ha! Ha!
Ha! Ha! Ha!
The lion's prowling for a treat
In a jungle far away.

    (*Stalk on all fours, call out "Ha! Ha! Ha!" in time to music.*)

The animals all run to hide
Sh! Sh! Sh!
Sh! Sh! Sh!
The animals all run to hide
In a jungle far away.
SH! SH! SH-H-H-H!

    (*Curl up into a ball, whisper "Sh! Sh! Sh!" in time to music. Then rest.*)

Circle Time Opposites (moving cars)

Make clear to the children which way they should move (clockwise, counter clockwise). Stand on the circle. Stretch out arms so that no one is touching; this should provide each child with enough space. Children can move their body when the car directions are given. Teacher demonstrates the motions throughout. As children become more familiar with "Moving Cars" during the year, background music can be playing, as if on a car radio.

Children follow the directions as they are called out by the teacher:

Open your car door.	(*standing position, twist the wrist*)
Get inside.	(*lift up right knee, then left knee*)
Close the door.	(*move left arm out and in*)
Put on your seat belt.	(*twist upper body right/left*)
Start the ignition.	(*twist wrist*)
Put the car in gear.	(*make fist with right hand, move toward body*)
Check the rear-view mirror.	(*move head around, left/right*)

You're off.	(*children begin moving slowly around circle by shuffling feet*)
Steady on the wheel.	(*children make rotating hand motions*)
Yellow light—caution!	(*slow down the hand motions*)
Red light! Foot on brake!	(*lift right foot, press down, freeze*)
Yellow light—caution!	(*look left, look right*)
Green light!	(*lift right foot up/down, rotate hands slowly, move forward*)
Go a little faster.	(*increase speed around circle*)
Go under the bridge.	(*duck down*)
Go over the bridge.	(*stand tall*)
Make a right turn.	(*move wheel to right*)
Make a left turn.	(*move wheel to left*)
Drive down a narrow street.	(*squeeze body together*)
Drive down a wide street.	(*elbows up, move wheel*)
Move faster.	(*increase speed*)
Pass a car carefully.	(*move wheel left, then right*)
Keep moving.	(*teacher can gauge the number of times students move around circle*)
Look up ahead! Yellow light.	(*slow down*)
Red light. Stop!	(*move right leg up/down; freeze*)
Yellow light—caution!	(*look left, look right*)
Green light!	(*move right leg up/down, move slowly around circle*)
Speed up a little.	(*move faster*)
There's the school up ahead.	(*slow down*)
The yellow light is blinking.	(*slow down even more*)
Flick on the directional signal.	(*left hand moves up*)
Turn right.	(*arm movements to right*)
Turn left into a parking space.	(*arm movements to left*)
Stop!	(*move right leg up/down; freeze*)
Put the gear in "Park."	(*fist forward*)
Turn off the key.	(*twist wrist*)
Put the key in your pocket.	(*key in pocket*)
Unclick your seat belt.	(*twist upper body, left/right*)
Check your rear-view mirror.	(*twist head around*)

Open door.	(*twist and push left arm out*)
Get out.	(*lift left leg, then right leg*)
Lock the car.	(*push down door lock*)
Close the door.	(*wide swoop of hand*)
Congratulations! You made it!	(*children say: "I'm a safe driver!"*)

Note: Teacher serves as a model for the motions. After doing this several times, children will begin to ask to do it during movement time.

Doing "The Humpty-Dumpty"

Teacher reads slowly, while children do accompanying motions. Teacher demonstrates throughout until children learn what to do. Start out in standing position (can be done on circle, or anywhere in room).

Humpty Dumpty	(*stand tall, feet together*)
Sat on a wall	(*bend knees*)
Humpty Dumpty	(*stand tall*)
Had a great fall.	(*bend knees*)
All the king's horses	(*stand tall*)
All the king's men	(*bend knees*)
Couldn't put Humpty	(*stand tall*)
Together again.	(*bend knees, then slowly crumple to the floor and freeze*)

While children are very still (resting after deep knee bends), the teacher picks up the toy telephone and announces that he or she is going to call Dr. Humpty Dumpty Doctor to put Humpty Dumpty all together again. Teacher speaks into toy telephone, as follows:

"Hello, I'd like to speak with Dr. Humpty Dumpty Doctor." (*pause*) "Yes, I'll wait." (*pause*) "Hello, Dr. Humpty Dumpty Doctor. This is _____ calling from _____ School. Humpty Dumpty fell off the wall. What should we do?" (*pause, nod, say, "Ok . . . uh-humm." then . . .*) "OK, thank you. We'll follow your directions." (*set aside toy phone*).

Turn to children, and tell them that these are the directions you were given. Everybody ready? Here we go.

Wiggle your right thumb.	(*wiggle right thumb*)
Wiggle your left thumb.	(*wiggle left thumb*)
Wiggle your toes.	(*wiggle toes*)
Blink your eyes.	(*blink eyes*)
Twist your right wrist.	(*twist right wrist*)
Twist your left wrist.	(*twist left wrist*)
Open shut, open shut hands.	(*open and shut hands*)
Touch hands to knees.	(*touch hands to knees*)
Now slowly sit up.	(*slowly sit up*)
Cross your legs.	(*cross your legs*)
Hands in lap.	(*hands in lap*)
Smile.	(*smile*)

Teacher picks up telephone again and says, "Oh, thank you, Dr. Humpty Dumpty Doctor. We've put Humpty Dumpty back together again! Yes, I'll be sure to tell the boys and girls that they should exercise every day. What's that? Have them stand up very very slowly and stretch? We'll do that. Good-bye." (*Hang up telephone, stretch, and go on to next activity.*)

Jack and Jill Jump-Ups

Read: Jack and Jill went up the hill
To fetch a pail of water
Jack fell down and broke his crown
And Jill came tumbling after!

Teacher reads each direction and demonstrates motions until children become familiar with this exercise and chant, as they do it repeatedly through the months. It will be a favorite they'll ask for.

Jack and Jill, reach up high.	(*reach high*)
Jack and Jill, touch the sky.	(*stretch higher*)
Jack and Jill, hands on hips.	(*hands on hips*)
Jack and Jill, move your lips.	(*exercise mouth muscles*)
Ready, Jack?	(*Boys say, "yes."*)
Ready, Jill?	(*Girls say, "yes."*)
Here we go up over the hill:	

Jump 10 times on both feet.

Jump 5 times on right foot.

Jump 5 times on left foot.

Jump and turn around in a circle.

Crouch down low and j-u-m-p up high!

Jump on left foot, holding right foot with left hand (3 times).

Jump on right foot, holding left foot with right hand (3 times).

Deep knee bend, grab your ankles, jump 5 times.

Ok, Jack?   (*Boys say, "ok."*)

Ok, Jill?   (*Girls say, "ok."*)

Good for you! You jumped over the hill.

Now sit down,

rest,

be quiet,

be still.

Clickety Clack, the Tongue Is Back

There once was a tongue named Clickety Clack. He lived inside a big red and white house. (*mouth*)

He liked to roam around inside the house. (*move tongue all around but keep lips together*)

He inspected the roof. (*move tongue along roof of mouth*)

He inspected the cellar floor. (*move tongue along bottom of mouth*)

He inspected the furniture upstairs. (*move tongue along upper teeth, slowly*)

He inspected the furniture downstairs. (*move tongue along lower teeth slowly*)

One day there was a knock on the door. Clickety clack peeked outside. (*open mouth and let just tip of tongue show*)

No one was there.

He came out just a bit more. (*slowly move tongue out*)

He looked up. (*move tongue up*)

He looked down. (*move tongue down*)

He looked all around. (*encircle lips with tongue*)

Then he saw who knocked on the door—the postman!

But the postman was leaving.

He would have to go after him.

Here he goes. (*make clicking sound with tongue*)

Faster. (*speed up*)

Faster. (*speed up*)

Slow down. (*slower speed*)

Go up to the postman and stop. (*tongue at rest*)

The postman gave him a package and he went back home. (*make clicking sound with tongue*)

There's his house. (*slow down*)

Open the door. (*open mouth wide*)

Go inside and shut the door. (*mouth shut*)

Lock it! (*tongue at rest*)

Well, Clickety Clack opened up the package, and guess what was inside? Something to clean his furniture! A toothbrush! Oh, what a lucky day for Clickety Clack.

Mary Had a Little Lamb

This is a childhood favorite and kindergarteners like to sing it regularly. Provide them with this opportunity to enjoy using their voice for pleasure.

Mary had a little lamb
Little lamb
Little lamb
Mary had a little lamb
Its fleece was white as snow.

It followed her to school one day
School one day
School one day
It followed her to school one day
Which was against the rules.

It made the children laugh and play
Laugh and play
Laugh and play
It made the children laugh and play
To see a lamb at school.

Mary took the lamb back home
Lamb back home
Lamb back home
Mary took the lamb back home
And no more it did roam.

Making Musical Instruments

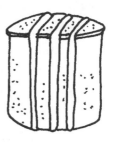

Students can help make a variety of instruments for the classroom to accompany songs. They can be decorated with paint, prepasted paper, feathers, and so on. Here are some suggestions:

- rhythm sticks—Use two wooden spoons.
- bell—Use a plastic flower pot with a hole in the bottom. Insert string, wrapped around a pebble, through the hole. This makes a clanging sound.
- drum—Use a metal coffee can with plastic lid and dowel rods.
- drum—Stretch a balloon over a metal can and secure it with a rubber band. Tap the balloon with the eraser on a pencil.
- sandpaper blocks—Wrap sandpaper around blocks of wood. Glue in place.
- rhythm instruments—Fill empty cardboard milk containers with a variety of seeds, grains, beans for different sounds.
- glass bottles on table—Fill with water to different heights for variety in pitch. Blow across top of each bottle or strike bottles with a pencil.

Making Music Instruments Naturally

The Native Americans made musical instruments from items found in nature—twigs, stones, reeds, dried grasses for lacing, seeds, gourds, and so on. Let's use our imagination and do the same thing. The book *Music Crafts for Kids*[*] (see page 397) by Noel and Phyllis Fiarotta invites children to go on a sound safari in nature, and to meet storybook musicians such as the Pied Piper and Pan.

The Marching Band

Play a tape with band music for this experience, and have students stand tall and high-step around the circle in time to the music. They can pretend to be holding and playing the instruments, such as the trumpet, flute, trombones, horns, clarinet, and so on. Those playing the same instrument should be together. The leaders are the drum major or drum majorette (diagonal arm motions across upper body).

This is good exercise and can be done more than once per day, especially on days when the students are restless and seem to need to give their muscles a work-out.

After children have mastered this, the drum major/majorette can alter the routine, leaving the circle and marching around the classroom, and then returning to the circle. The trick is to have everyone back on the circle when the band stops playing.

For patriotic holidays throughout the year, students can march out on the playground (chanting 1,2,3,4). They can make three-cornered hats from newspaper, and make red, white, and blue flags to carry. If music can be taken outside with a cassette recording, this will add to the festive celebration.

For a musical parade cassette treat that lets you hear 32 different instruments marching by one by one, be sure to get *Music Maestro Parade*[*].

Bounce 'Em, Throw 'Em, Catch 'Em

Balls are used the world over and children find no end of enjoyment with them. Some children are well coordinated already, while others need more time for development. Some simple activities with balls include:

- Bouncing the ball _____ times.
- Rolling a ball to another during Circle Time.
- Bouncing a ball with one hand.
- Bouncing a ball, alternating hands.
- Throwing the ball up and catching it.
- Kicking the ball (outdoors).
- Throwing underhand; throwing overhand.
- Practicing with a variety of sizes—cloth ball, small rubber ball, tennis ball, large beach ball, medicine ball.

---

[*]*Music in Motion, A Music Education and Gift Catalog for All Ages,* 783 North Grove Road, #108, Richardson, Texas 75081.

Play "Hit the Tree" (Native American)

This game is played outdoors with two or more players, a ball, and a sturdy tree. Tie a bright colored piece of yarn around the trunk about 2 feet up from the bottom, and tie another about 15 inches above that. Then, the ball thrower, who is standing 3 to 5 feet away from the tree, must hit the tree between the yarn. When this is accomplished, a point is scored. First player to get 10 points wins. All chime in: "You're the winner, hug the tree!"

Can You Catch a Bag of Sand? (island game)

Place some sand in a container (bag, baggie) and wind twine around it. Children can stand in a circle and throw the bag of sand to each other. The one who "catches" the bag when it bursts open must run to the nearest tree, touch it, and hang on, before being tagged by a member of the circle.

All chime in: "You're the winner,
we'll count to ten
Don't let go
'Til we say when!"

Creative Movement—Kung Fu (Asia)

The Chinese martial arts are a form of self-discipline and rigorous body training that make for a physically and spiritually healthy person. The martial arts traveled from China to Okinawa to Japan and then to Korea. Many children receive training in school because it helps build stamina, balance, and coordination. Try some of these:

The Stance. This is the body position just prior to the time when an athlete is going to begin her or his sport. For example, the diver assumes a *stance* prior to getting ready to dive into the swimming pool, the football players assume a *stance* prior to a play, and so on. A *stance* may be assumed by the ballet dancer just about to begin, or even the tightrope walker. Have children practice the stance—steady, no motion, for 20 seconds, and then relax. Begin to build up stamina to assume the stance for a longer period of time.

The Horse Stance. Have the students stand erect, arms at sides, feet apart, and bend their knees. This is one of the first sets of exercises to master. Students can try it for one minute (or half a minute depending upon the group).

For some children who are physically challenged, it may be necessary to have them try this individually before they are able to join the group.

Mawira Maitu Ni Ogwo
(This is the way our work is done) (Africa)

This is similar to the traditional chant, "This is the way we wash our clothes, wash our clothes, wash our clothes. This is the way we wash our clothes, so early in the morning." Children sing and use accompanying motions.

In this version players sing, "This is the way we chop our wood, here in the land of Kikuyu," and make appropriate motions. Other lines to act out include, "This is the way we grind our corn," "This is the way we carry our water," "This is the way we oil our bodies."

Pahlito Verde (Latin America)

This is a south-of-the-border version of "Drop the Handkerchief." Everyone gets into a circle and the one who is "IT" stands outside the circle behind the players, and holds a little green tree branch. As the one who is IT circles around the outside of the ring, the players chant:

"Pahlito Verde" (pah-LEE-toe VER-deh) and IT answers "Romero" (Ro-MER-oh), which means the herb, Rosemary. Again the players chant and IT answers; this continues until IT has made a complete circle. Then the chanting stops. IT drops the branch behind a player who must pick it up and chase after IT. If IT can successfully return to the spot vacated by the chaser before being touched, the person with the little branch is the new IT. The cycle of chant-and-chase begins again.

Mother, May I? (traditional North American)

This game activity is similar to Simon Says, where the person giving the command also has to give permission to carry it out. Students have to listen very carefully and ask, "Mother may I?" The response must be, "Yes, you may." *If* the response is only "Yes," then the persons may not carry out the task. (If they do, they sit down, and the last one standing wins the game.)

Jumping Rope

This is best done on the playground, unless you have a physical education room available with lots of space. Children can jump using a length of clothesline rope. (Some may benefit from practicing the jumping without the rope, at first.) Have children jump in a variety of ways, such as:

* forward with feet together

- forward on one foot, then the other
- forward by alternating the feet
- backward with feet together
- backward on one foot, then the other
- backward by alternating the feet

The Jumping Clock

Two players hold the jump rope at the end and keep it swinging. One player jumps once when "one" is sung out, one player jumps twice when "two" is sung out, and so on, up until the clock chorus sings out "twelve." Then, begin again.

Did You Ever See a Lassie?

This song can be continued for quite some time, with children taking turns as leader. The movements vary with the words "go this way and that way" every time a new person leads the tune. Here are the words to this familiar rhythm:

Did you ever see a lassie, a lassie, a lassie,
Did you ever see a lassie go this way and that (*demonstrate*)
Go this way, and that way, go this way, and that way (*all join in*)
Did you ever see a lassie, well how do you do (*bow*).

Some accompanying motions include:

- hand and arm motions (windshield wipers)
- crossing one foot in front of the other, then alternate
- hands on hips, swinging left, then right
- jump from one foot to the other
- circular hand motions, forwards, then backwards
- arms up, arms down
- "shovel" dirt, throw it over shoulder

On the Beam

Using the balance beam is excellent for gaining coordination skills and visual-motor integration. Here are some suggested activities:

- walk sideways, arms out at sides, weight on ball of feet
- walk forward, first one foot and then the other
- walk forward, with the right foot always in front
- walk forward, with the left foot always in front
- walk forward/backward with hands high overhead
- walk forward/backward with arms clasped behind back
- walk sideways, crossing one foot over the other
- walk halfway, pick something up (ruler) and then continue
- put a brick under one end of the beam and do the activities walking up and down

Walking a Pattern

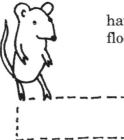

Scatter several rug squares in one area of the room, and have students walk the pattern. Also, put masking tape on the floor and have them "walk a shape":

- walk on a square
- walk on a rectangle
- walk on a circle
- walk on a triangle
- walk on a hexagon

Alexander's Band Music

The leader of the marching band can wear a special hat. Everyone is at attention in the circle with instruments poised, until the first note, then ready, go—march around the circle and play the instruments in time with the beat. "Stars and Stripes Forever" is a good tune for this activity. (*Marching Band Rule:* When the music stops, so do the instruments.)

Composer's Corner

Secure an old violin, a music stand, sheet music, cassette recorder and headphones, classical cassette recordings, and a straight-backed chair (*sources:* garage sale, flea market, parent donation). In the Composer's Corner, one child at a time can tune in to a symphony and "play the violin" along with the string quartet, string ensemble, or as a general accompaniment. Some children are attracted to this area repeatedly.

Occasionally, for the master musicians, change the instrument. Musical percussion instruments can be made from items in the environment. Decorate your instruments with paint, feathers, and beads as people have been doing for centuries. Remember, music is considered to be smooth and regular. "Noise" is made up of a jumble of different vibrations with no regular pattern.

Play a musical recording and have students accompany the recording. This is a good way to get started with a rhythm band in the classroom.

Play Background Music

While students are busy during playtime or worktime, play soothing background music. Tell them that you are going to do this, and ask them to keep their voices low enough so the music may be heard and enjoyed. The same recording each day during rest time becomes a soothing sound cue for children.

An excellent musical rhyming and counting book to read aloud is *Zin! Zin! Zin! a Violin* by Lloyd Moss, with illustrations by Marjorie Priceman.

Here We Go 'Round the Alphabet Bush

During Circle Time give each student an object that begins with a letter of the alphabet (have the letter pinned or taped to the object). You will also need a tub in the middle of the circle. To the tune of "Here We Go 'Round the Mulberry Bush," substitute the word *alphabet* for *mulberry*. Then call out a letter, and have the student with that letter place the object inside the tub by saying the letter and object name ("t—towel," "b—brush," etc.). Students enjoy the singing and the active involvement, and improve their letter–sound relationship skills through repetition of the song throughout the early months of the year.

Where Is Mary?

Incorporate singing with taking attendance. Teacher and students sing to the tune of "Frere Jacques." (Some children are shy at first with this, so you may want to appoint a partner; or have a child choose a partner to sing along with him or her.)

Teacher:	Where is Willie? Where is Willie?
Willie:	Here I am. Here I am.
All:	How are you today, sir?
Willie:	Very well, I thank you.
All:	We are glad. We are glad.

Music Patterns

Have children clap their hands in time to music that you provide. The speed and pattern can be varied. Also the sound may be soft or loud. Alternate clapping of hands with tapping of toes or clicking of the heels.

Here are some possible patterns. Do each one three times:

Clap, clap, tap	(A,A,B)
Clap, tap, tap	(A,B,B)
Clap, clap, click, click.	(A,A,C,C,)
Clap, click, clap, click	(A,C,A,C)

If You're Happy and You Know It

This is a familiar song, and there are many variations for the rounds:

If you're happy and you know it, clap your hands	*(clap, clap)*
If you're happy and you know it, clap your hands	*(clap, clap)*
If you're happy and you know it and you really want to show it	
If you're happy and you know it, clap your hands	*(clap, clap)*

Other verses:

- wiggle your toes
- blink one eye
- tap your toes
- click your heels
- turn your head (left)
- turn your head (right)
- beep your horn (tweak nose and say "honk, honk")
- reach up high

- bend your knees
- turn around
- click your tongue

(See reproducible activity pages for song so children can practice at home.)

The Bells Are Ringing

Wrist Bells. String two or three little bells onto a loopy piece of yarn, and tie it around the wrist for rhythmic movement along with the bell sound.

Bell Mittens. Sew two or three little bells on the fingertip ends of garden mittens. Wear one mitten and clap both hands together.

More Instruments to Make

Sandpaper Blocks. Glue sandpaper onto wooden blocks. Children can rub them together in time to the music.

Maracas. You will need two paper cups and some rice. Pour two tablespoons of rice into one cup, turn the other cup upside down on top of the first one, and tape them together. (Use heavy-duty packing tape.)

If you use white styrofoam cups, have students decorate their own cups prior to filling them. Other fillers include: beans, sand, lentils, peas, paper clips, and other items in varying amounts for different sounds.

Tambourines. You will need a flat stick, hammer, nails, and bottle caps. Hammer several bottle caps onto the stick with flat side up. Play the instrument by tapping the unnailed side against the palm, or by shaking the stick.

Musical Chairs

This game is played the world over, and is still played today in many Eastern European schools. Line chairs up back to back in a row for as many players as you have, minus one. Put on a record or play an instrument. As soon as the music stops, everyone must find a chair. The one left standing is out and joins an outside circle while clapping in time to the rhythm. Start the music again, remove another chair; when music stops, everyone scrambles for a chair. Last one left standing is the winner!

Special Olympics

Children with various handicaps are helped to play sports throughout the school year. Many individuals or teams are sponsored by businesses within the community and a national olympics is held on a regular basis. Learn more about opportunities for physically challenged children who are in your classroom. Inform parents of opportunities that are provided in the school district and in the community.

Down by the Station with "Puffing Billy"

In England, "Puffing Billy" or "Puffer Belly" is another name for the steam locomotive. Children can sing this song while standing in a row (facing the same direction) and then go shuffling around the circle (track) in time to the tune as they sing it once again.

Down by the station
  early in the morning
See the little puffer bellies
  all in a row.
See the engine driver
  pull the little throttle
Puff, Puff! Toot! Toot! *(make fist, raise arm up/down twice)*
  Off we go! *(shuffle along the track, turn around go back)*

A Woman's Work Song—Colonial Times

Sing this to the tune of "Here We Go 'Round the Mulberry Bush." It's a good sing-and-stretch song, and reflects by-gone days, before we had electricity to help with the household chores.

This is the way we wash our clothes, wash our clothes, wash our clothes
This is the way we wash our clothes, so early Monday morning.
  (scrub board motions)
This is the way we iron our clothes iron our clothes, iron our clothes
This is the way we iron our clothes, so early Tuesday morning.
  (ironing motions)
This is the way we scrub the floor, scrub the floor, scrub the floor

This is the way we scrub the floor, so early Wednesday morning.
(*on hands and knees, scrubbing motion*)
This is the way we mend our clothes, mend our clothes, mend our clothes
This is the way we mend our clothes, so early Thursday morning.
(*hand sewing motions*)
This is the way we sweep the house, etc. (*broom sweeping motions*)
This is the way we bake our bread, etc. (*kneading motion*)
This is the way we go to church, etc. (*hands folded*)

A Man's Work Song—Colonial Times

Men did not always have it easy, either. As an agricultural society, it took brains as well as brawn (strength) to keep a farm going. Here are some verses for the male:

This is the way we milk the cows, etc. (*pulling motions*)
This is the way we hoe the dirt (*bend forward and pull back*)
This is the way we plant the seed (*throwing motions*)
This is the way we weed the crops (*bend and pull*)
This is the way we build the barn (*pounding motions*)
This is the way we pull the reins (*pulling motions while jiggling in a wagon*)
This is the way we pump the water (*pumping motions*)

Music and Movement Survival Tips

Some Old, Some New

In music, often the children take cues from each other rather than from the teacher, so this can be a difficult type of experience to manage, especially with a variety of instruments. So go slowly.

1. **Introducing a Song.** Make sure you have everyone's attention. Tell the children you are going to sing a new song for them (a short one). Sing it through once. Then tell them you will teach it to them one line at a time.

   T: sing the first line alone

   C: join in

   T: repeat the first line again

   C: join in

   T: go to next line and sing it alone

   C: join in

   T: go to next line and sing it alone

   C: join in

   All: sing together what has been learned so far

   Follow this procedure for the entire song, or for just the first four lines, depending upon the complexity of the song and how well the group is catching on.

   Teach the song again the next day. By the end of the week, the children should be able to sing along with you. The teacher's voice must be strong and carry the tune, rhythm, timing. The children will imitate the leader.

2. **Sing Every Day.** Children enjoy music and you will want to build a time for singing and movement to music into your program. Have children hold hands and form a circle (all facing in). Then have them take a step back so that they have room to move around the circle. This is good exercise, and makes the children feel good.

   If teacher can play a musical instrument, this is an advantage (guitar, electric keyboard, etc.) because the teacher can then direct and control the singing more easily than with a recording.

   Check with the music supervisor for tapes, CDs, and other materials available within the district.

3. **Scheduled Music Classes.** Sit in on the music classes with the children and learn their songs so that you can use them in your own classroom with them. Also ask advice from the music teacher on songs and activities appropriate for kindergarteners.

4. **Play Background Music.** During rest time or quiet time, put on a soothing recording as background music. It makes for a relaxed atmosphere. When children repeatedly hear this music, they know what it means and what they have to do.

5. **Musical Instruments.** Children enjoy making them and using them. When working with instruments, do the following:

- tell the name of the instrument (have students say it)
- demonstrate how to play the instrument (give do's and don'ts)
- introduce children to the concept of the orchestra "conductor"
  —all eyes on the conductor
  —follow the baton of the conductor
  —musical instruments are not played when conductor's baton is pointing downward

Encourage the children to become good members of the orchestra team by following the rules; they will enjoy the experience. (It may be helpful to record a TV performance featuring a symphony orchestra, *for the purpose of observing the conductor.*)

6. **Music Appreciation.** Listening to regional music of the United States, as well as ethnic music, will expand the child's listening experiences. Many audiocassettes are available at the library. This is a good time to (first) listen to the music and (second) move to the music.

7. **For Restless Days.** Music is helpful for getting the wiggles out, so have children get into the Circle, take a step backwards for plenty of room, and then move clockwise around the circle to music for the elephant (*down on all fours, swaying imaginary trunk back and forth*), rabbit (*hopping*), bluejay (*arms up and gracefully flapping*), monkey (*fast footwork, toe tapping*), deer (*fluid body movement*), turtle (*bend knees, put hands around ankles, shuffle feet*), tiger (*hands on hips, swagger motion from side to side*), and so on. Follow this with a quiet activity.

8. **Just Moving Fingers and Hands**
   - Have children spread out their hands in front of them. Move the thumbs on both hands, then the forefinger, and so on until all fingers have been moved. Do this in time to music (1,2,3,4,5—5,4,3,2,1).
   - Form fists, then spread hands way out (repeat). Do this in time to music.
   - Form fists and alternate a hammer motion with one on top of the other (hammer once, twice, three times before alternating).
   - Make a music ladder. Place one hand on top of the other and then gently, and in time to the music, keep doing this until hands and arms are held high, then climb back down the ladder.

9. **Just Moving Feet**
   - March in place.
   - Pick up right leg 3 times; left leg 3 times in time to music. (Alternate the numbers.)
   - Make a circle with the right foot; a circle with the left foot.
   - Make a square with the right foot; a square with the left foot.

- Make a circle with the right foot; a square with the left foot.
- Right foot/left foot. Move feet to the side and back, side and back.
- Skip to the music (around the circle).
- Sit on circle, legs in front, and make circular ankle motions in time to the music (left foot, right foot).

10. **Simulating Motions to Music**
    - picking up a heavy load
    - riding a horse (gallop, trot)
    - floating like a feather
    - climbing a long ladder
    - swimming (arm motions)
    - riding a bicycle
    - kicking a ball
    - moving like a swivel chair (waist, shoulders)
    - head straight, head back, looking up, up, up at the sky; head straight, head down, looking down, down at the ground; head straight, pretend to be a cat looking over left shoulder and then right shoulder, and again
    - bending to touch toes (knees straight)

11. Children need to stretch, bend, and move their muscles throughout the day, so be sure to build movement and free play (preferably outdoors) into your program. It makes everyone feel better.

MUSIC and MOVEMENT ACTIVITY PAGES

Masks (*creative movement; music; drama*)

    Giraffe Mask

    Lion Mask

    Fox Mask

    Rooster Mask (*side view*)

Puppet Talk (*ways to make puppets*)

Goldilocks and the Three Bears (*finger puppets*)

Catch Me if You Can (*rhyme; game; decoration*)

Uncle Sam Says, "Move It!" (*playing with a ball*)

Shape Up with Yancy Yak (*exercise*)

Just Too Noisy for Bats! (*city sounds*)

Fairy Tale Puppet Set

(These can be used for a variety of characters, depending upon the decorations and colors used. They can be used as stick puppets, paper bag puppets, or in other effective ways.)

    Fairy Tale Princess Puppet (*little girl*)

    Fairy Tale Prince Puppet (*little boy*)

    Fairy Tale Queen Puppet (*adult woman character*)

    Fairy Tale King Puppet (*adult man character*)

    Fairy Tale Frog Puppet (*trickster or helper*)

    Fairy Tale Beast Puppet (*trickster, helper, or beauty and beast*)

    Fairy Tale Godmother or Helper Puppet

Yankee Doodle (*song*)

America, the Beautiful (*song*)

If You're Happy and You Know It (*song*)

Giraffe Mask

Lion Mask

Fox Mask

Rooster Mask (side view)

Puppet Talk

There are many ways to make puppets. How many can we make and use in our creative movement, stories, and music?

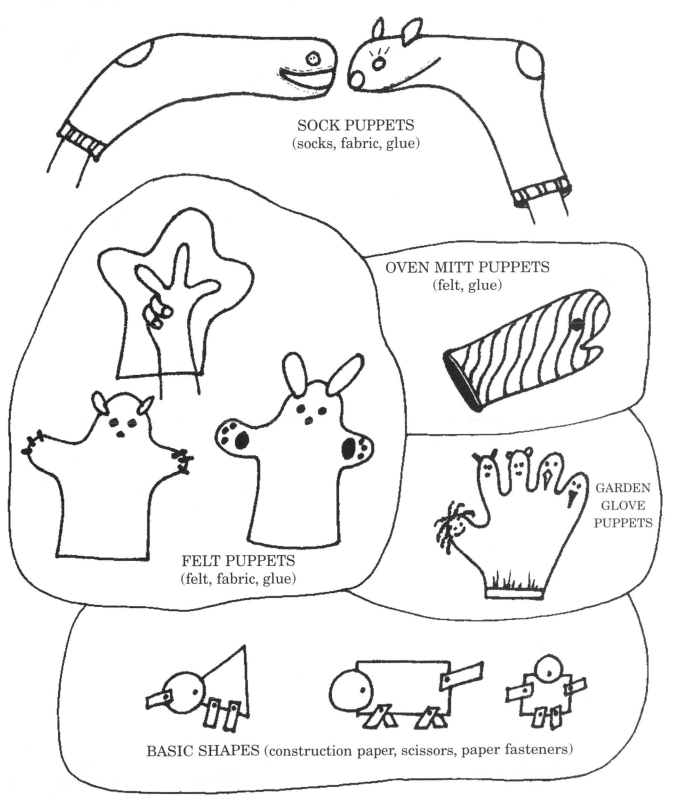

SOCK PUPPETS
(socks, fabric, glue)

OVEN MITT PUPPETS
(felt, glue)

FELT PUPPETS
(felt, fabric, glue)

GARDEN
GLOVE
PUPPETS

BASIC SHAPES (construction paper, scissors, paper fasteners)

Goldilocks and the Three Bears

Color, cut along dotted lines, and act out this story favorite.

Catch Me if You Can

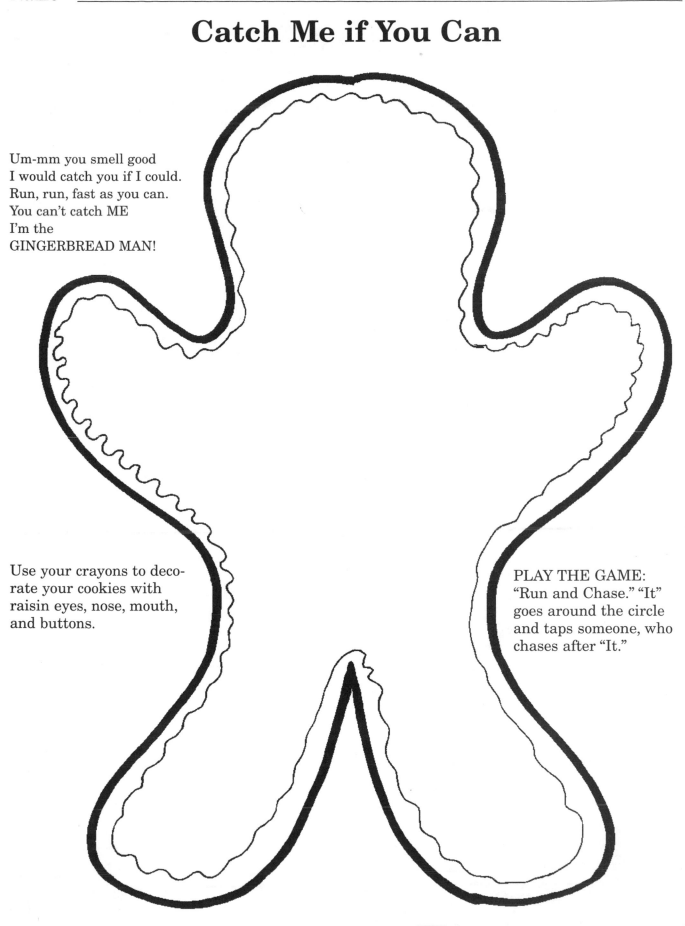

Um-mm you smell good
I would catch you if I could.
Run, run, fast as you can.
You can't catch ME
I'm the
GINGERBREAD MAN!

Use your crayons to deco-
rate your cookies with
raisin eyes, nose, mouth,
and buttons.

PLAY THE GAME:
"Run and Chase." "It"
goes around the circle
and taps someone, who
chases after "It."

Uncle Sam Says, "Move It!"

Bounce a ball ten times
(two hands).

Bounce a ball ten times
(one hand).

Play catch with a friend.

Roll a ball back and forth with a friend.

Run with a ball.

Dribble the ball.

Throw a ball into a wastebasket (outdoors).

Throw a ball in the air and catch it.

RUN   JUMP   ROLL   KEEP FIT!

Shape Up with Yancy Yak

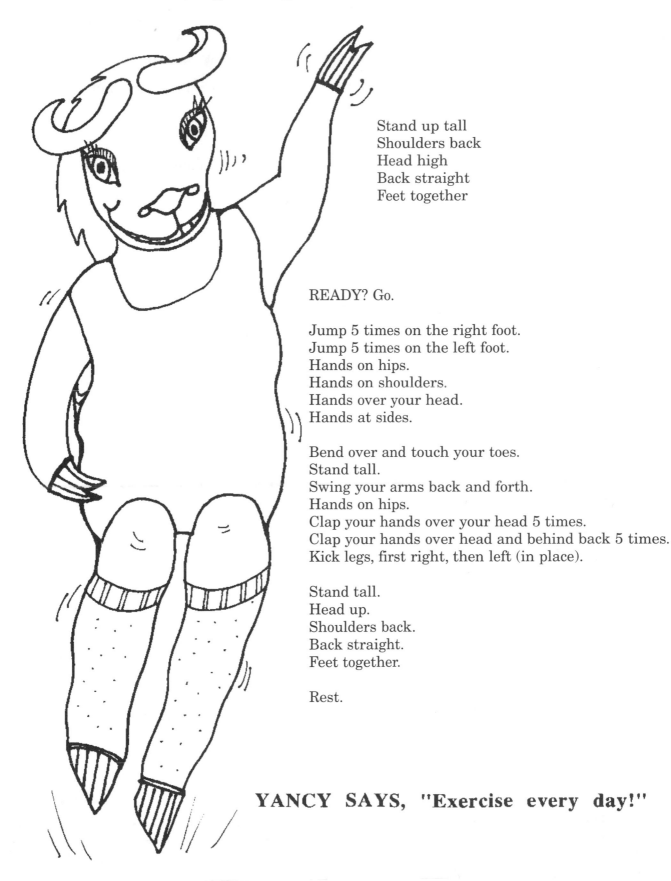

Stand up tall
Shoulders back
Head high
Back straight
Feet together

READY? Go.

Jump 5 times on the right foot.
Jump 5 times on the left foot.
Hands on hips.
Hands on shoulders.
Hands over your head.
Hands at sides.

Bend over and touch your toes.
Stand tall.
Swing your arms back and forth.
Hands on hips.
Clap your hands over your head 5 times.
Clap your hands over head and behind back 5 times.
Kick legs, first right, then left (in place).

Stand tall.
Head up.
Shoulders back.
Back straight.
Feet together.

Rest.

YANCY SAYS, "Exercise every day!"

Just Too Noisy for Bats!

Bats are nocturnal. That means, they sleep during the day and are awake all night long. But some days, it's difficult for a bat to get its much-needed rest, especially a "city bat."

(Call upon one child at a time to create the sound. Later, when children are familiar with the message, the class can be divided into different sound groups, all making sounds at the same time.)

Be sure that children understand the "Quiet Signal" at the end of the story.

NO SLEEP FOR B.J. BAT

B.J. Bat forgot to listen for his mother's signal, and he was left in the city while the rest of the family was sound asleep in a country barn.

"Well," said B.J. "I'll curl up on this window ledge and fall asleep." But all day long he heard the following:

"HONK, HONK, HONK," beeped the taxi cabs.

"A-R-EEEEEEEE," screamed the fire siren.

"PSSSSHHHHH," hissed the bus doors.

"R-R-R-ING," jingled the telephones.

"HA-HA-HA," laughed the people going by.

"SWISH, SWISH," sang the revolving doors.

"WOOF, WOOF," barked the playful dogs.

"CH-CH-CH-CH," sang the subway cars.

"TIP-TIP-TIPPETY-TAP," called out the computers.

B.J. got no sleep that day! When Mrs. Bat returned that night, he listened for her signal, and was glad to get back to the barn where he slept soundly all day long. "Z-z-z-z-z-z-z-z-."

Fairy Tale Princess Puppet

Fairy Tale Prince Puppet

Fairy Tale Queen Puppet

Fairy Tale King Puppet

Fairy Tale Frog Puppet

Fairy Tale Beast Puppet

Fairy Tale Godmother or Helper Puppet

Yankee Doodle

Yankee Doodle went to London
Riding on a pony,
Stuck a feather in his hat
And called it macaroni.

Yankee Doodle keep it up
Yankee Doodle dandy,
Mind your manners, be polite
And it will come in handy.

Show Yankee Doodle
on his horse

America the Beautiful

Oh beautiful, for spacious skies

For amber waves of grain.

For purple mountain magesties

Above the fruited plain.

America, America

God shed his grace on thee.

And crown thy good

With brotherhood

From sea to shining sea.

Memorize this song. Sing it with pride when
visitors come to your classroom.

If You're Happy and You Know It

If you're happy and you know it
    clap your hands (clap clap)
If you're happy and you know it
    clap your hands (clap clap)
If you're happy and you know it
And you really want to show it
If you're happy and you know it
    clap your hands (clap clap)

If you're happy and you know it
    tap your feet (tap tap)
If your happy and you know it
    tap your feet (tap tap)
If your happy and you know it
And you really want to show it
If you're happy and you know it
    tap your feet (tap tap)

If you're happy and you know it
    jump in place (jump up)
If you're happy and you know it
    jump in place (jump up)
If you're happy and you know it
And you really want to show it
If you're happy and you know it
    jump in place (jump up)

MORE VERSES TO PRACTICE:
tap your heels, twist your wrist, click your tongue, bend your knees, raise your arms, touch your head, snap your fingers, turn around, and you can think up more!

MORE INFORMATION
FOR THE TEACHER

Keeping the Kindergartener Happy
Keeping the Kindergartener Healthy and Safe
Home–School Connection
Transitions After Vacation
End-of-Year Assessment

Mr. Ratajczak

Keeping the
Kindergartener Happy

The Complexity of Kindergarten

Today a great many of our kindergarteners come to school after having been in a day-care environment since they were from three to six months old. They have been interacting with two's, three's, and four's as a group, and have their own set of rules and standards that stem from and reflect the quality of the environment in which they were growing and learning each day. Some kindergarteners have a "dress code" learned in preschool, and know just what kind of clothing and footwear are considered fashionable by their peers. This is no longer learned in the home by many children with working parents or a single parent.

Also, it is not unusual for kindergarten children to come directly to kindergarten from a preschool setting. Some children who attend *morning kindergarten* may be dropped off at a day-care center at 6 A.M. and are then picked up by a school bus later in the morning and brought to kindergarten. At the end of the morning, they are then picked up and returned to the day-care center for lunch and an afternoon program, and picked up by a parent or caregiver at 6 P.M. The children who attend *afternoon kindergarten* may also be dropped off at a day-care center at 6 A.M., where they spend the morning and have lunch. Then a school bus picks them up for afternoon kindergarten, and returns to pick them up and take them back to the day-care center until parents pick them up at 6 P.M. This makes for a long day away from home and a primary caregiver, and so children are being shaped and formed by each other in addition to the day-care givers and the setting in which they are placed.

Settle Down

The children often come to the school setting in an excited state from being with so many different children, from getting on and off a bus, from taking outer clothing on and off again. Others may come directly from a hurried wake-up-and-get-ready time at home. So, the kindergarten room needs to be quiet and unhurried, with a calm teacher. Sometimes having subdued lighting in the classroom (lamps) as children arrive has a settling effect.

When children arrive, only allow them to take a book and sit quietly . . . no building blocks, no housekeeping corner at the beginning.

Self-Esteem

Essentially, self-esteem is built by learning about things and gaining mastery over one's environment. Children feel proud when they can take care of themselves—mastery over buttons, snaps, ties, and zippers is a big hurdle. They also gain self-esteem from a job well done.

Self-Esteem Boosters

Carrying out expectations and being praised for it boosts self worth. For example:

- "You came down the hall much better than yesterday."
- "When we came in from recess, you remembered to . . ."
- "I was so proud of the way you listened to our guest speaker. This is the best kindergarten in the world!"

Reward Good Citizenship

When a child is polite and lets another child in front of him or her in line, recognize it. When a child picks something up off the floor and puts it where it belongs, recognize it. When a child is ready and waiting, recognize it.

- Give a "Good Citizen Badge" to wear.
- Put a sticker on the child's hand.
- Take a photograph of "Good Citizens" and make a display.
- Mention "Good Citizens" in your newsletter to parents.

Ultimately the reward is internal and the child cannot be made to be dependent upon material rewards forever. Some non-material awards to implement are:

- Appoint a child as the teacher-assistant for a task.
- Reward the child by having him or her select a favorite story or poem to be read aloud.

- Choose a child as the office messenger, and tell why you made that choice. ("Because Ramli started to clean up when the bell rang, he is our messenger today.")
- Put the child in charge of . . .

Keep 'Em Happy

Kindergarteners are kept happy by an environment that is stimulating and satisfies their natural curiosity and desire to learn. It's not chance—it's planning, anticipation, and preparation on the part of the teacher.

Accidents Happen

If a child accidentally knocks over a can of paint and it spills all over the floor, do not shame the child. It could happen to anyone. The teacher needs to let this attitude come through in his or her actions and words.

If two children are fooling around and paint gets spilled, that's another category. Refer to your room rules and consequences.

It's OK to Make a Mistake When You're Trying

Praise can be given for the trying, and knowing that you can try again. Risk taking, when it relates to learning, is something to be fostered. (Risk taking on the jungle gym on the playground is another matter, and children have to be told the behavior that is expected of them.)

Individual Differences Make a Difference

Performance expectations for children are regulated by knowledge of:

- different developmental levels
- different parenting styles
- different socio-economic levels

When the teacher recognizes this, he or she has something to work with.

Children who are behaviorally delayed, and thus developmentally delayed, because of their background (busy parents, overworked parents, parents who lack parenting skills, parents who are advocates of permissive parenting) require care, *firm guidelines*, and constant monitoring so that they become a happy, contributing group member.

This takes time and patience, but it is one of the roles of the kindergarten teacher and one of the purposes of public education.

The Feel Good Movement

The "I Am Special" movement has come into question in the late 1990s. Failure to correct children, making children feel good at all costs, accepting less than the child is capable of (and praising it), does not build self-esteem in the final analysis.

Positive feedback should be related to accomplishment and development, and not given indiscriminately regardless of what the child does. If the child is in charge, growth is diminished.

The child is in kindergarten to change and grow, under the guiding hand of a caring, thoughtful, knowledgeable teacher.

At Day's End

Gather everyone together and review the day. Talk about the good things that occurred, and mention what we need to work on.

Be sure to leave the children on a happy note, and give them something to look forward to the next day. Leave them in a state of anticipation. This can be done by saying:

- See this wonderful book with the goat on the cover? Tomorrow we'll learn about the day he went to the zoo.
- Tomorrow is a special day. We are going to make . . .
- Oh! Be sure to be here tomorrow! Perkins the Puppet told me he will have a special announcement! Wonder what it is? What could it be? We'll see tomorrow.
- Lucky us! Tomorrow our new pencils arrive.
- Tomorrow is Wednesday, and we know what that means. It's gym day!
- Carmen's mom says she will bring in their brand-new baby tomorrow to visit us. His name is Julius. We are so lucky.

Walk Them to the Bus

This is the time to informally have a kind word for each child as they leave for the day. Tousel their hair, pat them on the back, rub their cheek softly, give a wink, and let them sense how much you care for them. This is "caught not taught," and needs to be genuine on the part of the teacher.

Listen to Them

Be a teacher who looks a child right in the eye and listens as the child is speaking. If you are busy and a child needs to speak to you, cover their hand gently with your hand so they sense the "connection" and know they will soon have your attention.

Listen during Circle Time and during Show and Tell. This is not the time to be catching up on work or preparing a lesson. If you want to teach good listening skills, be a good listener yourself.

Each Child Is a Person

Regardless of race, color, creed, behavioral, physical, or learning disabilities, each child deserves to be treated fairly and with kindness. School is the finest experience in the life of some young children. The kindergarten teacher has an awesome responsibility in this area, and needs to be emotionally mature and resilient. The children are "on loan" for one school year. Make a little sign for the classroom door as a reminder:

RECIPE: CHILDREN GROWING HERE

Need: 1 cup warmth
2 cups security
3 cups safety
4 tbsp. playfulness
5 tsp. of challenges
generous sprinkling of laughter

Mix carefully for 10 months.
Hug good-bye in June.

Keeping the Kindergartener Healthy and Safe

Working with Parents

Keep parents apprised of health conditions in the classroom and school (outbreak of measles, chicken pox, flu). This information can be included in a "Health Update" section of your newsletter.

The Newsletter

This is a good opportunity to include information about new books for parents—include title and author. You may want to include a line or two from an article you read—cite sources such as journal/magazine, title of article, date.

If you have a number of parents who are not native-born speakers, it may be worth the effort to have a bilingual section in your newsletter that is short, succinct, and that gives a phone number to call for more information. Use the services of a community member or a high school teacher who speaks the same foreign language as the parents you need to address.

Have a Daily Healthy Snack Time

Discuss with the children some of their options for a healthy snack—fruit, crackers, raisins (rather than a candy bar a day). Put information in your newsletter regarding healthy snacks, and use pictures for parents who are currently limited in their ability to read English.

Keeping the Kindergarteners Safe

Be sure to discuss rules and regulations for acceptable behavior in the following areas:

- playground
- hallway
- bathroom
- bus
- walking to school (street crossing)

Basic Hygiene

Have a discussion with children about staying well. Be sure to cover the following points:

- Keep fingers out of your mouth.
- Wash hands after using the bathroom.
- Wash hands before eating.
- We don't share food from someone's plate.
- We don't share used tissues from our pocket.
- When you feel a sneeze coming on, cover nose with your hand.
- Know where the tissue box is kept in the classroom.

How Can Parents Help?

Aside from making sure that children get plenty of sleep (10 hours at least) and eat a variety of foods from the basic food groups, parents can donate items for the classroom such as:

- boxes of tissue
- paper cups
- band-aids

- handi wipes
- small paper plates/napkins
- crackers for snack (for those who forget)

Medicine for Special Needs

If a child is taking prescription medication, find out the procedure to be followed in your school building for administering the medication. Usually this is done by the school nurse or the office personnel. This medication should *not* be kept in the classroom.

Check School Health Records to Determine Special Needs

This should be done before the first day of school. Some children get an allergic reaction if stung by a bee, for example, and you need to know what procedure to follow. Some children may be subject to epileptic seizures but are not on medication. Find out what to do if the child should have a seizure.

For those children who are on medication and need to take it during the school day, place a small cardboard clock at their workplace in an effort to remind them that "when the clock on the wall looks like this," that's the time for your medicine.

Become an Advocate for a Full-Time Nurse in the Building

In some states, a full-time nurse is on duty, and that makes everyone feel secure and ready to carry on the work of the school day. However, in some states, a visiting nurse may be on duty only two mornings per week. Bring up the issue at faculty meetings, with other teachers, with the principal, and with parents. Maybe this should be brought to the attention of the Board of Education. Perhaps the services of a retired nurse-volunteer could be sought. (It is interesting to note that in some underdeveloped countries, a nurse is on daily duty. Some schools also have a dentist in the building one day per week, as well as a dental hygienist.) This is something to address through your teacher's association. Why not strive to be *above minimum standards* rather than *at* minimum standards.

The Miracle Cure—Cold Water

When a child comes to you with a complaint, such as a bump on the arm, a finger that doesn't feel good, a knee that got scratched, an ankle that pinches, be sure to look the child right in the eye and listen attentively. It requires a split-second decision about whether this is major or minor. For the minor category, take the child to the sink, run the cold water on a folded piece of paper toweling, place it on the spot that hurts, and have the child hold it there until it feels better. Tell them you want to know when they're feeling okay again. Often, this bit of time out and attention makes the hurt go away.

Wear a First-Aid Fanny Pack on Field Trips

Keep these items in your pack: school I.D. card, latex or plastic gloves, tissue, moist tissue, Band-Aids, whistle, coins for the phone or a cellular phone, and a list of names for everyone on the trip.

Out-Patient Clinics

Be sure to include information in your newsletter about the services available at the local Out-Patient Health Clinics. Some clinics in the area may administer shots free of charge. Include adult health-screening information that will be helpful for parents from diverse ethnic groups who are newcomers, and also for the parents from a lower socio-economic level.

Home–School Connection

Send Home a Newsletter

On a regular basis (weekly or bi-monthly), send home a short newsletter to keep parents apprised of what's going on in your classroom, to ask for assistance, and to inform them of things that are going to be happening soon.

Keep it short because parents are busy. Also, remember that some parents will not be able to read it with ease, so use Rebus picture clues. Go over the newsletter information with your class so some students can help their parents. Consider a bilingual corner if the population warrants this.

Connect Parents with One Another

Ask parents during Open House at the beginning of the year to sign up if they would be willing to assist others (newcomers, immigrant parents, caregivers who are not parents) by being willing to contact them when newsletters and other information go home to make sure they understand what is being requested. (For example, requests for field trip forms might be confusing to some parents from a different ethnic background.)

Plan a Multicultural Food Experience for Parents

One of your kindergarten meetings could be a dinner where parents are invited to sign up for and bring their favorite ethnic dish. Children can be included for the event. This would be a wonderful time to get to know each other just a little bit better, and to exchange favorite recipes. Invite the principal and special teachers to this as well. (Room mothers will be extremely helpful here for telephoning and helping to set up the menu.) It will help parents feel as though they "belong" to the school community.

More Connections—ADD/ADHD/Special Needs Children

Have a meeting for parents of your children with special needs. Invite the school psychologist or a physician or nurse from the community to give a brief address. Other parents may be interested in attending and are certainly invited, especially if there is an older or younger sibling with special needs in the family.

Since some parents are quite sensitive about asking questions before the group, distribute small squares of notepaper and have them write one question on each sheet that they would like the speaker to address. Keep circulating through the group to collect the questions. Encourage parents to hold up their paper square during the speech so that it can be collected and put on the podium for the speaker.

Conferencing with Parents from Foreign Countries

Some parents will need to be made very comfortable during parent/teacher conferencing because the parents may come from countries where they only go to school if there is a problem. Some parents are not used to having to divulge personal information about the home, such as "What type of discipline do you use in your home?" Some parents may feel ashamed because of their verbal English skills. It is up to the teacher to put them at ease and to reassure them that they are both there for the purpose of helping the child.

Invite Parents into the Classroom to Share Ethnic Holidays

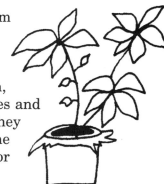

A parent may enjoy coming to class to share items from their culture (paintings, art work, clothing, etc.). Some may explain how a piece of clothing is worn, and demonstrate this before the class. Some may explain the customs during their holiday time, and share a song, a poem, or even food with the class. Some may show 35mm slides and take the students on a journey to a foreign country. They may teach the children a simple dance. This makes the youngsters feel good, especially the one whose parent or relative is doing the sharing.

The Room Mother Team

Instead of one parent, see if you can have several people sign up and then divide the tasks. Room mothers need to circulate sign-up sheets and make calls to parents to determine the following:

- who can assist at parties
- who can accompany the class on field trips
- who can aid with communication to parents
- who can help in the classroom

- who can help with transportation
- who can take photographs or make the videotape of special events

Do We Want to Form a Kindergarten Coffee Group That Meets Once a Month?

This has been done successfully in some schools in a variety of ways. It can be done as an after-school meeting, an evening meeting, a Saturday morning meeting, or as a meeting held in the multi-purpose room one morning a month (when a substitute teacher is provided and the teacher is released to present and officiate at the program). Topics can be planned and guest speakers can be invited, or it can be open forum.

Should we meet on the first Tuesday of each month?

Children's Books

Explain the importance of reading aloud. Reading aloud to the child daily can have a beneficial effect—not only does it create a bond between the parent and child, but there is a positive correlation with success in learning to read. Have a variety of picture books on hand that you borrowed from the local library so that busy parents can catch up with what they have missed. Encourage them to take their child to the library regularly and to apply for a library card if they have not already done so. (A supply of applications from the library would be helpful.)

Explain that the library has a wide variety of read-aloud books in *categories* that may be extremely helpful for them, such as:

- new baby in the family
- divorce
- death/illness
- love
- hospital visit

How Can I Help My Child at Home?

Many parents ask this during parent-teacher conference time and it is good to have something general to suggest, if you have no specific items to work on. Young children can be helped in many ways. Here are some general suggestions for starters:

- Set up a special area just for your child for reading, crayoning, writing.

- Subscribe to a newspaper and call interesting information to the attention of the child.
- Play card games with your children. This helps them to recall the numerals, the four suits (shape), and is good for strengthening memory, recall, and problem solving.
- Set up a cardtable with a jigsaw puzzle on it, and then work on it daily, a little at a time. This is something the entire family can do, and for young children it develops location skills and identification of shapes (which helps with reading).

- Take the child grocery shopping and let him or her be involved in finding specific items. (Take labels to match.)
- Let child help you put items away, and categorize them (all of the soups, the cereals, the cleaning supplies, etc.).
- Let the child sort the clean socks (good categorization skill).
- Teach the child the proper way to answer the phone and take messages.
- Take out a public library card and bring your child to the library regularly. (The library often has special events.)
- Talk with your child; spend some quiet time together.
- Enjoy learning about what your child is doing each day.
- Let the child know how you use math in daily life (putting gallons of gas in the car, writing out checks for the monthly bills, counting out money, programming the VCR, keeping track of time, checking the temperature, making out an order and adding up the items, and so on).
- Read a good book on parenting skills.
- Make sure the child has a warm family (or friends) link.
- Give the child responsibility and follow through to see that the job is done.

Transitions After Vacation

General Information

After the children have been away from the routine of daily kindergarten, you need to go back to square 1. The children will not have been together for quite some time, especially at Christmas holiday and spring break, and memories will need to be refreshed. The rules and expectations need to be reviewed (and perhaps some can be added or changed, especially for New Year's resolutions). Routines need to be re-established, and the children need to be made to feel secure in their environment once again.

- Begin the session quietly and on a low key, as many children will be subdued for the first session especially.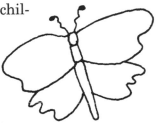
- Review your classroom rules.
- Do not introduce new work.
- Start way back at the beginning for some good review opportunities.
- Read familiar and well-loved stories, and add a new one.
- Play a familiar group game.
- Have an extended rest period, as the children are apt to be quite tired.
- Sing together and relearn some favorite finger plays or movement exercises to songs.

Refresh the Environment

This calls for fresh nametags, new labels for the classroom if old ones are faded or dog-eared, and fresh smocks at the easel.

New Pencils, New Crayons

Especially to begin the new year, these items will help to get the class off to a good start for learning.

New Items in the Environment

Reminders of holidays and seasons past should be removed before the students return. Perhaps you have a new theme for

your reading corner; that will need to be introduced. Perhaps the cut-out letters are already up on a new bulletin board that you will be working on this week. That new project can be explained to the students in an effort to give them something to look forward to.

Give Children an Opportunity to Draw and Talk About Their Picture

This can be a picture of something the children did during the vacation break if they would like to share it with the group. It helps them to reconnect with one another.

End-of-Year Assessment

Measuring Growth and Accomplishments

Some school districts will have testing procedures to follow to determine the level of growth the student has attained in academic areas, as well as their social development. Become familiar with them.

Office Records

Get on top of this early, at least a month before the end of school, so that you will know what it is you need to report in writing for the first-grade teacher, as well as required information that will help with making first-grade placements.

Keep a Calendar

Have a special monthly calendar just for due dates of items for the office, as well as special end-of-the-year events. You will need to be especially well organized, well planned, and rested.

Final Information Will Need to Be Gathered, Assessed, and Recorded

Here are some examples:

Reading/Writing/Speaking/Listening

- knows full name, address, age, and phone number
- recognizes beginning sounds
- recognizes capital letters
- recognizes lower-case letters
- recognizes some sight words and number words
- recognizes words/sounds that rhyme
- can write phonetically
- enjoys writing
- understands the purpose of writing

- can relate ideas in writing
- can pronounce letters and sounds
- can communicate with words (articulation)
- can make ideas understood when speaking
- waits for her or his turn to speak
- is able to listen attentively
- can gain information from listening
- can follow verbal directions
- enjoys listening to stories
- can make story predictions
- enjoys books and storytime

Mathematics

- recognizes numerals 0–10
- recognizes numerals 0–25
- likes to count and can rote count to _____
- knows basic shapes
- can recognize a visual and/or auditory pattern
- is comfortable with one-to-one correspondence
- can do simple addition
- can do simple subtraction
- can sort objects with like attributes
- can categorize objects into sets

Motor Skills

- can grasp and hold a pencil with appropriate grip
- can use scissors independently
- can trace around a pattern
- can make a pattern from a visual model
- can walk on a balance beam (or floor tape) with good balance
- can skip, march, hop, jump
- can button, zip, and tie clothing
- can form letters correctly
- can form numerals correctly

Social/Emotional Growth

- can engage in play with others
- can listen while another is speaking
- can share toys and equipment
- can wait for her or his turn
- gets along well with others
- is cooperative within a group
- likes to engage in a variety of activities
- knows difference between right and wrong
- obeys rules willingly
- understands the need for rules (firedrill, playground)
- shows emotion (laughing, crying) at appropriate times
- shows leadership qualities/is content to be a group member
- has a developed sense of humor
- acts appropriately for her or his background experiences
- is on target when describing characteristics of this age level

This assessment can be used at the beginning of the school year and at specific check points throughout the year.

End-of-Year Activities

Some teachers plan a tea for the parents, along with the children, for an end-of-the-year celebration. Art work that has been saved during the year is on display as well as other work completed by the children. There also can be singing and dancing performed by the children.

It's Pretty Hard to Say Good-Bye

So, let's agree not to say good-bye, but to just say farewell until next September when the children will be first graders and can come to visit you. Tell children that you will be sure to be in touch with them over the summer (a postcard will be welcomed), and encourage them to write to you.

An envelope, addressed to you and stamped, will assure that you get one note at least over the summer.

Bring Your Backpack Today

Make sure children bring their backpack for their last day, because there are last-minute items that will need to go home. Perhaps you plan to "auction" some of the chart stories that can be folded and put in their pack. Perhaps you plan to send home extra activity pages to work on over the summer, or a Summer Idea Sheet of things to do to keep those skills current.

Have extra bags available for those who do not bring a backpack. And if the stuffed animals have not gone home already, this is the very last chance to send them off.

Happy Birthday to Our July and August Friends

Have all of the July and August birthday people get an opportunity to stand tall and have the birthday song sung just for them. Parents may wish to bring or send some edible treats for their child's *special* day.

Many Schools Have a Checklist of What's Due, What Needs to Be Accomplished, and When . . .

- complete permanent record cards
- complete portfolios
- complete parent/teacher conferences
- final newsletter due

. . . And Specifically for Kindergarten This Might Help

- Sort and categorize all game items (with children's help) and return to proper boxes and containers.
- Decide whether smocks will be washed and saved or discarded.
- Clean out scrap box. (Some children like to take scraps home.)
- Cover shelf spaces with kraft paper.
- Wash and scrub easel and brushes.
- Take down all bulletin board materials.
- Remove all items from cubbies.
- Clear desk top.
- Leave inside of desk clean and well organized.

- Clean and organize items under the sink and in cupboards.
- Leave files in good order.

. . . and enjoy the summer months to rest, rejuvenate, and to reflect. When September arrives, you'll be refreshed and ready for the active kindergarteners!

BIBLIOGRAPHY

Mrs. Katz

Bibliography

Alphabet Books

Anno, Mitsumasa. *Anno's Alphabet.* New York: Thomas Y. Crowell & Co., 1975.

Azarian, Mary. *A Farmer's Alphabet.* Boston: David R. Godine, 1985.

Bannatyne-Cugnet, Jo. *A Prairie Alphabet,* illustrated by Yvette Moore. Canada: Tundra, 1992.

Crews, Donald. *We Read: A to Z.* New York: Greenwillow, 1967.

Ehlert, Lois. *Eating the Alphabet.* New York: Harcourt Brace, 1989.

Emberley, Ed. *Ed Emberley's ABC.* Boston: Little, Brown & Co. 1978.

Feelings, Muriel. *Jambo Means Hello, Swahili Alphabet Book,* illustrated by Tom Feelings. New York: Puffin Pied Piper, 1974.

Hoban, Tana. *26 Letters and 99 Cents.* New York: Greenwillow, 1987.

Loebel, Anita. *Allison's Zinnia.* New York: Greenwillow, 1990.

Mayers, Florence Cassen. *ABC, Museum of Fine Arts, Boston.* New York: Harry N. Abrams, Inc. 1986. (**an introduction to the world of art with actual photos**)

Mullins, Patricia. *V for Vanishing, An Alphabet of Endangered Animals.* New York: HarperCollins, 1993.

Pallotta, Jerry. *The Icky Bug Alphabet Book,* illustrated by Ralph Masiello. New York: The Trumpet Club, 1986. (**also in this series:** *The Spice Alphabet Book, The Furry Alphabet Book, The Desert Alphabet Book, The Underwater Alphabet Book*)

Rosen, Michael. *Michael Rosen's ABC,* illustrated by Bee Willey. Brookfield, CT: Millbrook, 1996.

Tapahonso, Luci and Eleanor Schick. *NAVAJO ABC, A Dine Alphabet Book,* illustrated by Eleanor Schick. New York: Simon and Schuster, 1995.

Zabar, Abbie. *Alphabet Soup.* New York: Workman, 1990. (**multicultural food experience**)

Board Books

Dubov, Christine Salac. *Ding Dong and Other Sounds.* New York: Tambourine Books, 1991.

___. *Oink and Other Sounds.* New York: Tambourine Books, 1991.

Johnson, Angela. *Rain Feet,* illustrations by Rhonda Mitchell. New York: Orchard Books, 1994.

McKee, David. *Elmer's Colors.* New York: Lothrop, Lee & Shepard, 1994.

Rylant, Cynthia. *Everyday Garden*. New York: Bradbury Press, 1993. (***in this same series, books include:*** *Everyday Children, Everyday House, Everyday Pets, Everyday Town*)

Snapshot Series. New York: Covent Garden Books, 1995. Titles include: *Going Places (Transportation), Giant Machines, Emergency*, and *Around Town*. (***simple text; bright colors***)

Witt, Dick. *Let's Look at Animals*. New York: Scholastic Inc., 1993.

Color Books

Brunhoff, Laurent de. *Babar's Book of Color*. New York: Random House, 1984.

Carle, Eric. *The Mixed-Up Chameleon*. New York: HarperCollins, 1991.

Heller, Ruth. *Color, Color, Color, Color*. New York: Putnam & Grosset, 1995.

Hoban, Tana. *Is It Red? Is It Yellow? Is It Blue?* New York: Greenwillow, 1978.

Imershein, Betsy. *Finding Red, Finding Yellow*. New York: Harcourt Brace Jovanovich, 1989.

Lionni, Leo. *Little Blue and Little Yellow*. New York: Mulberry Books, 1959, 1995.

Martin, Bill, Jr. *Brown Bear, Brown Bear, What Do You See?*, illustrations by Eric Carle. New York: H. Holt, 1983.

Walsh, Ellen Stoll. *Mouse Paint*. New York: Harcourt Brace, 1989.

Fairy Tales and Folktales

Brett, Jan. *The Mitten*. New York: Putnam, 1989 (***Ukranian***)

Galdone, Paul. *The Three Bears*. New York: Clarion, 1972.

Hawkins, Colin and Jacqui. *The House That Jack Built*. New York: Putnam, 1990.

Kraus, Robert. *Strudwick, A Sheep in Wolf's Clothing*. New York: Penguin Books, 1995. (***variation on the Red Riding Hood theme***)

Lewis, J. Patrick. *The Czar and the Amazing Cow*, pictures by Friso Henstra. New York: Dial, 1988.

Little Red Riding Hood Rebus Book retold by Ann Morris, pictures by Ljiljana Rylands. New York: Orchard Books, 1989. (***excellent for the beginning readers who can rely on pictures and words***)

McKissack, Patricia C. *Flossie & the Fox*. New York: Dial Books for Young Readers, 1986. (***African-American version of Red Riding Hood***)

Opie, Iona (ed.). *My Very First Mother Goose*, illustrated by Rosemary Wells. New York: Candlewick, 1996.

Paterson, Katherine. *The Tale of the Mandarin Ducks*, illustrated by Leo and Diane Dillon. New York: Lodestar, 1990.

Tolhurst, Marilyn. *Somebody and the Three Blairs*, illustrated by Simone Abel. New York: Orchard, 1990.

Wildsmith, Brian and Rebecca. *Jack and the Meanstalk*. New York: Alfred A. Knopf, 1994. *(a spin-off of Jack and the Beanstalk)*

Young, Ed. *Lon Po Po, A Red Riding Hood Story from China*. New York: Philomel, 1989.

Cinderella Tales (multicultural)

Climo, Shirley. *The Korean Cinderella*, illustrations by Ruth Heller. New York: HarperCollins, 1993.

___. *The Egyptian Cinderella*, illustrations by Ruth Heller. New York: Thomas Y. Crowell, 1989.

___. *The Irish Cinderlad*, illustrated by Loretta Krupinski. New York: HarperCollins, 1996.

Louie, Ai-Ling. *Yeh-Shen, A Cinderella Story from China*, illustrated by Ed Young. New York: Philomel, 1982.

Perrault, Charles; retold by Amy Ehrlich. *Cinderella*, pictures by Susan Jeffers. New York: Pied Piper Printing (Dial Books), 1990.

Cinderella Videos

Cinderella. Faerie Tale Theatre Series. Producer: Platypus Productions; Director: Mark Cullingham. Playhouse Video, div. of CBS/Fox.

Mufaro's Beautiful Daughters. Directed by David R. Paight. Weston Woods. *(African-American Tale)*

Holiday Books

Adler, David. A. *A Picture Book of George Washington*, illustrated by John and Alexandra Wallner. New York: Holiday House, 1989. *(one in a series of books about famous Americans)*

Bernhard, Emery. *Happy New Year!*, illustrated by Durga Bernhard. New York: Lodestar/Penguin, 1996.

Bunting, Eve. *The Valentine Bears*, pictures by Jan Brett. New York: Clarion, 1983.

___. *The Mother's Day Mice*, illustrated by Jan Brett. New York: Clarion, 1986.

___. *A Perfect Father's Day*, illustrations by Susan Meddauth. New York: Clarion, 1991.

Cowley, Joy. *Gracias, the Thanksgiving Turkey*, illustrated by Joe Cepeda. New York: Scholastic, 1996.

Fox, Mem. *Wombat Divine*, illustrated by Kerry Argent. New York: Harcourt Brace, 1996.

Friedrich, Priscilla and Otto. *The Easter Bunny That Overslept*, illustrated by Adrienne Adams. New York: Lothrop, Lee and Shepard, 1957, 1983.

Howard, Elizabeth Fitzgerald. *Chita's Christmas Tree*, illustrated by Floyd Cooper. New York: Bradbury, 1989.

Hutchins, Pat. *Which Witch Is Witch?* New York: Greenwillow, 1989.

Johnston, Tony. *The Magic Maguey*, illustrated by Elisa Kleven. New York: Harcourt Brace, 1996.

Joseph, Lynn. *An Island Christmas*, illustrations by Catherine Stock. Boston: Houghton Mifflin, 1992.

Kimmel, Eric A. *The Magic Dreidels*. New York: Holiday House, 1966.

___. *The Chanukkah Guest*. New York: Holiday House, 1990.

Kroll, Steven. *The Squirrels' Thanksgiving*, illustrated by Jeni Bassett. New York: Holiday House, 1991.

Mathews, Mary. *Magid Fasts for Ramadan*, illustrated by E. B. Lewis. New York: Clarion Books, 1996.

Moore, Clement C. *Ke Ahiahi Mamura O Kalikimaka*; 'Twas the Night Before Christmas in Hawaii (based on the original poem by Moore). Illustrated by Barbara Ewald. Hawaii: Bess Press, 1994. **(children familiar with this poem can replace the Hawaiian words with English; helpful picture clues; Glossary at the end)**

Moss, Marissa. *The Ugly Menorah*. New York: Farrar, Straus, Giroux, 1996.

Pilkey, Dav. *'Twas the Night Before Thanksgiving*. New York: Orchard, 1990.

Pinkney, Andrea Davis. *Seven Candles for Kwanzaa*, illustrated by Brian Pinkney. New York: Dial, 1993.

Pfister, Marcus. *Wake Up, Santa Claus!* New York: North-South Books, 1996.

Polacco, Patricia. *Mrs. Katz and Tush*. New York: Bantam, 1992.

___. *The Tree of the Dancing Goats*. New York: Simon & Schuster, 1996. **(Christmas/Hanukkah)**

Ross, Kathy. *Crafts for Christmas*, illustrated by Sharon Lane Holm. Brookfield, CT: Millbrook, 1996.

___. *Crafts for Hanukkah*, illustrated by Sharon Lane Holm. Brookfield, CT: Millbrook, 1996.

___. *Crafts for Kwanzaa*, illustrated by Sharon Lane Holm. Brookfield, CT: Millbrook, 1996.

Stevenson, James. *The Oldest Elf*. New York: Greenwillow, 1996.

Vincent, Gabrielle. *Merry Christmas, Ernest and Celestine*. New York: Greenwillow, 1983.

Multicultural Books

Bartone, Elisa. *American Too*, illustrated by Ted Lewin. New York: Lothrop, Lee & Shepard, 1996.

Clifton, Lucille. *Everett Anderson's Goodbye*. New York: Holt, 1983.

___. *Everett Anderson's Nine Month Long*. New York: Holt, 1983.

dePaola, Tomie. *Fin M'Coul: The Giant of Knockmany Hill*. New York: Holiday House, 1981.

Ehlert, Lois. *Moon Rope, Un lazo a la luna*. New York: Harcourt Brace, 1992.

Fox, Mem. *Possum Magic*, illustrated by Julie Vivas. New York: Kane/Miller, 1989.

Grimes, Nikki. *Come Sunday*, illustrated by Michael Bryant. Grand Rapids, MI: Eerdmans, 1996.

Hall, Donald. *Old Home Day*, illustrated by Emily Arnold McCully. New York: Browndeer Press, 1996.

Lattimore, Deborah Norse. *The Dragon's Robe*. New York: Harper & Row, 1990.

Lester, Julius. *Sam and the Tigers*, illustrated by Jerry Pinkney. New York: Dial, 1996. (**A remake of Little Black Sambo**)

Lewis, J. Patrick. *The Moonbow of Mr. B. Bones*, illustrations by Dirk Zimmer. New York: Alfred A. Knopf, 1992. (**regional: Kentucky**)

Little, Mimi Otey. *Yoshiko and the Foreigner*. New York: Farrar, Straus, Giroux, 1996.

McDermott, Gerald. *Raven, a Trickster Tale from the Pacific Northwest*. New York: Harcourt Brace Jovanovich, 1993.

Nomura, Takaaki. *Grandpa's Town*, illustrations by Amanda Mayer Stinchecum. New York: Kane/Miller, 1991.

Norworth, Jack. *Take Me Out to the Ballgame*, illustrations by Alec Gillman. New York: Four Winds Press, 1992.

Polacco, Patricia. *Chicken Sunday*. New York: Philomel, 1992.

Say, Allen. *Emma's Rug*. Boston: Houghton Mifflin, 1996.

Schroeder, Alan. *Minty: A Story of Young Harriet Tubman*. New York: Dial, 1996.

Wallace, Ian and Angela Wood. *The Sandwich*. Ontario, Canada: Kids Canada Press, 1975.

Wheeler, Bernelda. *Where Did You Get Your Moccasins?*, illustrated by Herman Bekkering. St. Paul, MN: Pemmican, 1986.

Number Books

Barnes-Murphy, Rowan. *One, Two, Buckle My Shoe: A Book of Counting Rhymes*. New York: Simon & Schuster, 1987.

Barry, David. *The Rajah's Rice, A Mathematical Folktale from India*, illustrated by Donna Perrone. New York: Scientific American, 1996.

Carle, Eric. *The Very Hungry Caterpillar*. New York: Philomel, 1983.

___. *1, 2, 3, to the Zoo*. New York: Philomel, 1996.

Chandra, Deborah. *Miss Mabel's Table*, illustrations by Max Grover. New York: Browndeer Press, 1994.

Ehlert, Lois. *Fish Eyes*. San Diego: Harcourt Brace 1990.

Feelings, Muriel. *Moja Means One, A Swahili Counting Book*, pictures by Tom Feelings. New York: Puffin, 1976.

Gretz, Suzanna. *Teddy Bears 1 to 10*. New York: Macmillan, 1986.

Grossman, Bill. *My Little Sister Ate One Hare*, illustrated by Kevin Hawkes. New York: Crown, 1996.

Hague, Kathleen. *Numbears*. New York: Henry Holt & Co., 1986.

Hoban, Tana. *Circles, Triangles, and Squares*. New York: Macmillan, 1974.

___. *Shapes, Shapes, Shapes*. New York: Greenwillow, 1986.

___. *Dots, Spots, Speckles and Stripes*. New York: Greenwillow, 1987.

Kitchen, Bert. *Animal Numbers*. New York: Dial Books, 1987.

The Lifesize Animal Counting Book. New York: A Dorling Kindersley Book, 1994.

Rosen, Michael. *We're Going on a Bear Hunt*, illustrations by Helen Oxenbury. New York: McElderry, 1989.

Russo, Marisabina. *The Line Up Book*. New York: Greenwillow, 1996.

Wallwork, Amanda. *No Dodos: A Counting Book of Endangered Animals*. New York: Scholastic, 1993.

Winter, Jeanette. *Josefina*. New York: Harcourt Brace, 1996. **(Spanish setting)**

Picture Books (General)

Ackerman, Karen. *Song and Dance Man*, illustrated by Stephen Gammell. New York: Knopf, 1988.

Barracca, Debra and Sal. *The Adventures of Taxi Dog*, pictures by Mark Buehner. New York: Dial, 1990.

Brett, Jan. *Comet's Nine Lives*. New York: Putnam/Grosset, 1996.

Brown, Marc. *Perfect Pigs*. Boston: Little, Brown, 1983.

Brown, Margaret Wise. *The Diggers*, illustrated by Daniel Kirk. New York: Hyperion Books, 1958, 1960, 1995. *(animals and machines that dig)*

Carlstrom, Nancy White. *Moose in the Garden*, paintings by Lisa Desimini. New York: Harper & Row, 1990. *(Alaska setting)*

Catalanotto, Peter. *Dylan's Day Out*. New York: Orchard Books, 1989.

Cohen, Caren Lee. *Pigeon, Pigeon*, pictures by G. Brian Karas. New York: Dutton, 1992. *(a zoo trip)*

Conrad, Pam. *The Rooster's Gift*, pictures by Eric Beddows. New York: A Laura Geringer Book (HarperCollins), 1996.

Crews, Donald. *Parade*. New York: Greenwillow, 1983.

___. *School Bus*. New York: Greenwillow, 1984.

Cousins, Lucy. *Za-Za's Baby Brother*. New York: Candlewick Press, 1995.

Degan, Bruce. *Jamberry*. New York: Harper & Row, 1983.

Deming, A. G. *Who Is Tapping at My Window?*, pictures by Monica Wellington. New York: E. P. Dutton, 1988.

dePaola, Tomie. *Strega Nona*. New York: Simon and Schuster Books for Young Readers, 1975.

___. *Strega Nona's Magic Lessons*. New York: Harcourt Brace Jovanovich, 1982.

Egielski, Richard. *Buz*. New York: A Laura Geringer Book (HarperCollins), 1995. *(cop pills chase a bug through the human body; large, bright bold colorful teaching book)*

Ehlert, Lois. *Feathers for Lunch*. New York: Harcourt Brace Jovanovich, 1990.

Florian, Douglas. *Vegetable Garden*. New York: Harcourt Brace Jovanovich, 1991.

Garland, Michael. *Circus Girl*. New York: Dutton, 1993.

Graves, Margaret. *Henry's Wild Morning*, pictures by Teresa O'Brien. New York: Dial, 1990.

Hazen, Barbara Shook. *The Gorilla Did It*, illustrated by Ray Cruz. Hartford, CT: Connecticut Printers, Inc., 1974. *(an imaginary gorilla gets blamed for messes and spills)*

Henkes, Kevin. *Julius, the Baby of the World*. New York: Greenwillow, 1990.

___. *Lily's Purple Plastic Purse*. New York: Greenwillow, 1996.

Henley, Claire. *Jungle Day*. New York: Dial Books for Young Readers, 1991.

Hennessy, B. G. *Road Builders*, pictures by Simms Taback. New York: Viking, 1994. *(big machines at work; road sign endpapers)*

Hest, Amy. *Baby Duck and the Bad Eyeglasses*, illustrated by Jill Barton. New York: Candlewick, 1996.

Johnson, Angela. *When I Am Old With You*, illustrated by David Soman. New York: Orchard, 1990.

Kasza, Keiko. *The Wolf's Chicken Stew*. New York: Putnam, 1987.

Keats, Ezra Jack. *Pet Show!* New York: Macmillan, 1972.

Keller, Holly. *Horace*. New York: Greenwillow, 1991.

Kelley, True. *Hammers and Mops, Pencils and Pots, A First Book of Tools and Gadgets to Use Around the House*. New York: Crown Publishers, 1994.

Kraus, Robert. *Whose Mouse Are You?*, pictures by Jose Aruego. New York: Macmillan, 1970. *(a reassuring tale)*

Krause, Ruth. *The Happy Day*, pictures by Marc Simont. New York: Harper & Row, 1949. *(a delightful surprise during winter)*

Lillie, Patricia. *Everything Has a Place*, pictures by Nancy Tafuri. New York: Greenwillow, 1993.

Lindgren, Astrid. *I Want a Brother or Sister*, pictures by Ilon Wikland. New York: R & S Books, 1988.

Lucas, Barbara. *Cats by Mother Goose*, pictures by Carol Newsom. New York: Lothrop, Lee & Shepard, 1986.

Maris, Ron. *I Wish I Could Fly*. New York: Greenwillow, 1986.

Martin, Bill, Jr., and John Archambault. *Chicka Chicka Boom Boom*, illustrated by Lois Ehlert. New York: Simon & Schuster, 1989.

McCutcheon, John. *Happy Adoption Day!*, illustrated by Julie Paschkis. Boston: Little, Brown, 1996.

McKee, David. *Elmer Again*. New York: Lothrop, Lee & Shepard, 1991,

McMillan, Bruce. *Sense Suspense, a Guessing Game for the Five Senses*. New York: Scholastic, Inc., 1994. *(a concept book that goes from part to whole)*

Maestro, Betsy and Giulio. *Traffic, a Book of Opposites*. New York: Random House, 1981.

Moss, Thylias. *I Want to Be*, pictures by Jerry Pinkney. New York: Dial Books, 1993. *(career choices)*

Numeroff, Laura Joffe. *If You Give a Mouse a Cookie*, illustrated by Felicia Bond. New York: HarperCollins, 1985.

___. *If You Give a Moose a Muffin*, illustrated by Felicia Bond. New York: HarperCollins, 1991.

Polacco, Patricia. *Babushka's Mother Goose*. New York: Philomel, 1995.

___. *Rachenka's Eggs*. New York: Philomel Books, 1988.

Raschka, Chris. *Yo! Yes?* New York: Orchard Books, 1993.

Rayner, Mary. *Mr. and Mrs. Pig's Evening Out*. New York: Atheneum, 1976.

Rey, H. A. *Curious George Gets a Medal*. Boston: Houghton Mifflin, 1957. **(there is a wide variety of books in this series)**

Richardson, Judith Benet. *Old Winter*, pictures by R. W. Alley. New York: Orchard Books, 1996.

Rylant, Cynthia. *The Relatives Came*, illustrated by Stephen Gammell. New York: Bradbury, 1985.

Sloats, Teri. *The Thing That Bothered Farmer Brown*. New York: Orchard Books, 1995.

Stevenson, James. *That's Exactly the Way It Wasn't*. New York: Greenwillow, 1991.

Stolz, Mary. *Storm in the Night*, illustrated by Pat Cummings. New York: HarperCollins, 1988.

Turkle, Brinton. *Deep in the Forest*. New York: E. P. Dutton, 1976.

VanAllsburg, Chris. *The Polar Express*. Boston: Houghton Mifflin, 1985.

___. *Two Bad Ants*, Boston: Houghton Mifflin, 1988.

Waber, B. *Do You See a Mouse?* Boston: Houghton Mifflin, 1995.

Waddell, Martin. *When the Teddy Bears Came*. Cambridge, MA: Candlewick, 1995.

Wilder, Laura Ingalls. *My First Little House Books, The Deer in the Wood*, illustrated by Renee Graef. New York: HarperCollins, 1995. **(an introduction to the famous prairie books; for the beginner; also in the series,** *My First Little House Books* **and** *Christmas in the Big Woods)*

Wildsmith, Brian. *Squirrels*. New York: Oxford University Press, 1974.

Wormell, M. *Hilda Hen's Happy Birthday*. San Diego: Harcourt Brace, 1995.

Wynot, Jillian. *The Mother's Day Sandwich*, pictures by Maxie Chambliss. New York: Orchard Books, 1990.

Yolen, Jane. *Owl Moon*. Weston, CT: Weston Woods, 1988.

Zieffert, H. *Oh, What a Noisy Farm!* New York: Tambourine, 1995.

Zion, Gene. *Harry the Dirty Dog*, pictures by Margaret Bloy Graham. New York: Harper & Row, 1956.

___. *Harry by the Sea*, pictures by Margaret Bloy Graham. New York: Harper & Row, 1965.

Poetry Books

Charles, Donald. *Paddy Pig's Poems, A Story About an Amusing Fellow and His Friends*. New York: Simon & Schuster, 1989.

Downes, Belinda. *A Stitch in Rhyme*. New York: Random House, 1996.

Hoberman, Mary Ann. *A House Is a House for Me*, illustrated by Betty Fraser. New York: Viking, 1978.

Kennedy, X. J. *Talking Like the Rain*, illustrated by Jane Dyer. Boston: Little, Brown, 1992.

Lear, Edward. *The Owl and the Pussy-Cat*, illustrations by Paul Galdone. New York: Clarion Books, 1987.

Lewis, J. Patrick. *A Hippopotomusn't*, illustrations by Victoria Chess. New York: Trumpet Club, 1990.

___. *Earth Verses and Water Rhymes*, illustrations by Pamela Paparone. New York: Atheneum, 1991.

O'Neill, Mary. *Hailstones and Hailibut Bones*, newly illustrated by John Wallner. New York: Trumpet Club, 1989.

Pomerantz, Charlotte. *The Tamarindo Puppy and Other Poems*. New York: Greenwillow, 1993.

___. *If I Had a Paka, Poems in Eleven Languages*, illustrated by Nancy Tafuri. New York: Greenwillow, 1982.

Prelutsky, Jack. *Something Big Has Been Here*. New York: Greenwillow, 1990.

___. *It's Snowing! It's Snowing!*, pictures by Jeanne Titherington. New York: Greenwillow, 1984.

___. *The New Kid on the Block*, drawings by Janus Stevenson. New York: Greenwillow, 1984.

Ray, Karen. *Sleep Song*. New York: Orchard, 1995. **(rhyming text)**

Strickland, D. S., and M. R. Strickland (eds.). *Families: Poems Celebrating the African American Experience*. Honesdale, PA: Boyds Mills, 1994.

Thomas, Joyce Carol. *Gingerbread Days*, illustrations by Floyd Cooper. New York: HarperCollins, 1995.

Yolen, Jane. *Alphabestiary: Animal Poems from A to Z*. Honesdale, PA: Boyds Mills, 1995.

Science Books

Agee, Jon. *Dmitri the Astronaut*. New York: Michael di Capua Books, 1996.

Aliki. *My Visit to the Aquarium*. New York: HarperCollins, 1993.

___. *My Five Senses*. New York: Trumpet, 1989.

Bender, R. *A Most Unusual Lunch*. New York: Dial, 1994.

Catherall, Ed. *Wheels*. East Sussex, England: Wayland Publishers, Ltd., 1982.

Cole, Henry. *Jack's Garden*. New York: Greenwillow, 1995.

Evans, David and Claudette Williams. *Make It Balance (Let's Explore Science Series)*. New York: Dorling Kindersley, Inc., 1992. **(this series contains books entitled** *Make It Change, Make It Go,* **and** *Me and My Body)*

Horvatic, Anne. *Simple Machines*, photographs by Stephen Bruner. New York: E. P. Dutton, 1989.

Pettigrew, Mark. *Music and Sound (Science Today Series)*. New York: Gloucester Press, 1987.

Taylor, Barbara. *Focus on Sound*. New York: Gloucester Press, 1992.

Webb, Angela. *Air (Talk About Series)*, photography by Chris Fairclough. New York: Franklin Watts, 1986. **(this series contains books on** *Water, Soil* **and** *Sand)*.

Audiotapes

A Kid's Eye View of the Environment. Michael Mish. Mish Mash Music Records; dist. by Alcazar. **(concerns, nature sounds, and suggestions)**

Alphabet Operetta, The. Mindy Manley Little, MVO. **(an original tune for every alphabet letter)**

Animal Crackers and other Tasty Tunes. Kevin Roth. Sony Kids' Music. ALA Notable Children's Recording, 1990. **(an award-winning children's performer with other fine audio-tapes)**

Camels, Cats and Rainbows. Paul Strausman, A Gentle Wind. **(singer/songwriter is a former preschool teacher)**

Everything Grows. Raffi. A&M Records. ALA Notable Children's Recording, 1988. **(repeated verses, nonsense, fun)**

Growing Up Together. Gemini. Gemini Records; dist. by Alcazar. ALA Notable Recording, 1990. **(the song "Hello" teaches greetings in several languages)**

Peter and the Wolf Play Jazz. Jon Crosse. Jazz Cat Productions; dist. by Alcazar. ALA Notable Children's Recording, 1990. **(a new approach to Prokofiev's tale; on the reverse side: "Cool Mother Goose Suite")**

Where Do My Sneakers Go at Night? Rick Charette, Pine Point; dist. by Alcazar. **(everyday problems and answers)**

You Sing a Song, and I'll Sing a Song. Ella Jenkins. Smithsonian/Folkways; dist. by Rounder Records. *(children experience new musical and cultural experiences)*

Music Distributors

Alcazar, P.O. Box 429, Waterbury, VT 05676; (800) 541-9904

BMG, One South 450 Summit, Oakbrook Terrace, IL 60181; (708) 268-6400

The Bumblebeez Records, 859 N. Hollywood, Suite 115, Burbank, CA 91505; (213) 654-9187

Videotapes

Eyewitness Video Series. New York: Dorling Kindersley Publishing Inc., 1996. There are twelve videotapes in this series: *Amphibian, Cat, Dog, Dinosaur, Elephant, Horse, Fish, Insect, Jungle, Reptile, Shark, Skeleton.*

Harry Comes Home. Producer: Pete Matuvalich. Barr Films. ALA Notable Children's Film, 1990; Andrew Carnegie Medal 1991. This is a sequel to *Harry, the Dirty Dog* and *Harry and the Lady Next Door* by Gene Zion. *(read the book series, and then enjoy this video)*

Maurice Sendak Library, The. Children's Circle. This includes many of Sendak's tales, including *Where the Wild Things Are* and *In the Night Kitchen.* At the end, there is an interview with the author that can be used with parents.

Robert McCloskey Library, The. Children's Circle. Five story favorites are on this video, including *Make Way for Ducklings* and *Blueberries for Sal.*

Squiggles, Dots, & Lines. KIDVIDZ. Ed Emberly shares his drawing skills with an enthusiastic group.

Strega Nona and Other Stories. Children's Circle. This videotape can be played after children listen to *Strega Nona* by Tomie dePaola. Another favorite here is *Tikki Tikki Tembo.*

Video Producers and Distributors

(The materials listed above were found in these resources.)

Children's Circle, Division of Weston Woods, C.C. Studios, Inc., Weston, CT 06883; (800) 243-5020

National Geographic Society, Educational Services, Washington, D.C. 20036; (800) 368-2728

Weston Woods, 389 Newton Turnpike, Weston, CT 06883; (800) 243-5020

Computer Software

Katie's Farm. Lawrence Productions. Apple II, IBM/Tandy, Macintosh, Amiga. *(participate in farm chores while learning)*

Kidsmath. Great Wave Software. Macintosh. Technology & Learning Software Award, 1990–91. *(difficult words can be translated into picture messages)*

Letter Go Round. Hi-Tech Expressions. Apple II, IBM/Tandy. *(an alphabet game played on a ferris wheel)*

Muppetville. Sunburst. Apple II, IBM/Tandy. *(Kermit the Frog introduces children to a shapes game, number recognition, and music)*

Picture Chompers. MECC. Apple II. *(a large set of chomping teeth direct children to "chomp all the green things," etc.)*

Talking First Reader. Orange Cherry Software/Talking Schoolhouse Series. Apple IIGS. *(stories, animation, sound)*

Computer Software Distributors

Broderbund Software, Inc., P.O. Box 6125, Novato, CA 94948; (800) 521-6263

The Learning Company, 6493 Kaiser Drive, Fremont, CA 94555; (800) 852-2255

Tom Snyder Productions, Inc., 90 Sherman Street, Cambridge, MA 02140; (800) 342-0236

Teacher Resource Information

All Ears: How to Choose and Use Recorded Music for Children, Jill Jarnow. New York: Penguin, 1991.

American Library Association Best of the Best for Children, Denise Perry Donavin, ed. New York: Random House, 1992. *(reviews of books, magazines, videos, audio, software, toys, travel)*

Booklist. Twice monthly with single issues in July/August. American Library Association, 50 E. Huron Street, Chicago, IL 60611. *(reviews of new software appear regularly)*

Borman, Jami Lynne. *Computer Dictionary for Kids . . . And Their Parents*, illustrated by Yvette Santiago Banek. Hauppauge, NY: Barron's Educational Series, Inc., 1995.

Buy Me! Buy Me! The Bank Street Guide to Choosing Toys, Joanne Oppenheim. New York: Bank Street, 1987.

Frazier, Deneen, Barbara Kurshan and Sara Armstrong. *Internet for Kids*. San Francisco: Sybex Publishing, 1994–1995.

Freeman, Judy. *More Books Kids Will Sit Still For*. New Providence, NJ: R. R. Bowker, 1995.

KIDSNET: A Computerized Clearinghouse for Children's Television and Radio. Suite 208, 6856 Eastern Avenue, NW, Washington, D.C. 20012.

Mudworks: Creative Clay, Dough, and Modeling Experiences, MaryAnn F. Kohl. 1989. Bright Ring Publishing (Dist. by Gryphon House, 3706 Otis St., P.O. Box 275, Mt. Ranier, MD 20712).

Multimedia Home Companion, Rebecca Buffum Taylor, ed. New York: Warner Books, Inc., 1994, 1995.

NAPPS Directory of Storytellers. National Association for the Preservation and Perpetuation of Storytelling, P.O. Box 309, Jonesborough, TN 37659.

New York Times Parent's Guide to the Best Books for Children, Eden Ross Lipson, Children's Book Editor. New York: Times Books, a Division of Random House, 1988.

Only the Best: Preschool-Grade 12: The Annual Guide to Highest Rated Software, Shirley Boes Neill and George W. Neill. New Providence, NJ: Bowker, 1996.

Rief, Sandra F. *How to Reach and Teach ADD/ADHD Children*. West Nyack, NY: The Center for Applied Research in Education, 1993.

Schecter, Harold. *KIDVID, A Parents' Guide to Children's Videos*. New York: Pocket Books, a Division of Simon & Schuster, 1986.

Stull, Elizabeth Crosby. *Multicultural Discovery Activities for the Elementary Grades*. West Nyack, NY: The Center for Applied Research in Education, 1995.

Technology and Learning. Peter Li, Inc., 2451 E. River Road, Dayton, OH 45439.